Dedicated with Love

To my three daughters,
Kerry, Kristy,
and Kim (in Spirit);

To my husband Doug
for all his patience and support

# Contents

# Acknowledgments

I wish to acknowledge the many people without whom this book would never have come into being. I am deeply grateful to all the wonderful people who have influenced my life and helped me along my spiritual journey.

I would like to thank my three friends: Heather Currie, Judy Piers, and Jane Cookson, who were the first to reach out to help me during my time of intense grief. Thank you for your part in my journey and for listening to my "miracles." I will forever be indebted to each of you for your support, compassion, and caring.

I wish to thank my friends Judy Hunt and Sue Stone and my sister-in-law Ruth Ryan for listening and opening their hearts to the truths we were discovering together and for encouraging me to move forward into this world of the unknown. You gave me the courage and support I needed to continue and pursue my journey into the Light.

To all the new friends who have entered my life and have been part of my miracles, I thank you. Each and every one of you entered my life at exactly the right time. I truly believe we were fated to meet and that we were meant to be part of each other's destiny.

Among them I thank:

Bonnie Jordan: For sharing your deep compassion and quiet wisdom. I couldn't have walked this path without you.

Joanne Rankin: For your friendship and courageous spirit.

Jeanne Lightheart: For your gift of laughter, which I so much needed.

Susan Williamson: For teaching me through your kind actions the importance of reaching out to others with love and caring.

Velma Campbell: For your support, encouragement, and friendship.

Connie DaCosta: For sharing your spiritual wisdom and unwavering faith.

I am deeply indebted to all those online people who helped to lighten my burdens during the earliest stages of my grief and the darkest moments of my life.

I gratefully thank Ann Booth for all your help, support, and patience with the original organization of this book. Thank you for caring.

And to the numerous others with whom I now share my journey, including David and Elyse Chapman and all my friends who work at Purity Life Health Products Limited. I am glad we are united in friendship and purpose.

I wish to say a special thank you to Karen Green, Sharon Kerr, and Sylvia Christenson for sharing your personal journeys with me and for reaching out to help me with mine.

To my teachers and mentors: Shawna Ross, Hazel McGuiness, Marlene George, Carol Baltkalns, Lou Baccash, and Scott, I thank you. Without your love and knowledge, I could not have awakened my soul. Together we can soar.

To the families who graciously allowed me to share their personal stories of loss in this book, it is an honor to pay tribute to your loved ones on the other side.

To Rob and Wendy Lindsay: I honor your courage and pay tribute to your children, Tim and Laura (both in spirit), who helped guide my book to its publisher.

To my publisher Karla Wheeler: Thank you for finding value in my journey and my story. I am grateful to you and Quality of Life Publishing Company for taking on the momentous task of editing and publishing my work.

I thank Doug's brothers and sisters for their continued support. I thank my family for understanding how important to my survival this journey has become and for not placing judgment on where my journey has taken me.

I wish to extend a very special thank you to Sharlette Pumphrey for being one of the greatest gifts in my life. You opened my soul to the truth of the other side. It was you who gave me 100% proof of the afterlife and that Kim was in it. Thank you, Sharlette, for being my lifeline when I so desperately needed you to be, for being my contact through which Kim could send her messages to me, for being my spiritual mentor as I grew in my beliefs, and for being the friend that you have become.

To Sharon Sauer and her daughter Kandi (in spirit): Our meeting was definitely beyond chance. We are forever linked together.

To my grandmother, Gladys Gallant, who is now on the other side, thank you for your love and continuing guidance. Grandma, you always knew this to be true!

To my daughters, Kerry and Kristy, whom I love deeply: Thank you for understanding the importance of this book to me.

To my husband Doug: Thank you for being my partner and my confidant. I am so grateful that I share my life with you.

To Kim who is guiding me and teaching me to understand that death, as I always feared it, is really nothing to fear. I love you.

— *Sandy*

Chapter 1

# REMEMBERING

*I am not now*

*that which I have been.*

— Lord Byron

At 9:20 p.m. on the evening of October 27, 1998, I was awakened by a loud pounding on our front door. I wasn't expecting anyone. My husband Doug was at work. Twenty-year-old Kerry was away at school, 18-year-old Kristy had been doing homework when I had last seen her, and Kim had said she was going to the gym after work and would be home late.

As I stood half-dazed at the top of the stairs, trying to make sense of the intrusion, I stared down at the stone-faced police officer. I tried to comprehend the words coming out of his mouth as I walked down the stairs toward him.

"Mrs. Wiltshire?"

My heart leapt into my throat. This was no mistake. He knew my name. "Yes. What is it?"

"Do you have a daughter who drives a red car?"

Kim. He must mean Kim. I nodded, struck speechless with horror.

"I'll drive you to the hospital."

"Is Kim okay?"

His eyes locked on mine. "It's bad."

The officer escorted Kristy and me to the hospital after asking for Doug's work phone number. Kristy and I were directed to a little room in the hospital and told we had to wait there. As soon as Doug arrived from work, he joined us. By then, we'd learned that a truck had swerved over the centerline into Kim's lane, colliding with her vehicle.

A few minutes later, we were told that our beautiful, vivacious daughter had died of the injuries she sustained in the accident. We did not get a chance to see her or say goodbye.

❋ ❋ ❋

Prior to the tragic evening of October 27, 1998, my life at age 47 was good. I had a wonderful husband and three beautiful, happy, and well-adjusted daughters. Doug and I owned a lovely home and lived a comfortable life. We were a close and loving family.

I was proud of the part I had played in the raising of our girls. From the day I gave birth to my first daughter, Kim, I knew that staying home and being a mom was my first priority and the most important job I would ever have. I chose to set aside my professional teaching career to stay home with the girls while they grew up.

When Kim entered first grade, I began babysitting so I could continue to stay at home with my girls yet earn some income at the same time. Once Kim was in the fifth grade, I put my name on the supply list to do occasional substitute teaching. I thoroughly enjoyed having contact with children without the responsibility that came with having my own classroom. As a substitute, I could be home for the girls at lunchtime and after school.

As they grew older, I spent many hours sitting in gymnasiums, happily cheering on the three of them. Their teachers were glad to call on me as an available volunteer to chaperone a social event or to drive a group of students to a neighboring town for an after-school activity. I loved being part of it all.

When Kim was about ten years old, we bought a trailer and a plot of land near Peterborough, Ontario, on Pigeon Lake. These were contented times in our lives that hold exceptional memories for us. Each summer we spent almost every weekend at our trailer. The girls took swimming lessons and loved being in and on the water. As soon as we bought a motorboat, the girls learned to water-ski. Doug and I made lasting friendships, as did the girls, so they were always eager to go to Pigeon Lake when Friday night arrived. Many good times were had sitting around the campfire, roasting wieners and marshmallows, and sharing stories.

As a teenager, Kim did a lot of growing up on Pigeon Lake with her little sister Kerry tagging along, trying to mimic her big sister. They often returned from an evening with their friends, laughing and joking with one another. Kerry followed suit a few years later when her younger sister Kristy tagged along.

Pigeon Lake was a safe place; even so, Kim, Kerry, and Kristy were never very far from Doug or me. As the girls grew older and started part-time jobs, we were not able to go to the trailer park as often, but the girls continued to maintain their Pigeon Lake friendships through phone calls and occasional visits.

Summers were always an active time for us. Between swimming and baseball, we kept busy. My husband had been her T-ball coach when Kim was five, and he loved it. After watching years of baseball, I became a coach myself for the younger two girls. As they grew older and changed leagues, I changed leagues with them.

When Kim was about seven, my husband Doug surprised us with a huge trampoline. I remember a brief moment of absolute panic as he set it up in our backyard while the girls screeched with excitement. I worried they were too young. I was thankful we already had a fence encircling our entire yard. We hosted many trampoline parties while I sat outside supervising excited children eagerly awaiting their turns.

Our trampoline continued to be a big attraction as the girls grew into their teens. All three were trained in gymnastics, so it was not unusual to see them doing back flips or some such acrobatic stunt — as I held my breath. Later, when Kim started to host parties of a more adult nature where alcohol was served, I worried even more. I was thankful no one ever got hurt.

I loved spending time with all three of the girls. They knew they could always count on me when they needed a ride. I was happy to chauffeur them and their friends to a variety of activities. I was one of those doting mothers you see portrayed in movies who beamed with family pride.

When all three girls were home, it was not unusual to find them sitting cross-legged on one of their beds, talking and giggling together. Since I did not have a sister myself to share secrets with as I grew up, I had hoped my daughters would be friends as well as sisters. My wish came true, and watching them grow close truly warmed my heart.

I honestly can't remember many times when they were angry with each other. As individual as each one was, our girls were very devoted to each other and forged a tight bond. I was quite aware they kept secrets from their father and me, as all teenagers do, but I remained glad they had each other to confide in. Hearing teenage giggling behind closed bedroom doors would bring a smile to my lips. I knew we were doing a good job of rearing our children.

*If someone had asked me about my religious beliefs, I would probably have said I was an agnostic.*

By the time the girls were 18, 20, and 22, they had matured into responsible, caring adults. All balanced school and part-time jobs. The girls were rich with friends who lived in our small town. My husband and I, as well as the girls, were very close to both sides of the family. Our family ties were strong.

I had never been a religious person. If someone had asked me about my religious beliefs, I would probably have said I was an agnostic. I didn't feel I needed to go to church to be a good person. I believed by being a good wife and mother and by setting a good example, I would impart to my children the values that were central to living a happy and successful life.

As a fourth-year student at Wilfrid Laurier University, Kim had recently moved back home to begin her co-op placement at Microsoft in Mississauga, Ontario — a job she loved. After work, she often went from her job directly to the gym before heading off to meet friends or coming home to eat. She loved being busy as much as she loved to work out. Kim had recently been bustling about getting ready to leave for France in January. She had been accepted into the International Business Program at Wilfrid Laurier University. She was excited about going, and we were thrilled for her.

I was contented with my own life. Because the girls were basically grown, I did not feel the need to be so available to them at this point in their lives. I was reassessing my career options. I had begun to teach on a more regular basis but still as a substitute teacher, although I was contemplating applying for a full-time position starting the following September.

But that was before our world radically changed forever.

❋ ❋ ❋

During the early days after Kim's passing, I walked around in a zombie-like state, rooted in a deep abyss of denial. How could this tragedy have happened? These things happened to other people, didn't they? Not to happy families like ours. I felt helpless and so incredibly angry.

The details of the next few days following Kim's passing remain sketchy in my memory. My parents and Doug's cousin Bruce and brother Murray arrived immediately. My aunt and uncle were also at our house, as they had picked up our middle daughter Kerry from school and brought her home. The rest of the family arrived in stages as they learned that our beautiful daughter Kim was gone.

The day of the funeral arrived. Things somehow got organized, an avalanche of food arrived, and hundreds and hundreds of people came to honor our precious Kim. She had a heart as big as her smile; it was for her that they came. Over and over we were reminded that Kim had a way of

*Mourners said Kim was like an angel who had come to spread her love to all she met.*

making everyone she met feel important. I heard repeatedly as mourners came to pay tribute that she was like an angel who had come to spread her love to all she met.

Kim had touched many lives in such a positive way that my heart screamed out in pain with the unanswerable question: Why our daughter? Why Kim? She loved life and lived it to the fullest. She was a happy young woman with a plan for her life. It just didn't make sense that Kim was gone. She was too driven, too loving, and had too much yet to do.

After the service, despite our families being downstairs, I barricaded myself in my bedroom. I could not stand the incredible pain. I felt as if my heart was being ripped right out of my chest. The torturous, unendurable pain just would not stop. I existed in a state of shock. We all did.

Shortly after Kim's passing, her fellow students at Wilfrid Laurier University in Waterloo, Ontario, held a special memorial service in the school's chapel. During this service the friends with whom she had shared the last four years of her life poured out their feelings and memories of our cherished daughter through tributes, a slide show, and tears. Lots of tears. As we listened to stories of their times at school, we were reminded of how much Kim had enjoyed her life and how much she was loved.

Within days of her passing, the tributes to Kim began streaming in. A scholarship fund was set up at her former high school, initiated by her longtime friend Andrea, to "continue the commitment to excellence that Kim lived in every way."

Another tribute was set up in her name by her university. As one of a group of student volunteers during the summer of 1998, Kim helped to establish a literacy program. The focus of this program was to make visits to the Courtland Shelley Community Centre near the university where student volunteers worked with children struggling with various aspects of learning. Kim's fellow volunteers, with the approval of Wilfrid Laurier University, established a Resource Centre in her memory at this location. In a letter we received, her fellow volunteers shared their personal feelings: "It is our belief that this project symbolizes what Kim stood for. Her love of learning and belief in the ability of others was evident in everything she did."

The outpouring of love was immense, as cards, tributes, and personal letters continued to arrive. People we didn't know — some of whom had met Kim only once — took the time to write and express their feelings about our daughter. One such letter read in part, "If I had a daughter, I would have wanted her to be just like Kim." Someone else wrote, "I would be so proud to have my daughter grow up to be like Kim." People dropped in and brought food. Her friends came by to talk and cry with us. Unable to do little else, I spent time reading and re-reading the mountain of cards and letters.

Her boss from Microsoft paid us a visit the day after her passing. He conveyed his shock and the immense sadness he felt when he was informed of her death as he arrived at work on the morning of October 28. He came, he said, because of Kim and the extraordinary impression she had made on him. He wanted us to know the impact Kim had made on the lives of his employees in the short time she had worked with them.

An employer who hired many co-op students, he told us how he ended up hiring Kim. She was the final student to be interviewed. He had pretty much made his decision to hire someone else when in walked Kim. "She lit up the room," he told us. Her maturity and self-confidence impressed him so much that he changed his mind and hired her.

He felt it was important to share this story with us. To show us just how unique Kim was, he said that his story about her didn't end with the job offer. Kim surprised him by responding she would be happy to accept the position, but it just didn't pay enough. If she were to accept the job, she would need an increase in salary.

I knew that Doug and Kim had discussed the issue of money in relation to this co-op job. Kim had enjoyed an earlier placement with Microsoft the year before. When they approached her the second time with a new offer and more responsibility, she confided in us that, although she loved working there, the company just did not pay enough. I am sure she was thinking about saving money for her upcoming trip to France.

This was the Kim we knew and loved.

Once her employer agreed to a salary increase, she accepted the job. Kim, however, was not finished. Her boss told us how Kim confidently informed him it wouldn't be fair for her to be the only student to have an increase. As a result, every present-day and future co-op student working at Microsoft would earn a little more money.

This was our daughter! We were grateful that he took the time to share with us this heartwarming story about our Kim.

Soon after this visit a book of tributes arrived from Microsoft, delivered by a neighbor who worked there. It had started out, he stated, as a way for them to share with us how sorry they were for our loss, but it ended up being an outpouring of their love for Kim and messages to Kim. As I turned the pages, I realized that both men and women — co-workers, supervisors and district managers — had all taken time to express their personal feelings about the woman Kim was and how much she would be missed. Some people had written poems. A few detailed their final moments with Kim. Still others had written how Kim had touched their lives in some memorable way.

We will treasure these tributes forever.

Shortly after we received this book, a letter from Microsoft arrived, informing us: "During the unveiling of our new auditorium at our Mississauga office last week, we announced 'The Wiltshire Room' in dedication and memory of Kim." The letter continued, "Kim was recognized as a rising star in our organization. She was a warm and caring individual who touched everyone she met and worked with."

Kim was a warm, loving person and, we were discovering, the love she gave was returned by all who knew her.

I could not stand it that Kim was gone. For the next two months I couldn't function. I couldn't eat. I slept for days at a time; to be awake hurt too much. I couldn't face being a mom of just two. To make my heart complete, I needed all three of my daughters.

I couldn't deal with the loss and the all-encompassing pain, so I was put on medication and slept even more. I secluded myself in my bedroom. I had very little awareness of my surroundings. People telephoned. Some I talked to, some I didn't. Often, I just couldn't compose myself enough to speak in logical sentences.

How could this have happened to Kim when she loved life more than anyone else I knew? How could her life end when the promise of great things was at her fingertips?

About two weeks after the accident, we had to go to court. The individual who had caused the accident had been charged, and we needed to be there. As I looked at this person who had robbed Kim of her life, I can honestly say that, at this stage of my grief, I felt hatred. He was living. Kim was not.

I came home and headed for my bedroom. I started flinging books at the wall, every book I could find, as hard as I could. I didn't know what else to do. The pain was excruciating. I wanted someone to take it away.

We went to see about her headstone. All I could think was how wrong this was. We should be thinking about planning her wedding, not selecting a headstone to mark her grave. Once I returned home, I again retreated to my room, took my medication, and went to sleep.

During this initial stage of my grief, I have whole blocks of time that I cannot remember. I literally dropped out of life. To wake up was too painful because then I would have to face the day without Kim.

*My heartache was so intense I thought someone had taken a knife and thrust it into my chest.*

It was when the shock started to wear off, however, that the real pain began. My heartache was so intense I thought someone had taken a knife and thrust it into my chest. The pain was continuous and invaded everything I did or tried to do. On my stronger days, I made the effort to leave the safety of our home — to purchase everyday things we needed — but often returned empty handed. I felt suffocated by crowds of shoppers and couldn't breathe. My physician explained that these episodes were panic attacks. I had always been in control of my emotions, but I had never experienced a loss, certainly never a loss of this magnitude. I didn't know how to deal with the emotions I felt. I was a stranger to myself and thought I was going crazy.

My whole world changed the day I came face to face with the unexpected tragedy of Kim's death. How I perceived everything and everyone — my family, my home, my job, and my friends — changed. As the weeks passed and I had to accept the physical reality that Kim was gone, I began to question my entire belief system. My old values didn't fit or make sense anymore.

*I began to question my entire belief system. My old values didn't fit or make sense anymore.*

I would go to the cemetery everyday and talk to Kim. Was it possible she was listening? It gave me strength to believe she heard my cries, because the alternative was just too heartrending to think about. Was she lying in the ground or was she with God? Was she in some other world watching our tears, aware of our unabated sorrow without her?

In an attempt to find some answers to my questions, I began my journey into the Light, one that would take me through many highs and lows and much soul searching. It has not been an easy pilgrimage, but it has been an enlightening one.

My wish is that the ideas presented in this book bring some measure of solace and healing to others who have lost loved ones. May this book help you along your own personal journey for answers: Do we really have eternal life? Are we here to learn lessons and to help advance our souls? Do we survive death? Is it possible to contact our loved ones who have gone on to another realm of existence? Can we lift the veil that exists between our two worlds?

It is my hope that in sharing my journey of pain and enlightenment, you, too, may find comfort in your quest for the meaning of life and death. I will guide you through each stage of my incredible pilgrimage, one I began as a skeptic. I will describe the events that awakened me to the realization of this belief: When we leave this physical plane, we move on to another plane of existence.

As I fought my way from overwhelming grief to the renewing Light, I discovered reading books of a spiritual nature brought me some measure of comfort. It was my first step on a very long road to learning how to cope with my devastating loss. When I completed one book, I searched for another. As the famed theologian Teilhard de Chardin said, "...we are spiritual beings having a human experience." The meaning of these words was a common thread woven throughout the pages of every book I chose. As I progressed through my pilgrimage to the Light, opening to the miracles around me, I began to believe de Chardin's words to be profoundly true.

This is the story of my journey: *My Gift of Light.*

Chapter 2

# My Journey Begins

*May the God of hope fill you with*

*all the joy and peace in believing,*

*so that you will abound in hope. . .*

—Romans 15:13

**January 1999.** After losing Kim, I was afraid to live. I didn't know how I could survive without her; yet I was afraid to die because my other two daughters needed me.

The panic attacks kept me confined to the house. These attacks were a whole new experience for me. I didn't understand them. They made it extremely difficult for me to enter a store. Before going out, I would make a detailed list of all the items I required. Sometimes I was able to purchase what I wanted, but more often I would be in the middle of an aisle and suddenly feel a compulsion to leave. My heart pounding, I'd have a hard time catching my breath. When this happened I desperately needed to return to the sanctuary of my home.

When I was out of the house, I couldn't bear to see all the happy people. I was quick to notice that life for others didn't stop just because I had lost

Kim. It was unbearably painful for me to face the reality that their lives went on without skipping a beat. Only *our* lives were forever changed.

I felt like the entire world should be thunderously changed just as our world had been. How could life go on as if catastrophe had not struck? Nothing made sense any more, including the unpredictable onset of these panic attacks, which would hit without warning. Sometimes I didn't even answer the door. At the time, I wasn't aware of what was happening to me. Thanks to counseling, I eventually came to understand more about these sudden and debilitating attacks.

It had been two agonizing months since Kim had passed. To me, however, it felt as if time stood still. When you're in the grip of such pain, the mind seems to shut down.

❋ ❋ ❋

The first Christmas without Kim had come and gone. Normally, Christmas had always been a momentous time for the five of us. Each Christmas morning, all three girls would pile into bed with their dad and me. No one was allowed to go downstairs before waking us up. Each year, Doug and I would hear scurrying around as the girls woke each other then, in unison, jumped into our bed with excited anticipation. As the years passed and the girls grew, the five of us plus our dog Buddy didn't fit so comfortably in our bed, but we loved the fun of it anyway.

Now Kim was gone, nothing was the same, and I couldn't stand it.

*Only someone who has lost a child can fully understand the depth of this despair and its complex ramifications.*

My younger brother Randy had invited the family over for Christmas. Heavily medicated, I shuffled around his house like a zombie.

Only someone who has lost a child can fully understand the depth of this despair and its complex ramifications. Of course, each person grieves in his or her own unique way. Most, however, experience exhaustion, sleeplessness, panic, and inertia. They quarrel with partners and find horror —

and guilt — in laughter. Many of us who grieve feel powerless over our bodies and our feelings. I was definitely no exception.

Without realizing it, in a desperate effort to survive this crushing grief, I put up a lot of emotional walls and separated myself from the people I loved most. What I really craved was that my husband and two remaining daughters be immersed in this pain with me. If I could have locked them in the bedroom with me, I really believe I would have.

In retrospect, I realize how much I let them down and am so very sorry I was not able to be stronger for them. Doug, while engaged in his own struggle for survival, had to deal with so much alone. I am grateful he was there for Kerry and Kristy, because I was not. They not only lost their sister but also the mom who had always been there for them. My husband lost his partner in marriage. Today, I still deal with this reality and, undoubtedly, will regret it forever.

By the time I was ready to talk and cry with my family, I was hit with the awareness that they were not wanting or able to share their grief with me. I had barricaded myself inside my own little world and had ultimately created a rift I would have to work hard to repair. We all had changed. We were a family in pain — a family of four, not five.

I made a conscious decision to be present as much as possible when the girls were at home. I talked to Kristy about her final year at high school and helped her arrange to get a special letter written by her guidance counselor to send with her university applications. I tried to re-establish and repair our once close relationship. Doug and I began to worry about Kerry away at school. I called her more often — just to talk — and ask how she was doing. When she came home, I made myself more available. In between these times I would still retreat to my room. Sleep was my only break from the unbearable ache weighing down my heart.

The absence of Kim was evident everywhere. Everyday chores that used to be routine were now incredibly painful. Setting the table for four, not five, was something I was unable to do for a long time. When I'd see a certain food that only Kim would eat, I would suddenly realize I didn't need to buy it any more and the tears would come. I reeled around the house, a house that reminded me of Kim everywhere I looked. Each time I went upstairs, I passed her empty room. I'd think about cleaning the bathroom, but before I could get at the job, I would see something that had belonged to Kim sitting on the counter, and I would collapse in tears.

Everywhere I went and everything I did brought me back to the reality that Kim was not coming back to us.

It was at this time — mid January — that I received a telephone call from Heather. Her son Shaun had been Kim's boyfriend for about three years. During that time, Heather and her husband David had come to know and love Kim. When she called, Heather asked me if she could come over for a short visit. She arrived with a book in her hand titled, *Talking to Heaven*, by James Van Praagh. The author was a world-famous medium who claimed to be able to communicate with those who had died. The book had become a bestseller.

Heather softly assured me that she didn't want to upset me but hoped I might read it. The book had brought her some comfort. One of her neighbors had given it to her in hopes of helping her through some of her pain. By passing the book on, she wanted to do the same thing for me.

Over a cup of tea we talked about Kim and cried.

As soon as Heather left, I opened the book and began to read. Even though I had picked up a few other books, this extraordinary one really marked the start of my journey. As I pondered the information presented, I felt a glimmer of hope.

The author, James Van Praagh, conveyed the message that death is not the end. Our loved ones who have died are still very much around us. He explained that when we die we will be reunited with our loved ones who have passed before us.

I wanted to believe in such reunions. I needed to believe there were people who could communicate with Kim. I desperately needed to believe that Kim, even though she was gone from us, still existed somewhere and was okay. This book emphasized, for me, one central point: No one ever truly dies because life is eternal.

I telephoned Heather and expressed my gratitude for both the book and the visit. We began to spend more time together and had many discussions about the various books I was reading. Heather would listen and let me ramble on about some interesting point I had discovered in this book or that one. She helped me more than she realized just by listening and letting me pour my heart out about Kim. For that I am eternally grateful.

*I desperately needed to believe that Kim, even though she was gone from us, still existed somewhere and was okay.*

Prior to Kim's passing, I had seen a woman named Sylvia Browne on television. What she had to say interested me. She was introduced as a clairvoyant who had used her "gift" to aid the police in solving missing person cases.

Now I had an urgency to find out more about what she did. I quickly finished the Van Praagh book and immediately went to the bookstore in search of others. I picked up Sylvia Browne's book titled, *Adventures of a Psychic.* As I wandered through the bookstore, I noticed one written by George Anderson, another renowned medium. His book, *Lessons From the Light: Extraordinary Messages of Comfort and Hope from the Other Side*, looked like another book I should read.

Anderson's book proved to be quite thought provoking. As I read his background, I learned that for 25 years George Anderson had worked with bereaved families to facilitate communication with their loved ones on the other side. He had the support of many professionals in both medical and scientific fields. Doctors — and others — considered George to have a true and genuine method of communication with souls in the afterlife.

Reading now filled my days. I located another book about George Anderson himself entitled, *We Don't Die: George Anderson's Conversations with the Other Side,* written by Joel Martin and Patricia Romanowski. I felt drawn to a second book written by Joel Martin: *We Are Not Forgotten.* I went to the local library to see what other books were available on the subject of life after death. As I visited bookstores in and around my area, I became like a sponge trying to absorb the information contained within the pages of these books.

One afternoon I happened to catch Sylvia Browne on the Montel Williams television show. I sat riveted to the set. This day she was talking about the presence of angels around us. Her comments on this show piqued my interest to read more on the subject of angels, but that agenda item would have to be placed on hold for a while.

Sylvia Browne, George Anderson, James Van Praagh, and a young, up-and-coming John Edward all claimed to communicate with loved ones who had passed on. This was definitely my focus at the present time. I thirsted for knowledge and understanding about this form of communication. My search for answers became my lifeline.

My sister-in-law Ruth took on a major role in my journey. Intrigued by my spiritual quest, Ruth called to tell me that James Van Praagh was going to be a televised guest on *Larry King Live* that evening. I watched in wonder as he delivered messages to callers from their loved ones who had passed on to what they called "the other side." He gave details about their loved ones to validate who was "coming through" or communicating with him. Sometimes the validation came in the form of a name or information on how they passed. Sometimes he gave information about another member of the family they wished to say hello to. He explained that he was just a vessel for the souls to come through.

For the entire hour, I repeatedly hit the re-dial button of the telephone trying desperately to get through. I was more than a little disappointed as the end of the hour approached and I realized that I would not get a reading. It did help, however, to be able to watch others receive the messages they needed so much.

Shortly after this, John Edward, who wrote the book *One Last Time*, was a guest on another TV talk show. He delivered spontaneous messages to members of the audience. I stared in fascination as he startled a young lady in the audience with a detailed message from her father. As I watched her break into tears, I shed some of my own and wondered how I would be able to arrange a reading with this remarkable man. When he delivered a message to a family who had lost their son, I felt compelled to contact a medium.

While I tried to figure out how to accomplish this connection, I wondered what my husband and daughters would think. How could I explain to them what I wanted to do? I desperately needed some kind of sign or message from Kim.

Our child was not supposed to die. I was supposed to die first. That is the natural order of life and death, the way it is supposed to be. I needed to know why this natural order had been turned upside down!

Toward the end of January, I received a call from my good friend, Judy Hunt. I had known Judy and her husband Gary since Kim was a baby. They had rented the basement apartment in our house almost two decades earlier. Judy was pregnant when they moved in downstairs and Kim was just a baby, so the two of us easily bonded. We often spent time in the backyard that first summer getting to know each other. Our connection remained strong over the years.

The January afternoon Judy called was a particularly difficult day for me. I was crying when I picked up the phone. Judy explained that she had a strong impulse to call me at that specific time. She urged me to sit down because she had something important to tell me.

My friend began by emphasizing that she was a confirmed believer in heaven and angels. She revealed she had a strong belief that each of us had a mission to complete here on earth, and, when our lessons were over, we returned to our true home on the other side. Since she was about nine or ten years old, she had an inner feeling that this was true. Her mother, she explained, had a near-death experience many years earlier. As soon as Judy matured and could better understand, her mom told her about the wondrous experience.

As I sat and listened attentively to the details of her mom's illness that caused her to have this out-of-body experience, I became hopeful. What I was reading might really be true! I knew Judy, and I knew her mother, Pat. These weren't just strangers describing an extraordinary experience. They were friends I had known for years, people I knew to be totally credible.

Somewhere along my journey I read that earth angels are beautiful people who touch our souls and make us better people just because they are part of our lives. For me, Judy Hunt is one of those earth angels. This beautiful friend handed me a lifeline of hope at a time when I didn't feel I would ever be hopeful again.

I wanted to know why she had never shared her spiritual beliefs with me in all the years we had known each other. Judy's explanation was that she never felt the necessity to discuss her beliefs with me before this. She felt confident now was the perfect time to tell her story and said she hoped it would help me cope with Kim's death. She kept assuring me that Kim was just fine and was looking down on all of us, trying to help us through the pain of her loss.

Judy definitely was a believer in the afterlife.

Judy and I started discussing some of the spiritual beliefs that I was beginning to open up to since Kim's passing. She helped me develop some perspective on the startling information I was getting from books and television programs. I had read about those who found themselves floating out of their bodies during near-death experiences. Now I personally knew someone who had done just that!

*At that time, I didn't have many friends with whom I could discuss spiritual issues.*

At that time, I didn't have many friends with whom I could discuss spiritual issues. I was hungry for such conversations. Fortunately, this was only the first of many discussions Judy and I were to have on the subject. From that day on, Judy encouraged me to talk about Kim, share my grief, and continue my pilgrimage to spiritual awareness.

One day while standing in my kitchen, I felt the sudden urge to go and visit my grandmother. Although I wasn't sure I was strong enough to drive the 45 minutes it took to get there, Doug encouraged me to go. He knew we had always been close. I had not seen Grandma since Kim's funeral.

My grandmother Gladys was a unique lady. She was the only spiritual person I knew as I was growing up. For years, Grandma had given psychic readings to friends and family members. She used regular playing cards with a big "G" for Gladys on them. I didn't understand how she derived information from the cards, but I was pretty amazed, especially when she gave an accurate reading to one of my friends whom she did not know. In addition to doing readings, Grandma would tell us about dreams in which she said she would have visitations from loved ones who had passed away. She believed in angels, and she believed in God.

I didn't understand this part of her life, but I loved her. Over the years, I sometimes felt that we humored Grandma and her eccentricities. Now, of course, I was prepared to see her in a different light.

I really needed to talk to her! Grandma, however, had suffered a recent stroke, and communicating with her was often difficult if not impossible. Nonetheless, I drove down to see her. She recognized me, and we talked about how she was doing. It was sad to see her mouth droop on one side and hear her struggle for words. I asked if she remembered Kim had died, and she quickly responded, "Hazel [her older sister who had died a few years earlier] and Kim came and sat at the end of my bed and told me that they were both okay. Kim told me to tell you she was fine."

I honestly didn't believe her, even though I had started to open to the possibility that this sort of visitation could happen. After all, such confirmation was one of the reasons I had come. Yet my skepticism kicked in. Was Grandma just trying to make me feel better?

Grandma fell asleep exhausted, and I was left alone to wonder. I tiptoed out of her room, leaned against a wall and cried because I so much wanted her words to be true. My emotional meltdown left me shaken. I tried to calm myself with a cup of coffee and regain my composure before I felt competent to drive home.

As I continued to investigate the possibility of an afterlife, my grandmother's words echoed in my ears. I struggled with the probability that my family and friends would think my grief had sent me over the edge into irrationality. Nonetheless, my search for Kim and my connection to her had become my top priority.

I knew I had to continue.

Besides the message given to me by my grandmother, I had other reasons to persevere on my quest for spiritual understanding. I vividly recalled that about an hour before the accident on that fateful evening when Kim died, I had experienced a deep sense of dread. I began to feel sick and, by about 8:00 p.m., had to lie down and close out the world. Fully clothed, I stretched out on top of my bed and shut my eyes. That is where I was when I heard the loud knock of the police officer at our door. I intuitively knew without consciously knowing that something had radically changed in my world.

Words defy explanation of the heaviness I felt and the panic that welled up from deep within me when I heard the incomprehensible news. Months later, here I was, still fighting for equilibrium and answers to the unanswerable. My quest just had to continue.

The next book I was drawn to read was John Edward's, *One Last Time*. I was fascinated by his story. When I discovered he was from New York, which was not that far from us, I wondered how I could get a reading. It was a secret mission, however, and I was very hesitant to tell others what I was trying to accomplish.

I didn't yet realize that the solution to my determination to find a credible medium was already staring me in the face: computer technology.

❋ ❋ ❋

**February 1999.** Early in the month I sat myself down in front of our computer. I had, of course, worked with word processing programs to type letters and such, but now I was venturing into the world of the Internet. What especially excited me was finding a website listed in the back of John Edward's book.

It was thanks to Kim that I was even able to go online. Kim, as a business student, had routinely carried her own laptop computer and, with her connections to Microsoft, often laughed and teased us to "get with the program" and get hooked up with an Internet service provider. Because our computer was an older model, it wasn't ready for Internet usage. Besides, the Internet was not something Doug and I ever felt we needed. But because of Kim's insistence, we had taken our computer to a local company to see what it required in order for us to go online. The date was October 23. We arranged to pick up our upgraded computer at 6:00 p.m. on October 27, only a few hours before Kim's accident.

While we were driving home with the computer, my feelings of heaviness began. I remember I snapped at Doug, and he asked me what was wrong. I responded that I wasn't feeling well and just wanted to get home. By the time we arrived home, I was feeling very ill. Neither of us knew that in the next few hours our safe, ordered world would disappear forever.

Now, four months later, I realized that were it not for Kim's insistence, I would not be sitting in front of the computer, surfing the web, looking at John Edward's website, and reading about what to expect during a reading. Posted on this website were comments by people who had read his book *One Last Time*. I spent several minutes poring over their thoughts about his book.

Then I saw it. Wow! An email address was staring back at me. Was I brave enough to actually send an email to him? I worried about being disappointed if Kim did not come through during any reading I might have. My concern was so great that I could not bring myself to send an email and make contact. I didn't realize it at the time, but I was still so rocked by grief that I simply could not think anything through in a logical manner. I was confused and felt utterly alone. I would have to decide what to do — later.

In the meantime, while on John Edward's website, I went onto a chat line for the first time in my life. I followed the instructions, hesitated for a moment when they asked me for my name, then typed in the fake name "Holly." I did not feel comfortable using my own name, and the name

Holly just popped into my head. I figured it was as good as any.

So there I was being welcomed into this chatroom as Holly. I sat back quietly at first, reading the dialogue that was taking place. I quickly became aware I had a strong desire to actively participate in the discussion. I began to ask questions about some of the spiritual concepts I had read about. These strangers from different parts of the world were patient with me as I asked my questions. I was told that this was a place where people come together to share their spiritual beliefs as well as their feelings of grief after suffering the loss of a loved one. We were all there to help each other.

I could have listened for hours to these wonderful strangers. Some were still searching for answers, while others, already believers in the afterlife, imparted both their wisdom and their sympathy. Eventually, as heartening as it was, I became emotionally drained, said goodbye, and signed myself off, promising to return. Afterward I reflected on the experience. Blessedly, I had found a place where I felt comfortable and could ask questions from the privacy of my own home — the safest of all venues in which to continue my search.

During subsequent visits to the website chatroom, I met and talked with other bereaved parents. They talked about their deceased children, sharing the events that had charted their own routes to spiritual awakening. I read their comments and listened quietly with tears streaming down my cheeks.

*Many. . . had experienced similar premonitions before their children had passed.*

Finally, I no longer felt so alone. I began typing. I had so much to say, but I'm not sure I made a lot of sense. I began to describe for this group of strangers my sudden and tragic loss of Kim. I took a leap of faith and revealed the feeling of dread I experienced before being informed about the accident and how this was a catalyst for my spiritual quest. Responses came flooding back. They understood exactly what I was saying, since many of them had experienced similar premonitions before their children had passed.

I sat glued to the computer screen, reading a litany of personal tragedies.

There are two I remember most vividly. A gentleman told how his seven-year-old son came up to him one day and frankly announced he would never reach nine years of age so he wanted a big party for his eighth birthday. Sadly, the little boy was killed when a car in their neighborhood struck his bicycle. Just as he predicted, he was only eight years old. The father didn't know what to do after the death of his son, and so, with his son's prophetic words ringing in his ears, he began his own quest for answers.

A mother who had lost her son when he was in his early twenties, like my daughter, explained that her son had come over one afternoon just to say he loved her. She thought at the time how nice a gesture this was but recognized it as uncharacteristic of him. Usually, he arrived with his arms full of laundry or in search of a home-cooked meal. But not this day. Unfortunately, this mission of love was the last time she saw him alive. Inexplicably, he went missing. It was a few days before he was found. He had slipped, fallen into a pond, and drowned.

Through my tears I asked, "Could Kim have known she was going to die?" A consensus came back to me. "Yes, her soul knew." This was an emotional experience for me. I was completely exhausted and needed to think about everything I had just learned. I signed off and went to bed, but it was hours later before I fell asleep.

I was surprised and thrilled that bereaved parents from all over the world were using the Internet to connect with each other. Now I was a part of that group. Talking on the Internet to people who believed in an afterlife, and the connection we can have to it, brought me a great sense of calmness and some much-needed peace. I was able to share the pain of losing Kim and the extreme anger I felt about the accident. This wonderful band of so-called strangers validated my sense of loss, my horrid feelings. They opened me up to the idea that Kim was still very much around me. When I cried, which seemed constant, my newfound Internet friends comforted me.

I spent hours — probably too many hours — listening and conversing with my new chatroom buddies. I continued to use the pseudonym of Holly when I signed on and was happy with my new identity. As I continued to listen to their stories of loss and their own spiritual awakenings, I realized I had an urgent need to believe, with confidence, that Kim still existed "somewhere" even if she couldn't be with us physically.

All my alone time was spent either on the Internet or reading something of a spiritual nature. The chatroom I used most often was linked to the John Edward web page, but it was actually a site set up by Bill and Judy Guggenheim, authors of *Hello From Heaven.*

When I first saw the book title on their website, I felt I should read it. I found the book to be filled with a series of firsthand accounts from people who believed a deceased loved one had contacted them. These contacts were called ADCs by the authors, short for "After-Death Communications."

Bill and Judy Guggenheim had interviewed 2,000 people from across the United States and Canada and published a variety of these true accounts in their book. I loved reading about how others were able to sense, feel, smell, and sometimes receive physical signs from their deceased loved ones. As other bereaved parents described details of their personal ADCs, I desperately wanted at least one of my own.

The advantage of a chatroom is your ability to ask questions. When I finished reading *Hello From Heaven*, I went online to find the site extra busy that evening. How, I wanted to know, does someone open to signs from those we love who are on the other side? I really opened up a door to a major discussion when I asked if anyone logged on that night had experienced an ADC after the loss of his or her loved one. I wondered if Kim had given me a sign and, blind with grief, I had missed it.

I started by asking Kim to give me a sign I could understand.

According to Judy and Bill Guggenheim's website, signs from the other side or ADCs are spontaneous and direct communications that may occur anytime and anywhere, but no third parties such as psychics, mediums, or hypnotists are involved.

Based upon their research, the most frequent types of after-death communication people report having with their deceased loved ones are sensing a presence, hearing a voice, feeling a touch, smelling a fragrance, visual experiences and visions, and electronic communication that can include telephone calls and/or physical phenomena like electric lights and appliances being turned on and off. Symbolic ADCs include the meaningful appearance of butterflies, rainbows, birds, animals, flowers, and a variety of inanimate objects such as coins and pictures.

According to the Guggenheims' research, the purpose of these visits and signs by those who have died is to offer comfort, reassurance, and hope to their loved ones. According to the authors, ADCs confirm that "life and love are eternal."

I wanted my own personal confirmation from Kim.

I had heard that pets sometimes give us signs when our loved ones are around. Kim had dearly loved our dog Buddy whom we had gotten as a pup 14 years earlier. I started watching Buddy to see if there was any significant shift in his behavior at various times. While Kim had been away at school the last three years, Buddy had avoided her room except when she was home. He had gotten out of the habit of sleeping on Kim's bed and instead would join one of the other girls who was home.

Strangely, since Kim's passing, I had noticed how often he tried to get into her bedroom. Was it really possible that Buddy could see Kim or feel her presence? I watched him look past me sometimes and wondered. At times Buddy seemed to be "licking the air," yet according to the naked eye, no one was there.

I walked around the house talking incessantly to Kim. Since I had not yet returned to work and was accustomed to spending my days home alone, I was free to look for signs from Kim. Every time a light flickered, I would look around and wonder if Kim was responsible. If the phone would ring and no one appeared to be on the other end of the line, I felt this could be my sign. I sometimes thought I might drive myself insane. Every time I got discouraged, each time my doubting mind intervened, I would remember that others had received messages of love from their children on the other side.

I deserved one of my own.

I was constantly being challenged through the books I was reading to re-examine my past beliefs. Could I free myself from my old belief system? I realized our belief systems create the way we see the world. Mine, like most people's, was deeply rooted, created by past relationships and experiences. Although I was discovering it was not an easy task to free myself from these old agnostic beliefs, I strongly felt I must. Because past views no longer fit, I made the conscious choice to remain open to new concepts and ideas. Kim's passing demanded a new way of looking at life. My conscious choice to remain open brought with it a new feeling of hope.

It was the middle of February when an astonishing occurrence took place that led me to believe Kim may have given me her first sign, or at least the first sign I recognized. I was on the Internet with one of my new friends, Abby, a bereaved parent herself. She told me I could create a memorial in honor of Kim and have it posted on a web page for people to visit. I was such an Internet novice and my grief was still so intense that I felt overwhelmed by the notion of doing this. How would I ever adequately describe the person Kim was? I wondered what kind of things others included in their memorials and felt the urge to have a look at some. Abby was happy to direct me to one of these sites.

This particular site was set up alphabetically. One could click on any letter in the alphabet and a series of names would appear. I recall feeling shocked and saddened at how many memorials were listed at this one site alone. Looking at the letters highlighted on the web page, without giving it a second thought, I automatically went to the "W" and scanned the list for girls' names. I followed the instructions and instantly was staring at a memorial for a young lady named Kandi Willis Webb. As I quickly scanned the memorial, I was stunned by what I read. I couldn't breathe as I stared at the dates before my eyes. This young lady was born on March 15, 1967, and died on October 27, 1988.

My mind raced and I recall thinking, this is not possible! Kim was born on March 15, 1976, and died on October 27, 1998. Although the birth and death years were different, dates for the month and day were identical!

I sat mesmerized, staring at the computer screen. My mind tried to comprehend what I was looking at. I must have re-read those dates at least a hundred times. One date coinciding exactly with Kim's could be a coincidence, my logical mind told me, but *both* of the dates? Suddenly I realized another fact. Both Kim and Kandi had the same initials. They were both "K.W." This fact was not nearly as significant as the corresponding dates, but it sent my mind reeling once again.

One of my first thoughts after staring at this memorial was how would I be able to find out more about Kandi? Could I contact her mom? Would she want to hear from me? After all, Kandi had passed in 1988, almost 11 years earlier. Nowhere on this memorial was there a contact number or even an email address to write to her family. I just kept staring at those dates, my mind unable to embrace this as a mere coincidence. Afraid I might not remember how to find this memorial again, I decided to print it out and put it away for safekeeping. I was determined that someday I would find a way to make a connection with Kandi's mom.

*This was just the first of a string of mystifying events that I now call "my miracles."*

Even in this early stage of my spiritual journey, I realized this had to be more than just a coincidence. Winning the lottery was more probable than my randomly clicking on the name of a girl with identical birth and death dates and initials to Kim. I marveled at the fact that I had chosen to open this particular memorial first — out of the hundreds that were listed. Maybe I was guided to open it up. Maybe Kim had her hand in this. Well, if Kim helped me to do this, then I would place my faith in the fact that one day Kim would help me find a way to connect to Kandi's family.

This was just the first of a string of mystifying events that I now call "my miracles." By definition, miracles are events that occur in ways contrary to what we would expect based on our own experiences and are inexplicable using the known laws of nature. Miracles were the perfect description of the experiences that were beginning to happen around me. Yet it wasn't until over a year later, through another miraculous event, that I had my first contact with Kandi's mom, Sharon.

Toward the end of February, Doug and I decided to contact Bereaved

Families of Ontario. As important as my spiritual quest had become, we as a couple needed to share our feelings with others who were grieving the loss of a child. The closest office was about a half-hour away. We arranged a meeting with a husband and wife who volunteered their time to help the newly bereaved. They also had lost their daughter, some years earlier. We shared our mutual losses, talked about our girls, and Doug and I learned a little about the organization.

I urgently needed to spend time with other parents who had lost a child. They were the only ones who could understand the depth of our loss. I reasoned, if I was able to reason at all, that I would not have to act "normal" with them but could display my feelings and tears honestly. Toward the end of the meeting, we were informed that all the groups for bereaved parents had already begun but they would put our names on the list for the next group that would start. Disappointed and heartbroken, we went home to wait for their call.

In the meantime, I became aware that it was necessary for me to seek professional help to cope with Kim's death. I missed Kim so desperately that some days I thought I would not survive the pain. It was a deep, physical ache that debilitated me. I needed to scream and yell. My husband and daughters had their own grief to deal with. But I needed to deal with mine, so I set up an appointment with a local psychiatrist. After the first few visits, I felt comfortable enough with him to talk about the spiritual journey I had begun.

When I came for my first appointment, I met the psychiatrist's wife, Bonnie, who helped run the office for him and scheduled his appointments. This lovely and very spiritual lady entered my life just at the point when I was wondering what other avenues I might take to further my spiritual journey. I felt an instant connection to Bonnie, as if I had known her for years. She later shared, as we became friends, that she felt the same immediate connection. Was it a coincidence that I met Bonnie when I did or was it pre-destined? Bonnie and I talked about this over coffee more than once as we got to know each other better.

It was the end of February when Bonnie suggested I make an appointment with a spiritual healer she knew. Her name was Shawna Ross. I wasn't even sure what a spiritual healer did. My spiritual knowledge consisted mostly of what I had read and what others had expressed to me in the chatrooms. Bonnie and I talked about what I could expect. It sounded pretty bizarre to me, but I knew I needed healing — any kind of healing. I agreed to make an appointment.

It was the last day of February when I found myself sitting in a pleasant room with a couch on one side and what looked like a type of massage table on the other. Some crystals lay on a shelf, and the room was filled with the heady smell of incense. Shawna and I talked for a few minutes as she helped make me feel comfortable. She knew I had lost my daughter because I had told her when I made the appointment. As she talked and I tried to comprehend what Shawna was explaining to me, I noticed that her eyes seemed to stare past me and around me. When I asked her about this, she quietly responded, "I am looking at your energy field, and it appears to be very greatly depleted." She reported she would work on that first. She said something about an aura around me and energy points called "chakras." Since I had no previous exposure to these terms, none of it really registered with me at the time.

I stood like a puppet in front of her as she worked on me. I didn't have the strength to question what she was doing. I just let it happen. During my two-and-a-half-hour session, Shawna used a few different healing methods on me, explaining the significance of each as she went along.

While she worked on me, she delivered a message from one of my spiritual guides and shocked me with the information that the guide's name was Holly — the alias I used in the chatroom! The healer said my guide was telling her I had the ability to put one foot into the spirit world and keep one foot here on planet earth if I chose to. I thought that was interesting but wondered what it meant. All I really wanted to do was connect to Kim in whatever way I could. Since I didn't know about spirit guides at this point, I decided to read up on this subject when I got home.

I tried very hard to stay focused on what Shawna explained to me during the healing. The experience was moving and cathartic, and I shed many tears that morning. Then, almost in a whisper, Shawna revealed the presence of a young woman who wore her hair in a ponytail. "She is in the room with us."

As she continued her healing, in a quiet voice Shawna described Kim bouncing up and down on a bed. "Her legs are crossed because she wants me to hurry up. She says she can't wait all day to talk to you."

I stared at her, dumbfounded. That was so much like Kim! She remarked that Kim was throwing colors at me to try to speed up the process. Again, I smiled through my tears.

It was her description of Kim hopping off the bed and doing a little dance that really got my tears and laughter flowing. Suddenly, she halted the healing and fixed her eyes to my left. She described a special, unique dance move, one that only Kim was known to do, a movement Kim's family and friends had always teased her about. Somehow, the dance got labeled the "running man," no doubt from the ridiculous way Kim flailed her legs and arms around when she was doing it.

This was Kim for sure!

How could she possibly know this unless Kim really was there? I wondered if Shawna could see her. I instantly swiveled around to look where she was gazing, but I could not see Kim, only an empty room behind me. Turning back to Shawna, tears streaming down my cheeks, I stared at her. She then lifted one arm and flipped her hand: "Poof, and now she is gone."

Shawna reassured me that Kim was not far away. She continued the healing session for another hour or so. At the conclusion of the morning, Shawna took the time to explain the benefits of spiritual healing.

She explained to me that spiritual healing works on mind, body, and spirit. Healers believe that in order to maintain good health, all of these must work in harmony. Understanding more about this mind, body, and spirit balance helps one to be more receptive to the unseen energy around us. Shawna emphasized the importance of people taking responsibility for their own healing and that energy work can be a catalyst to be able to feel and sense those on the other side.

My mind raced as I drove home. I didn't understand much of what happened to me that morning, but I tried to absorb what I did understand. I was anxious to arrive home so I could write down all that happened. I urgently needed to get in touch with Bonnie, my spiritual confidant.

*This. . . planted a significant seed of hope that Kim still existed, that we could still communicate, and that all was not lost after all. This glorious hope began to grow in the darkest despair.*

When I got home, I immediately locked myself in my bedroom and meticulously recorded all the information I could remember and the messages I received from Kim and my guide, Holly. Because I was such an emotional mess at this time, I felt it was essential to record everything I experienced as soon as possible. I didn't want to risk forgetting even the smallest detail. The healing session that morning and the messages I received had planted a significant seed of hope that Kim still existed, that we could still communicate, and that all was not lost after all. This glorious hope began to grow within my darkest despair.

Once I finished writing, I ran to the phone to call Bonnie. I had to know if she had told Shawna any details about Kim. I still didn't know Bonnie all that well and wondered if she would do that. The skeptic in me was creeping in. I wanted to ask her what, if anything, she had told Shawna. I wanted to feel confident that the information relayed to me was authentically coming from Kim.

In retrospect, I realize I really wasn't thinking clearly because there actually was no way Bonnie could know those things about Kim — or the significance of the name Holly. I had never told her any of the details.

Bonnie and I met over coffee that afternoon and discussed my healing session. She reassured me she had merely set up the appointment and had not told her friend anything about Kim, my loss, or me. With this out of the way, she encouraged me to relate the events that had taken place in the healing room that morning.

Over time our friendship grew, and Bonnie, with her quiet wisdom and virtuous nature, became one of my confidants and a mentor. I learned I could trust that whatever I said to Bonnie would remain confidential between the two of us.

I had come to a place in my spiritual journey where I sensed it was essential to surround myself with people who had a true belief in the existence of "the other side." Bonnie was one of these people. She would listen quietly as I poured out my feelings of loss and pain and then, in my calmer moments, discuss with me some new spiritual concept I was trying to understand. Because Bonnie played an intrinsic part in my awakening to the spiritual beliefs I presently hold, she will always remain one of my dearest friends.

By this point, I felt it was time to share with Doug what had happened at Shawna's. I was timid and a bit nervous about telling him I went to a healer. I wasn't sure about it myself, so how could I expect Doug to understand? Sitting down together that evening, I eased into the topic and finally described the experience.

Doug definitely had his reservations and openly expressed his opinion that maybe I had made more out of the messages than they merited. How could I blame him? I would have thought the same thing. But I knew deep within my soul that it had really happened. Kim had, almost certainly, made contact with me.

❊ ❊ ❊

**March 1999.** After the spiritual contact Shawna received from Kim during my healing session, I was ready to believe that connecting with Kim might be possible. I recall going into Kim's bedroom, sitting on her bed, and crying out to her silently, "Okay Kim, if this is true, if you exist, I need proof!" I walked around the house repeating these words over and over, day after day. I asked Kim to give me some message that would prove without a doubt that she was still around us.

This was the month that I began, thanks to my husband's suggestion, to meticulously record every step of my miraculous spiritual pilgrimage.

March was also the month that Kim would have turned 23. Her birthday was fast approaching and with it my ever increasing need to hear from her. I frantically pleaded with her, "Please let me know before your birthday that you are okay." I repeated this silent plea over and over while I waited to see if Kim would send me another "miracle."

I spent a considerable amount of time at Kim's gravesite, sitting quietly on the still-brown grass, talking to her about many different things. I asked her to watch over her father and sisters. I needed to feel they would remain healthy and safe. I asked her to help me feel confident that something beyond our present awareness exists so I would know she was safe.

Reading about it was not good enough. I needed to receive something tangible to strengthen the spiritual beliefs I was trying so desperately to understand and embrace.

Despite my having embarked on this spiritual journey, my intense pain and inconsolable grief following Kim's passing remained unrelenting. I struggled to get out of bed each morning. I often wanted to be alone. Solitude gave me time to read then reflect on the information. For the first time in my life, I couldn't handle being around people. I felt panic set in when everyone was "acting normal." I was a stranger to my family and myself. My grief had immobilized me in so many ways that I had distanced myself from the family I loved so much. Now I was beginning to feel the urge to draw family and friends in closer, but this urge was counter-balanced by many complex, unfamiliar emotions. Everything was push/pull in my world; nothing in my life made sense or seemed to fit any more.

I had a small, select group of family and friends who allowed me to share my spiritual awakening with them, for which I will be eternally grateful. I would have been quite easily discouraged without these special people. They had faith in me when I didn't always have faith in myself. This poem captures my feelings about these wonderfully supportive people.

SOME PEOPLE

*Some people come into our lives and quickly go.*

*Some people move our souls to dance.*

*They awaken us to understanding*

*with the passing whisper of their wisdom.*

*Some people make the sky more beautiful to gaze upon.*

*They stay in our lives for awhile, leave footprints*

*on our hearts, and we are*

*never, ever the same.*

—Flavia Weedn

*(© Weedn Family Trust. Reprinted with permission)*

My sisters-in-law, Carolyn and Ruth, encouraged me on my quest. Judy Hunt, my long-time friend who shared her mother's near-death experience with me, was another. Bonnie, my newest friend and mentor, was yet another. Their support gave me hope and solace.

There was no kinder, more compassionate friend to me since the tragic death of Kim than Judy Piers. She became an acquaintance of mine when Kim had dated her son Mike while she was in high school. Although the romance had ended years before, Kim had remained close to the entire family. Everyone in the Piers family was devastated over Kim's death. Just days after Kim's passing, Judy wrote some of her fondest remembrances of Kim — sharing some of Kim's antics in the form of one-liners — and dropped it by for us to have. The depth of Judy's feelings for Kim was evident on those pages. They made me both laugh and cry as I sat quietly reading through the memories.

Judy encouraged me to call her anytime and assured me that she would do whatever she could to help. I will never know how she was able to listen to my anguished cries and handle my incredible pain, but I know she is the person who saved me when I wasn't sure I wanted to be saved.

When I didn't know how I would handle another moment, I left the house and walked. As fall had turned into winter, I ventured out, often without a hat or gloves, to walk and walk. Then I would waken from my dazed state and realize that I had nowhere to go. It was at those times that I would call Judy who would, without asking any questions, hop into her car and come to get me.

During one of these times, Judy asked me where I wanted her to take me, and I just shrugged my shoulders. She drove me to her home, ushered me into her den and shut the door. No longer alone, I vented my anguished heartache safely, away from my family. Petrified to show my daughters and husband the magnitude of pain I suffered, for fear of distancing myself from them even more, I had bottled it up. Judy listened, comforted me, and cried with me as I released some of the pressure built up inside.

If a week would go by and I had not called her, Judy would phone to see how I was doing. She seemed to sense when I needed her to call. We spent more and more time together reminiscing about Kim. Naturally, as I began my spiritual awakening, I shared that with her, too. At the outset, I wasn't sure whether or not Judy might think my trying to find Kim was just plain crazy, but she sat silently and listened as I related some of the intriguing events that happened.

I continued to find great comfort talking to my new chatroom friends, too. My own beliefs were often challenged as I sat at my computer tuning into discussions on some aspect of spirituality. Angels were often discussed. One evening I observed three different people discussing what they felt was a personal experience with an angel. Two of them expressed the belief that an angel warned them of an upcoming danger, saving their lives. Sometimes what I heard angered me. "Where was Kim's angel?" I thought mournfully. "Why didn't an angel save her life?"

On the evening of March 9, I entered the chatroom once again. The discussion topic was "automatic writing." My curiosity turned to intense interest as I heard that some people had experienced success connecting to loved ones on the other side through this form of communication. They discussed the automatic writing technique and how it was accomplished. Although I was somewhat apprehensive, I decided to give automatic writing a try. As crazy as it sounded, I had nothing to lose and everything to gain if I was successful.

On March 10, 1999, I let go of my fear, went into Kim's bedroom with paper and pen, and sat on her bed. "Okay, Kim," I pleaded with her, "write to me." I sat there feeling quite out of my element. Quickly my intellect took over and I convinced myself that I had really gone too far this time. Dropping my notepad and pen, I shuffled downstairs to let Doug know that nothing had happened. Of course nothing happened, I thought to myself, I didn't give the process, or Kim, a chance before I retreated.

Despite such a dismal outcome on my first attempt, Doug encouraged me to give it another try. For several nights, for about 20 minutes each session, I would sit in Kim's bedroom hoping to receive some written communication from Kim while struggling to keep my skepticism out of the way.

As mid-March arrived, I felt a surge of panic as I waited for some "miracle" that I would recognize as a message from Kim. On March 14, one day before Kim's birthday, I drove to the cemetery, blanket in hand, to sit there for a while. I had no idea I was about to have an experience that would bring me one step closer to believing that Kim was reaching out from wherever she was to give me the message that she was indeed okay and lived on.

As I parked the car, I noticed a lady I did not know placing flowers on Kim's grave. She stood up as I approached, and we introduced ourselves. Her name was Susan and she was bringing flowers from her daughter, a friend of Kim's, who was away at school and had asked her mother to visit the cemetery because she would be unable to come herself. Susan asked if I would consider having a cup of tea with her, as she lived only a few houses up the street. I declined at first, wanting to be alone with my own sorrow. As Susan took a few steps to leave, suddenly she turned back. It was obvious she had something she needed to say.

"I'm sorry," she murmured. "I don't mean to intrude, but if you would like to change your mind, I would love for you to come for that cup of tea. I will go home now and put the kettle on. Come at your leisure."

One glance at Susan as she took another step toward me persuaded me that I would feel comfortable with her. I decided to accept her offer. Reflecting back on that afternoon, I am so grateful Susan persisted.

"I have a friend who is a medium," Susan said without warning as she poured tea. "You know, a medium is someone who gets messages from those on the other side. I will call her, if you like."

Dumbfounded, I stared at her, not saying a word. Susan walked around the kitchen table and set down her steaming cup of tea. I could tell she was waiting for a reply. I don't recollect if I said anything at all, but I must have nodded my head because I watched Susan walk over to the phone and dial a number. My heart pounded and my mind raced as it became filled with a jumble of thoughts. I was pulled abruptly back from my reverie when I heard Susan say into the phone, "We will see you here shortly."

Within a half-hour of arriving at Susan's door, I was sitting in front of her friend Carol, who quickly started to relay messages from spirit to me. She began by saying a young female was around us and wasn't alone. I replied that my daughter had died and said, "Her name is Kim."

Carol continued: "Kim appears to be with an older lady. They are very close on the other side and are standing side by side."

I mumbled that I didn't know who this woman could be.

Carol proceeded to give me other snippets of information, which included the observation that Kim had a big smile and shoulder-length hair. The messages continued: "Kim had a bubbly personality and liked being busy. She wants to say hello to a sister. She liked school and loved learning. She is going to school on the other side."

Everything she was saying made sense, but nothing up to that point in the session really stuck out as positive proof that this woman was receiving messages from my Kim.

Then it came. "The lady with her might be a Rita or have a name similar to that. Would you know who that is?"

I was stunned. My favorite aunt, who had passed the year Kim was born, was named Rita. Kim was only three months old when Aunt Rita died quite unexpectedly. I had always felt sad that Kim had never met her.

I shared this information with Carol. Now I was sitting on the edge of my chair, hanging onto her every word.

She continued: "Kim is telling me she got you here today and you know it." Her final words to me were, "Tell Mom I am okay because she needs to hear that today!"

*Miracles really do happen! I received what I had pleaded for — a message from Kim before her birthday, saying she was okay.*

Miracles really do happen! I received what I had pleaded for — a message from Kim before her birthday, saying she was okay. Through my tears I hugged both Carol and Susan and told them. "I will have to process all this. I am now going home to do just that."

After struggling to regain some composure before arriving home, I raced into the house. I found Doug and his brother Murray sitting in the family room. I was not planning to tell anyone other than Doug what I had just experienced, but I was unable to stop myself.

I took a deep breath. It was now or never. I was bursting to share what had just taken place, so with the two of them staring at me, I recounted what had transpired in Susan's kitchen that afternoon. Doug listened intently, knowing how often I had asked for a sign from Kim.

I ended my babbling with, "Now all I need are more details. People call it 'verification.'"

Doug glanced at me, shaking his head. "Don't you have enough now? You want more?"

I responded excitedly, looking Doug directly in the eyes, "Yes! I am asking and I am getting, so I want it all!"

My logical mind couldn't get a grip on what had just occurred, but I tried not to let the skeptical side of me take control of my thoughts. Later, after recording all the details of the day in my journal, I sat and reflected on the events at Susan's. I was absolutely convinced time would prove to me that I had indeed experienced a genuine communication from Kim.

March 15 arrived, and Kim was not here to celebrate her 23rd birthday. I struggled through the day, but my mind was still very busy processing the mystical experiences of the day before. I had asked Kim for a message and had received one. This fact definitely gave me hope and renewed strength to get through the next few very difficult days.

I decided I would tell Judy Piers what had happened. I was unable to reach her during the day so it was evening before we were able to talk. I had seen her flowers at the cemetery and knew she had visited Kim's grave sometime during the day. After closing the door to my bedroom and dialing Judy's home, I related all that had transpired the day before. I really didn't know how Judy would respond but, as usual, she did not let me down.

We had an open and honest conversation about the information that came through during that short reading. She wholeheartedly agreed with me that something had occurred that could not logically be explained. Judy asked me if I ever just sensed that Kim was around me. Her words hit me like a thunderbolt! While I tried to receive messages through others, I might very well be missing the signs Kim was trying to give *me* directly.

So far, I had spent six evenings attempting to receive a message from Kim in the form of automatic writing. Nothing had happened yet, but I decided I would have more faith in the process. On March 16, I settled onto Kim's bed. Feeling more relaxed and peaceful than I had for other attempts, I just allowed myself to remain quiet. I silently asked Kim to write to me. Then, for the first time, I just let it be.

Unexplainably, my hand started to glide across the page from left to right. All calmness left me. I threw my pen down and bolted out the bedroom door, almost falling down the stairs in the process. I yelled for Doug, who poked his head around the corner. I showed him the page with only a wavy line across it and described the sensation I felt as my hand had moved across the page.

"I know that I didn't move my hand," I excitedly explained to him. Part of me was very wedded to my current reality. I liked my safe little world. This new turn of events was definitely not safe, and I was feeling tremendous fear about what I had just attempted to do. I had never been one to take chances, but the opportunity to connect with Kim had overshadowed my fear, at least for the moment. Now remembering the sensation of my hand's flowing movement across the paper, I was pulled back into that fear again. The experience was impossible to explain. I told Doug in the emotions of the moment that I should quit trying to do such a crazy thing.

*Even with all the other mystical experiences that had recently taken place, I still was allowing logic to invalidate them.*

Doug, being the adventurous person he always has been, grinned and said encouragingly, "This is exciting. Why would you want to stop?"

"Then you go up there and do it!" I snapped back. As my emotions calmed down, I tried to think rationally. Maybe I had moved my hand without realizing it. That, of course, was the logical answer. Even with all the other mystical experiences that had recently taken place, I still was allowing logic to invalidate them.

No! I thought. Doug was right. I yearned for a direct connection with Kim. If this was possible, why would I stop now?

I had persuaded myself to try once more, so the very next evening I found myself back in Kim's room. My sole purpose for attempting this connection through automatic writing was to communicate with Kim. It was beyond my comprehension that if I asked Kim to connect in this fashion it might be possible for someone other than Kim to come through, but that's exactly what happened.

On March 17, 1999, I had my first real, full-blown experience with automatic writing. In the darkened bedroom, I focused on my breathing and tried to relax as much as possible. After a few minutes, I felt a new and unusual energy in and around my hand. This time my hand moved ever so slightly; then I had the sensation of up and down movement. Next the sensation turned to circles. The whole episode lasted only a few seconds.

When I turned on the light and looked at the page, I saw an almost illegible handwriting with the words, "Sandy, you could help me." I was stunned but sure someone or some energy had guided my hand. I knew it definitely wasn't me!

I also knew Kim would not call me Sandy.

If it wasn't Kim, who could this writer have been?

I did not feel the same level of panic I had felt the night before, but I was puzzled as to who wrote the message. I wondered: Who needs my help, and what do they need help with?

*[Please see the Appendix beginning on Page 236 to learn more about this and other examples of automatic writing.]*

Interestingly enough, I did not doubt the message and quickly recognized this fact. There was a "knowing," an awareness within me that this was a true communication. It turned out to be just the beginning of my personal experiences with automatic writing. From that evening on, I began a series of communications with many souls on the other side.

As the month was drawing to a close, I finally felt prepared enough to connect to someone like John Edward for a reading. I was ready to find a medium who would give me absolute proof that Kim was fine and lived on. I began to research some of the more famous mediums I had seen on TV. I sent a few emails but was disappointed when I did not receive an immediate response. It didn't dawn on me that their fame had created an avalanche of requests like mine, and they were inundated.

While online one evening, I tried to find contact information for Rosemary Altea, a spiritual medium and author of the book, *Proud Spirit.* A woman in a chatroom said she couldn't help me with my search but told me about a reading she had with a medium in Arkansas named Sharlette Pumphrey. I asked if she received specific information in her reading that proved to her, beyond a doubt, that she was really talking to her loved one.

The woman emphatically stated that there were many such instances, creating a certainty she was hearing from her son who had passed in an accident a few years earlier.

My tears flowed freely as she described the contact she had with her son that day. Sharlette had done this for her, and I wanted her to do the same for me. I was ready to hop on a plane to Arkansas until the woman explained that Sharlette's readings took place over the telephone — and in designated chatrooms — all the time.

I chose not to allow myself to be overcome with the apprehension of venturing into this unfamiliar territory of requesting a reading with a professional psychic medium. My overwhelming need to make this connection led me to honor my inner feeling that I was doing what was right and appropriate for me at this time. This need gave me the determination to email Sharlette and ask her to explain what a reading with her entailed, the cost, and how to arrange one.

*The reading. . . would change my belief system — and my life — forever.*

Sharlette's reply was swift. As I read her response, I clearly felt she was a loving and compassionate lady.

Her reply will be etched in my heart forever. She wanted absolutely no information about the person with whom I hoped to connect. She talked a bit about her background and the loss of her own mother, which was the catalyst for her own journey. She explained the process that takes place during a reading and that there are never any guarantees as to who may come to talk. She confirmed she would be glad to give me the reading over the telephone. I could send her payment in the form of a U.S. money order and call her at a pre-arranged time. Then she said if my need was great, we could arrange for an immediate reading, and she would trust me to send payment after the fact. I earnestly wanted this medium to be the one to give me a reading, so I quickly sent an email back requesting an appointment as soon as possible.

My reading with Sharlette took place on March 26, only a few days after our initial contact. I had just sent the money order off to her that morning. I was grateful she trusted me enough to allow the reading to take place before she received her payment. I was secretly comforted by the fact that Sharlette knew nothing about me except my first name and the time of the reading. I still was somewhat of a skeptic and needed this assurance. The reading I received would change my belief system — and my life — forever, because Sharlette gave me 100% proof of Kim's continuing existence.

As I expressed this sentiment at the conclusion of my reading, Sharlette quickly corrected me. "Your daughter gave you the proof. I am just the vessel."

It was a reference to the automatic writing that significantly helped to convince me that Kim had been communicating with me that day.

The reading I received through the vessel Sharlette was tape-recorded. What follows is the verbatim transcription. Explanations needed to clarify the messages are printed in italics. Through the one-hour session, I expressed a multitude of emotions but said very little.

Sharlette: "You just need to give me yes or no answers. I feel that it is a daughter you want to contact today."

Sandy: "Yes."

Sharlette: "Sit back and relax because they work off your energy, too. There will be moments of silence while I focus. I am getting an impression of a female, but I'm only getting the bottom of her body. Her legs are very slim. She is not showing me the top half, which is strange. She is moving her legs around a lot which usually indicates that she was an active person or maybe a dancer."

Sandy: "Okay, yes."

Sharlette: "Please be open to other spirits coming through. I know you want your daughter but we never know."

Sandy: "Okay."

Sharlette: "She is starting to show me the rest of her body. She has shoulder-length hair, and it seems to be kind of medium brown.

Seems like highlights in it or something."

Sandy: "Yes."

Sharlette: "Oh, I'm getting chill bumps, which usually means it is her. I'm getting a K like a KA. A hard sound like a K."

Sandy: "Yes." *I wanted to start talking, but she stopped me.*

Sharlette: "Don't tell me because if I can get it or get real close to it, it is validation for you."

Sharlette: "Seems to be an impatient type person because it is like I interrupted her, and she's trying to tell me something."

Sandy: "Yes." *This sounded just like Kim.*

Sharlette: "Does her name have the same rhythm as Candy or Kinder? Two syllables? It sounds like she is saying Kenny."

Sandy: "No." *I was so nervous and was thinking of Kim or Kimberly that I forgot that she was often called Kimmy.*

Sharlette: "Maybe then we can work together and she will just slip it in later when I am not trying. If her name is unusual, I probably won't get it."

Sandy: "No, not unusual." *I did not have enough understanding of the process at this time to recognize the significance of the K name. All three of the girls' names started with Ks. As I did not want to give Sharlette any clues, I did not even acknowledge this fact, and now I realize how hard I made Sharlette work.*

Sharlette: "I'm seeing the numbers one and six. Do they mean anything to you?"

Sandy: "Six maybe, yes."

Sharlette: "Seeing the number three. Is this pertaining to the number of children you have?"

Sandy: "Yes."

Sharlette: "Getting another K."

Sandy: "Yes."

Sharlette: "Now she is giving me the letter B of someone close to her."

Sandy: "Yes, could be."

Sharlette: "She wrote the name Bob and is circling it… often means they are worried about that person."

Sandy: "Okay."

Sharlette: "She is saying uncle."

Sandy: "Really." *Kim has two Uncle Bobs, but one of them is always called Rob. Thinking afterwards, I remembered that Bob was out of a job at that time, and she would have been concerned for him.*

Sharlette: "She is writing 'car accident.' Is this how she crossed?"

Sandy: "Yes."

Sharlette: "She is showing me the inside of a car. One female in the driver's seat. She is alone."

Sandy: "Yes."

Sharlette: "She is writing this. 'Mom, I love you. Tell Daddy I'm here...not dead...see you all the time...all the time. Don't be upset. I'm fine.'" *Crying.*

Sharlette: "Does she have a grandmother there? Sounds like a grandma. Starts with 'M.' She tells me she is with a grandmother there, to give you comfort that she is not alone."

Sandy: "I wouldn't have thought a grandmother, maybe a great grandmother."

Sharlette: "Well, I don't know. Is there a Mary?"

Sandy: "I don't know." *I was thinking of my side of the family and forgot, in my excitement, about Doug's grandmother Mary. She was very old when she passed, and I have a picture of Kim with this grandmother and had just been looking at the photo recently.*

Sharlette: "She is showing me a picture of a lady in an apron and the lady reminds me of the lady Aunt Bea from the Andy Griffith show. The apron usually means grandmother."

Sandy: "Okay."

Sharlette: "Is she a young woman in her early 20s?"

Sandy: "Yes."

Sharlette: "But I am seeing an innocence and sweetness about her like a sweet sixteen. Sweet person."

Sandy: "Yes."

Sharlette: "I'm getting the impression of a ranch-type house. The brick has got a reddish tone to it. Is that your home?"

Sandy: "Yes."

Sharlette: "Now she is talking about her room. She is saying you haven't changed it. 'Thank you.'"

Sandy: "No, we haven't."

Sharlette: "Have you felt her presence there? Because she is saying, 'I stay there a lot.'"

Sandy: "Yes, I do."

Sharlette: "My Buddy. She is saying my Buddy!"

Sandy: "This is the sign I asked for. I told Kim if she would give me our dog's name, I would have to believe." *I am screaming and have completely lost my composure.*

Sharlette: "That's your dog?"

Sandy: "Yes, that's our dog."

Sharlette: "Wow!"

Sandy: "That's one of the signs I needed."

Sharlette: "Sends you lots of love. She is sending you so much love that it is coming up through my body and filling my heart. She is really excited right now because she knows you finally believe."

Sandy: "So am I."

Sharlette: "She has to calm down right now before we can continue."

Sharlette: "She is saying, 'Tell the boys, hi.' Does she have brothers?"

Sandy: "No, but I understand." *Kim had some close guy friends that she knew all her life. They were like brothers to her, and when she talked about them they were always "the boys."*

Sharlette: "Okay, now she is showing me someone with the letter 'A.' Amanda or Amelia."

Sandy: "Amanda, yes."

Sharlette: "Close friend?"

Sandy: "Yes."

Sharlette: "Does she call her Mandy?

Sandy: "Yes, Yes. She never called her Amanda, only Mandy. Wow!"

Sharlette: "'Tell Mandy, hi.' Tell her Kim's still here and saying something about all the good times they had at her place."

Sandy: "I definitely understood that sentence, as Mandy's was the party place."

Sharlette: "She likes to write when communicating with me."

Sandy: "Oh."

Sharlette: "Do you know what automatic writing is?"

Sandy: "Yes."

Sharlette: "She is good at it."

Sharlette: "It feels like someone was a cheerleader because I'm getting a feeling of a gym."

Sandy: "Not a cheerleader but a gym. Yes." *Later her friends said they understood this part of the reading, as the message was more for them than for me.*

Sharlette: "Bleachers. She shows someone standing in front of bleachers, cheering."

Sandy: "Don't know but she could be meaning something. She is so smart." *Again this was very significant for her circle of friends.*

Sharlette: "She is saying, 'Aw, thanks, Mom.' Has she been gone less than a year?"

Sandy: "Yes."

Sharlette: "I am getting the number six again. 'Important,' she says."

Sandy: "Yes." *We had talked about the three sixes on her license plates just weeks before she passed. I told her I didn't like it that it read 666 and that she should get new ones. Kim just laughed at me.*

Sharlette: "Now she is showing me a man about five foot ten or eleven with salt and pepper hair. Medium-sized man in weight. Solid looking, probably in his 40s.

Sandy: "If this is her dad, she has to say something else."

Sharlette: "Okay. I see a man with something in his right hand now. A cane. But I don't think this is about the same man. It is a man standing behind her. An older man."

Sandy: "Yes, her grandfather had a cane before he passed."

Sharlette: "Now back to the first man. It sounds like she is talking about her daddy. But she has to show me something else?"

Sandy: "Yes."

Sharlette: "Does he have a beard?"

Sandy: "Yes! Yes!"

Sharlette: "Because she is showing me a dark shadow on his face."

Sandy: "Yes, he always had it!" *I was crying again.*

Sharlette: "Does your husband's name start with a D?"

Sandy: "Yes."

Sharlette: "Is she your oldest daughter?"

Sandy: "Yes."

Sharlette: "Okay, now back to the K. She is telling me her sister's name. KA-sounds like Karen. Does her name start with K, also?"

Sandy: "Yes, and the other sister, too."

Sharlette: "Three girls and all Ks?"

Sandy: "Yes."

Sharlette: "No wonder I kept hearing all those Ks. Now let's see, sister…is her name Karen?"

Sandy: "No, but close enough. It is Kerry."

Sharlette: "Oh, I wouldn't have got that. Now I am just going to give you what she is throwing at me. She is saying Kenny very strongly."

Sandy: "Oh! Could she be saying Kimmy?"

Sharlette: "Oh yes, that is what she is saying. She said that at the very beginning, and we didn't get it. Oh! Her name is Kim. Now one more sister. She is saying K. Two syllables."

Sandy: "Yes."

Sharlette: "R in it too."

Sandy: "Yes."

Sharlette: "I will leave it for now because she is showing me the house again. Do you have a field behind it?"

Sandy: "Yes."

Sharlette: "Getting the impression of a horse."

Sandy: "No, cows. Oh, there may be a horse." *Actually there was a donkey, I remembered later, and that we often talked about the awful noise it made.*

Sharlette: "I'm getting a long distance view of a dog with light hair."

Sandy: "Yes."

Sharlette: "Like a setter or something. Slimmer. Now I can hear her say Kimberly. Now she is showing me a young man with short hair, slim, not tall, five foot eight or nine. Name starts with a S-Sh sound."

Sandy: "Yes."

Sharlette: "'Boyfriend.' she says. They were together a while, she says, but broke up."

Sandy: "Yes, exactly."

Sharlette: "She is acknowledging him. Now she is showing me another guy...B...Brett."

Sandy: "Yes! Yes! That's another verification I asked Kim for."

Sharlette: "Now she is giving me the impression of jumping on a trampoline. Do you have a trampoline?"

Sandy: "Yes! How did you know that?"

Sharlette: "She is telling me, of course. Wow! She is doing flips. Could she do that?"

Sandy: "Yes!"

Sharlette: "Now she is showing off."

Sandy: "She would do that."

Sharlette: "Now she is showing me your backyard."

*These next details were so specific that I was overcome with the realization that only Kim could be giving Sharlette this information.*

Sharlette: "From your back door, if you look out, there is a clothesline to the left."

Sandy: "No, no clothesline."

Sharlette: "She is saying, 'Yes there is, Mom!'" *And then I thought about our neighbor's clothesline just over the fence and to the left of our patio door. In the summer, spring, and fall, there were usually clothes on it. In fact, I used to comment about it and that I didn't have the patience to hang my clothes out each week.*

Sandy: "Yes. Wow, Kim."

Sharlette: "Garage to the right and trampoline is in the center."

Sandy: "Yes! Unbelievable!"

Sharlette: "I get the impression of a ring. She says, 'I have it with me.' She has it around her neck to keep it close to her heart. The ring is connected to a guy. M..Mike or Mark."

Sandy: "Yes, to a Mike, could be." *I didn't know this at the time but it was confirmed later that Kim was wearing this ring on the day of the accident and was buried with it. I guess I was so blinded by my grief that I hadn't noticed the ring.*

Sharlette: "Now she is giving me the impression of another ring around the neck. No, it is a necklace with three or four things hanging on it. I have the impression that it is heavy."

Sandy: "Yes! Her youngest sister put this around her neck."

Sharlette: "Keeps it with her, she is saying. Showing me a daintier ring now on the right hand. Gold with little stones all around it. It has a balance of color. All the stones are the same color."

Sandy: "Yes!" *This was a very special ring put on her finger by her close circle of girlfriends. They each wear a matching ring now.*

Sharlette: "Thank you. It is very special. She holds it to her heart. Kim is writing this to me. She is very good at it. She says, 'I can still write material stuff. Wow!' She is saying, 'All day, all night, Mom, practice; practice makes perfect.' Do you understand?"

Sandy: "Yes! Yes!"

Sharlette: "Okay, she is saying she stands behind you on the right so she won't get in the way. Oh! Are you trying automatic writing?"

Sandy: "Yes."

Sharlette: "Well, keep practicing because she says she will come through to you this way."

Sandy: "Okay. Wow!"

*"You know now, Mom. You must leave me be for a while, as I have many things to learn here. I will be with you. I love you all."*

The reading continued and more verification was given, but by this point there was no doubt in my mind that the messages were from Kim. She continued to talk about a building at her university and what it looked like. When I asked her friends about the inside hallways of this building, they confirmed the information for me. Kim talked about her love of jazz music. She told me about the library established in her honor at the university she attended and about the high school scholarship fund set up in her name. Sharlette identified the third — and youngest — sister's name as Christine. It is Kristy.

Kim's final message was: "You know now, Mom. You must leave me be for a while, as I have many things to learn here. I will be with you. I love you all."

My reading with Sharlette gave me the proof I needed to confirm that Kim was still around us. The reading revealed many details as verifications, and so much of Kim's personality came through. Sharlette had no way of knowing that I was experimenting with automatic writing, yet she had claimed Kim was "writing" and was very good at it.

I was astounded when Sharlette informed me Kim was encouraging me to continue writing, because she would come through to me in this way. Sharlette asked me if I had tried automatic writing — Kim made her feel that I had. How would she know that if Kim, or someone else, weren't telling her? Kim told her she was standing on my right so she wouldn't get in the way! Sharlette didn't know I was left-handed, but Kim knew!

This communication from Kim transformed me! It was this reading that opened my heart to the truth of an afterlife. I knew I would have to set aside my old beliefs — my skepticism — once and for all, and openly accept there was something more on "the other side" and that Kim was now there.

This astonishing connection sparked in me a need to know more, so I once again set aside that nagging fear of the unknown, understanding now that I would proceed on my journey into the Light. I would open the door to new and exciting possibilities.

My mind was full, and I was exhausted. I would think about all this tomorrow after a good night's sleep.

In the days immediately following this reading, I wanted to shout from the housetops the fact that I had received messages from Kim, but of course, I couldn't. I told Doug immediately. I mentioned that his dad had come through with Kim. I could see the pain in his face as I told him some of the details. I knew this was helping me to cope but wondered if it was as beneficial to Doug. I worried about that. I loved him too much to cause any more pain for him.

I called my friends Bonnie, Judy Hunt, and Judy Piers, and met each of them individually for coffee. I zealously shared my reading with them. It was a relief to talk about all the details that came through and to discuss it with these three dear friends. It wasn't long before I also played the tape for my sister-in-law Ruth.

In that one reading, Sharlette gave me a little bit of my heart back. Together, we have begun a personal journey of friendship. When I talk about the angels who walk among us, I think of Sharlette. In the book, *Are You Ready for a Miracle with Angels?,* Canadian author Angelica Eberle Wagner tells us angels can manifest change in our lives by giving us thoughts that cause us to rethink our direction and lead us by inspiration. Sharlette Pumphrey became my earth angel that day and has since touched my life in many ways.

Sharlette had been instrumental in opening my spiritual awareness, but now, how was I to expand my spiritual connection to the other side? Sharlette mentioned that meditation was the key to feeling the connection to those on the other side. How would I ever learn to meditate when I was engulfed by so many emotions? This, I steadfastly decided, would be a new avenue to pursue — and my next challenge.

Chapter 3

# SURROUNDED BY MIRACLES

*Fear not, the blackest holes of life...*

*may give birth to...the greatest miracles!*

—Author Unknown

**April 1999.** The warmer weather had arrived. I knew it was time to work in the gardens around our house, but my heart just wasn't in it. Obviously, the work had to be done, but I couldn't motivate myself to get started. I would think about gardening and even occasionally open the door and peek outside. I'd think, "Maybe today," but would shut the door just as quickly as the thought ran through my head.

One morning as I wandered through the study, engrossed in a jumble of thoughts, I paused to look around the messy room. It was as if I were seeing the room for the first time in months. Everything was laden with dust. There were piles of stuff in every corner that had never been put away. Clothes were strewn about waiting to be ironed. I put the book aside that I was planning to read and began to clean.

When I finished cleaning up the study, I headed into the living room. The first items that caught my eye were the newspaper clippings from our local paper reporting Kim's accident and death along with an article written by her friends that had been published in the university newspaper, *The Cord.* Staring out at me was a full-page picture of Kim. It was deeply challenging for me to stay focused on the task at hand, but somehow I summoned the strength, carefully moved the newspapers, and continued with my cleaning. When I was done, about three hours later, I dropped my head into my hands and broke down in tears, consumed by a wave of grief.

*. . . I had let my pain and anger immobilize me. I had set the physical world aside and immersed myself in the spiritual in an attempt to hide from life. I had let my family down.*

Gradually I became cognizant of the fact that I had let my pain and anger immobilize me. I had set the physical world aside and immersed myself in the spiritual in an attempt to hide from life. I had let my family down. It was like a light bulb suddenly turned on inside my head. I recognized the importance of re-establishing some balance in my life.

Awakening to this realization did not make it easy to turn my life around, because now I would have to face my grief head on. I had been selfish! Staying stuck in my shell — and taking care of my needs only — was hurting my family. I would have to learn to live again. I would have to find a way to bring balance back into my life. At last, I recognized that I had become too focused on matters pertaining only to my spiritual growth while leaving other aspects of my life unattended. I was determined to resume some semblance of the normalcy we enjoyed before Kim was so senselessly taken from us.

I went outside and pulled weeds and leaves out of the gardens. I dusted off my cookbooks and began to prepare hot meals for the family every night. I took my friend and neighbor Cathie up on her offer to walk with her. She had been trying to coax me into joining her for months.

I had good days and I had bad days, but I began to feel stronger.

One afternoon I decided I would crank up the riding lawn mower and cut the grass. I was having one of my bad days. It was in the midst of my inconsolable pain that I received what I believed to be a sign from Kim reassuring me she was okay. The message came in the form of a butterfly. While sitting on the riding lawn mower, I noticed a little white butterfly circling my legs. It proceeded to weave in and out around my head. It remained intertwined with me while I finished cutting the front lawn.

After watching this butterfly hovering around me for ten minutes or so, I recall thinking; "Kim, is that you doing this?" Not daring to think it really was, I put out a challenge to prove to myself that this butterfly was Kim's way of saying she was with me. "Let the butterfly stay a little longer," I pleaded silently with her.

I completed the entire back lawn, which took me about 45 minutes, with the butterfly swirling around me most of that time. As it finally fluttered away, I looked at my watch to discover this tiny white butterfly had remained with me for nearly an hour.

"Okay," I rationalized, "don't be foolish," as I returned the lawn mower to the garage. "You can't prove Kim was here!"

Over the course of the next couple of days my mind would often wander back to the unusual behavior of that butterfly. I wanted so desperately to believe that it was a sign from Kim.

Early one evening, only a few days after this incident, Judy Hunt called to see if she could coax me to come out for coffee. When we met at the coffee shop a short time later, Judy held in her hand a small gift bag decorated with angels. Placing the bag on the table in front of me, she quietly explained, "I just felt I had to buy this for you." As I opened the bag, I was stunned by what I saw. It was a tiny butterfly pin. I gave Judy a big hug and told her my experience with the tiny white butterfly.

Another morning, I decided to rejoin my exercise club. Sue Stone, the owner of the fitness center, had sent a beautifully written card inviting me back when I felt I was ready. Sue encouraged me to chat with her about

Kim, talk about my feelings, or just exercise quietly if that was what I needed to do. Once I returned, I got into the habit of arriving at the quiet time of the afternoon and quickly began looking forward to our talks. Sue never made me feel awkward or uncomfortable as I shared a story about Kim. She made me laugh — something I desperately needed to do.

Sue had her own story to tell about her first encounter with Kim. She had met Kim, unbeknownst to me, only a short time before her passing when she came in to tan one evening after work. She had a pre-arranged appointment but, as she bounced through the door, was informed that the lady ahead of her had arrived late. Kim would have to wait about 15 minutes. A few moments later, Sue glanced out of the corner of her eye to see Kim pacing back and forth. Ignoring her, she turned back to her work. Suddenly Kim was standing in front of her. "I am too busy to wait around like this." After Sue replied there was nothing she could do, Kim sat back down and waited. Sue revealed, with a smile, that Kim did return for a second tan later in the week.

Patience had never been one of Kim's stronger qualities.

Within the first few weeks of my return to the exercise club, we were discussing my new spiritual beliefs. Sue listened when I recounted the "little miracles" and my experiences with Kim. I gave her the details of my reading with Sharlette. She was non-judgmental and surprisingly supportive. Sue was being slowly drawn into my journey and, before long, would begin her own quest for enlightenment.

Late each evening when the house was silent, I would practice my automatic writing and allow the energy to flow through my hand. When I was finished, I would read the messages. My writings were becoming longer and contained more detailed information. I was still skeptical that these messages were actually coming from the spirit world, but as the verifications came, I gained more confidence that they were.

My mind would wander back to the idea of meditation and Sharlette's advice to learn a technique that worked for me. How would I ever quiet my chattering mind? This was going to be deeply challenging for me, but I imagined it would be tremendously gratifying if I were successful. I knew I must learn to rely upon myself. I was determined to do so.

Every time my doubting mind would intervene, some new "miracle" would transpire, and a sense of peacefulness would engulf me. Realizing that Kim was still around me, I yearned for more contact. Even though some of my family and friends believed I was losing my grip on reality, I felt myself being drawn further into my newfound spirituality. I knew this was my personal path to understanding and learning to cope with the incredible, heart-rending pain and emptiness I had to live with now.

"Coincidences" were happening in my life, and I was now open and aware of each of them — like when Hazel McGuiness came into my life. I was introduced to Hazel through my brother-in-law Murray. The day was April 12, 1999.

When the phone rang, I listened intently as Murray excitedly explained that Hazel had worked for him for a few years as a housekeeper. He had just found out she did spiritual readings at her home in the evenings and on weekends. He suggested that I talk to her about Kim, but before I could even get a word in edgewise, he handed the telephone to Hazel.

In a very comforting voice, Hazel explained that on her way to Murray's that morning she felt a tremendous push to talk to him about her spiritual work. At the time she didn't understand why she felt the urge to reveal this. Hazel recounted to me how there had been a pink light around her since early in the morning and that she now understood why she was moved to talk to Murray about this part of her life. Kim, she continued, was with her and had arranged this meeting. The pink light symbolized that Kim was in a very high level of heaven, in what Hazel called "The Angel Room."

I listened attentively but with some wariness. Was it a coincidence that Murray asked her to take a break and join him for a cup of coffee so soon after Kim's passing? Was it a coincidence that Hazel chose this time to share her "other job" with Murray? They had never discussed this side of her life before. Did Kim send Hazel to me as a new teacher on my journey into the Light? I believed, without a doubt, that it was a genuine and sincerely offered message of hope.

I didn't feel an urgency to receive another spiritual reading at the time so I asked Hazel if I could keep her number and call her at a later date if I felt drawn to do so. I carefully recorded her number and tucked it away for safekeeping. It wasn't until a few months later that I actually met Hazel in person.

I had just discovered places online where I could get free readings. These readings, although not private and not lengthy, contained details necessary for validation. Here was another way, I thought, I could get more messages from Kim. I spent my evenings online in search of the sites that offered readings open for all to see. I sat, as if hypnotized, as I watched others receive their messages and witnessed their reactions to the information.

On Friday, April 16, I put my name on a list to have a reading and then sat staring at my computer screen, anxiously waiting for my name to be called. Finally I was asked if I was ready.

Here is the reading I received that evening. I was sent a log of the reading by email.

> Online Medium: "Holly, did you lose a teenage daughter?"
>
> Sandy: "Yes." *In the emotions of the moment, I did not mention that she was a bit older than that. Kim often looked like a teenager, younger than her 22 years.*
>
> Online Medium: "Long dark hair?"
>
> Sandy: "Yes. Longish, fairly dark."
>
> Online Medium: "She said you know she loves you."
>
> Sandy: "Yes. I know." *Crying.*
>
> Online Medium: "She said, 'Please try not to worry.' She has made many friends."
>
> Sandy: "She always had lots of friends."
>
> Online Medium: "Was this an accident?"
>
> Sandy: "Yes."

Online Medium: "She said to tell you she is in a real cool place. She wants you to know so you will not miss her so much."

Sandy: "Okay."

Online Medium: "She said, 'I just couldn't stay, Mom. They told me I had to go.'"

Sandy: Oh! Why?"

Online Medium: "'But it was a cool trip.' Sounds like she has adjusted very well."

Sandy: "Yes. She always went with the flow. Nothing scared her."

Online Medium: "Great smile."

Sandy: "Yes."

Online Medium: "She says you cry too much. Makes her sad to see you cry."

Sandy: "Yes, I know. I am crying right now."

Online Medium: "She says if you could only see how nice it is here, you would be happy."

Sandy: "Tell her I am sorry I cry too much."

Online Medium: "She said to tell you she loves you. Something she took for granted before. She was always so busy."

Sandy: "I know."

Online Medium: "'Yes, I didn't realize the important stuff, Mom.'"

Sandy: "Yes. I can hear her say that."

Online Medium: "She said she visits you, and you can feel her there sometimes but are afraid to believe it is really her."

Sandy: "Yes, I can. I get chill bumps."

Online Medium: "Well, she said, 'Believe. I will not leave you. I will be there as long as you need me.' With that she flipped her hair and said she has to go now. She is gone now. She is so full of energy."

Sandy: "Yes. She always was."

I did not find a lot of verification in this reading, but if you had known Kim you would know that her words and the action of flipping her hair and making a fast exit was so much like her. I may have doubted the information if this reading had come before the others, but at this point in my journey I had no doubt that Kim was relaying the messages.

I read the words over and over, "I just couldn't stay, Mom. They told me I had to go." What did she mean by that, and *who* told her she couldn't stay? I thought she was referring to her accident and that a decision had been made whether to stay on earth or return to spirit. Apparently, the decision was not Kim's alone to make. I had to learn and understand more about this other world where Kim now existed.

I continued to search for messages from Kim over the Internet. It became my passion and my mission. Eventually, not only did I receive messages from Kim, but also other deceased family members began to step forward with their own communications. I recognized that I had not only found a link to Kim, but I had also found a link to many souls of loved ones on the other side.

*I recognized that I had not only found a link to Kim, but I had also found a link to many souls of loved ones on the other side.*

Amazingly, Kim spontaneously started making her presence known to the mediums whom I became connected with on the Internet. They would comment on how insistent Kim was that I get these impromptu messages. This was so much like Kim that, when they told me, I would smile with appreciation.

One of these unexpected messages came on April 15, as I was chatting online with a woman I had talked to a few times. Suddenly she announced, "Your daughter is here and wants to talk." I didn't know this online acquaintance did spiritual readings, and I told her so. Nonetheless, I replied that I would be happy to receive any messages from my daughter. As we were on one of the sites that did not allow online readings, the woman was kind enough to direct me to a site where she could bring through these messages. We quickly reconvened on the new site.

Here is the unplanned reading I received that day:

> Online Medium: "Your daughter really wants to talk to you. She has something important to say. She is a very bright spirit and sends a lot of love to her family, but that is not the reason she has come today. This message is to be given to the special boy in her life. 'Please tell him that I was with him when he wanted me to be.' That is why she has come today. He will understand what she says. 'Please tell him, Mom.'" *I didn't understand the message, but said I would.*
>
> Onlne Medium: "Now she is saying, 'Give my love to Grandma, too.'"
>
> Sandy: "Okay." *Which Grandma? I wondered.*

I really didn't understand the message. One of her grandmothers had been ill, and I thought she just wanted to acknowledge that. As I needed more verification of these messages, I began to silently ask, "Please give me details, Kim, so I can know it is you." I was astonished when the woman's very next words were:

> Online Medium: "She says she could give you lots of details, but what she wants to say is 'I love all of you.' She says: 'There are lots of things in my room to keep me forever in your hearts.' She is with you often. She says: 'Mom, talk to me.' She loves you. She says she is with a baby with the name of Rachel or April."
>
> Sandy: "Don't know. Maybe. I met someone recently who had just lost a baby named April."

After I thanked her and we said goodbye, I sat down and wrote details of the conversation from the notes I had scribbled during this reading. Then, as I re-read the message for the special boy in Kim's life, I wondered how I could possibly call this young man and give him this message. He would think I was crazy. Yet, I knew I had to because Kim wanted me to.

I picked up the phone and dialed his number. As I shared this information with him, he quietly replied that his birthday had just passed and that he had been talking to Kim on that day and saying, "I know you would call if you could, Kim."

I tearfully replied, "I think you just got your phone call!"

During our conversation, I discovered that his birthday was the same day as Kim's grandmother's. Now I understood why she had mentioned both of them. She wanted to let them both know she was thinking about them on their birthdays.

It all made sense to me. When one starts hearing messages that are just so right, one just has to believe. I definitely believed.

On April 20, I had another brief reading over the Internet. This time I was surprised by who came through. The medium for my reading began by announcing there were two women in spirit with messages for me. I was anxious to find out who these ladies were.

> Online Medium: "There are two women in spirit standing side by side."
>
> Sandy: "They must not belong to me."
>
> Online Medium: "Yes. They say they do."
>
> Sandy: "Okay. Ask them what they want." *I did not yet understand that they were not puppets for us to command and that just their stepping forward meant they had a message they wanted to get through.*
>
> Online Medium: "Who had the operation?"
>
> Sandy: "Wow. My mother-in-law had surgery, just this morning."
>
> Online Medium: "They say they belong to her."
>
> Sandy: "Wow."
>
> Online Medium: "They say she is in and out of it. Make sense?"
>
> Sandy: "Yes."
>
> Online Medium: "One is tall and one is shorter. The shorter one is sterner looking." *I suddenly realized who these ladies must be. One was Maggie and one was Mary, both Mom figures to my*

*mother-in-law.*

Online Medium: "I see an infant who died right around its birth."

Sandy: "Yes, I know my mother-in-law lost a baby at birth."

Online Medium: "Who is Irene?"

Sandy: "Don't know for sure but do know that is my mother-in-law's middle name."

Online Medium: "She is saying the baby is with them. Says the names 'William and Kathleen.' Mean anything?"

Sandy: "Don't know. This is my husband's side of the family."

Online Medium: "Now I am hearing the name Wilhelmina?"

Sandy: "Have to check."

Online Medium: "Remember it, please, and find out if there is someone with this name on the other side."

Sandy: "Okay. I will."

Online Medium: "They are fading now."

I thanked her for the information. I believe the two ladies stepped forward because of the illness that my mother-in-law had at this time. Later, I did get confirmation on one of the names.

On April 24, I went in search of some information about automatic writing. I had some questions and went online in hopes of getting some answers to my questions. I wasn't in the chatroom for more than a few minutes when I was told someone in spirit wished to give me a message. Thinking it was Kim, I said to go ahead.

Online Medium: "I see an older lady, and she wants to talk. Grandmother, I think."

Sandy: "Yes, I have a grandmother in spirit."

Online Medium: "Long hair, stern looking but loving."

Sandy: "Long hair, yes." *I was thinking this was my father's mother.*

Online Medium: "She is from a Scottish or English background."

Sandy: "Not my grandmother. Can you describe her?"

Online Medium: "Petite, five feet, grey hair."

Sandy: "Sounds like my husband's grandmother."

Online Medium: "Yes, she is nodding. She is showing me a hospital room and pink flowers."

Sandy: "Yes, this is Doug's family, as his mom has just had an operation."

Online Medium: "Yes. She is saying she will be fine now, saying intestines, a growth?"

Sandy: "Exactly."

Online Medium: "Removed some. Don't worry. It looks okay. She is showing me flowers on the window ledge to her left."

Sandy: "Yes! Wow."

Online Medium: "Has she had trouble with this for awhile? With bleeding and didn't know what it was."

Sandy: "Yes." *She had trouble with her blood count for a couple of years. The doctors had said she must be bleeding inside, but they could not find the problem. She had been back and forth to doctors for this.*

Online Medium: "She will be okay now."

I thanked her and was getting ready to leave when she added, "Guess I am not done yet. There is a young lady here now, longish brown hair with blond highlights."

Sandy: "Yes."

Online Medium: "She is laughing and says: 'With brown hair, please!' Looks like she is wearing shorts and running shoes. Does this make sense?"

Sandy: "Yes." *Kim was very fit and went to the gym on a regular basis. She was wearing her workout clothes at the time of the accident, as she was on her way home from the gym.*

Online Medium: "Is she late teens?"

Sandy: "No, just a bit older, but I have been asked that before."

Online Medium: "She has a nice smile, happy person, says there are three. Make sense?"

Sandy: "Yes."

Online Medium: "She sends her love to them. Are her siblings younger than her?"

Sandy: "Yes."

Online Medium: "Are they both girls?"

Sandy: "Yes."

Online Medium: "She is with them a lot she says." *I am crying at this point.*

Online Medium: "She is saying: 'Mom, I am okay. Believe it.'"

Online Medium: "Now she is saying the name of Brad. Is this her boyfriend?"

Sandy: "No. A friend, maybe."

Online Medium: "Okay, well she is saying: 'Betty's Brad.'" *I am speechless. This is someone in my bereavement group.*

Sandy: "Do you know why she is saying his name?"

Online Medium: "No, she is just saying 'Betty's Brad.'"

Sandy: "Okay, strange." *Amazingly this connection is validated later, much to my surprise.*

Online Medium: "Great smile. She is leaving now and blows you kisses and says that she is with you."

I could not begin to express the excitement I felt about this experience. I could hardly wait to tell my friends about it.

I instinctively knew my friends would fully believe that there was no possible way the online mediums could have learned about all the accurate facts about Kim, my family, and Doug's family through any of my chatroom discussions. After all, I was using a pseudonym of Holly, and many of the details that came through in online readings were not even known by me but were verified later by family members.

One day, quite soon after this conversation, I had lunch with my friend Bonnie. I was anxious to share the events that occurred earlier in the month. For the very first time, I began to feel goose bumps up and down my arms as we talked about Kim and about our spiritual progression. Sharlette had explained to me how goose bumps were a sign that someone from the other side was trying to make their presence felt. Both Bonnie and I could see the goose bumps on my arms. She had them, too. Bonnie said she felt Kim's presence as well as the presence of someone else. It was a tall, young woman with dark hair. I thought this must be my guide Holly. We both felt very strongly that Kim was with us that afternoon.

*I struggled to absorb the numerous mystical events that were happening. I was finding some much-needed comfort in the knowledge that Kim, although gone from our sight, still existed somewhere and was happy.*

We meet new people for so many different reasons. It was not a coincidence that Bonnie and I had met. She was to play a part in my spiritual growth in many more ways than I understood at that time. Likewise, I was to play a part in hers.

Could Kim have arranged our meeting the way she seemed to have done with Hazel? I definitely had a lot to think about — and much more to learn.

❊ ❊ ❊

**May 1999.** I struggled to absorb the numerous mystical events that were happening. I was finding some much-needed comfort in the knowledge that Kim, although gone from our sight, still existed somewhere and was happy. I now understood that contact with the spirit world was possible and that those on the other side also had a need for connection. I have come to believe such connections are our loved ones' way of helping us through our grief. Our loved ones on the other side want us to know they are still around us.

No matter what I believed, however, reality assaulted me with the fact that Kim was gone, and I was angry. We didn't want her *there*. We wanted and needed her *here* with us. I knew I would open any new door that offered me a way to Kim. The prospect of these personal contacts became my only comfort. During this month, Kim bombarded me with messages of her continuing existence.

*I had come to comprehend that love can reach across the veil between the two worlds.*

What I had originally believed to be "miracles" were now happening routinely in my life. When so much verification comes in such a short span of time, one can feel overwhelmed, but I knew in my heart that all the messages from Kim were true and real. My skepticism had disappeared.

First through books and chatrooms, then through personal experiences, I had come to comprehend that love can reach across the veil between the two worlds. Kim was doing just that with the spontaneous messages she was sending me.

On May 10, while standing in Kim's bedroom, I noticed a little dress she had purchased just before she passed. As I gazed sadly at the dress, I wondered if I should offer this dress to one of Kim's friends. I had not yet done anything with her clothes, but it seemed a shame to just let all her lovely things hang in the closet.

That same evening, after taking my position in front of the computer, I was shown again how thin the veil actually is between the two worlds. As I logged onto one of my regular chatrooms, I was informed that Kim was there once again and had something to tell me. She came across with, "Yes, Mom. You can give some of my clothes away now." Her next message set me back on my heels: "My little white dress with the flower on it. Go ahead, Mom. You know who to give it to for me." This encouragement ended the message.

The person giving me this information told me: "She is gone now. Boy, is she powerful. She gave her message and, poof, she was gone. Is she like that?"

"Yes," I answered. "That is exactly how she is."

The medium's communication completely addressed what my private thoughts had been while standing in Kim's room. No one else knew of them, not even my family. The "little white dress with the flower on it" was the dress I had focused on that afternoon. I wasn't sure, however, that there was a flower on it. But when I checked it out, sure enough, there was a little flower on the front.

Kim had heard my thoughts and given me her directive.

It seemed that I had my own connection to Kim; we were talking just the way we used to. I was dumbfounded by the reality of this. Then on May 14, I was given such a powerful message that any doubt I still had about the reality of all this just melted away. Kim came through on a website called "Spiritspace," even though I was not asking for her. Kim initiated the contact as she had done just four days earlier. I was told, "Kim is here. She is showing me a little gold angel and saying 'harp.' She is saying 'thank you.' Now she says, 'End of message. Bye, Mom.'"

*I truly understood that love is the reason such other-worldly connections are made — our love for them and their love for us.*

Stunned and speechless, I did not immediately respond to this message and was asked if I was listening. My mind raced and the tears flowed. Just the previous day at the cemetery, I had placed a little gold angel playing a harp at Kim's headstone. "This is for you, Kim," I had said. "I hope you are playing a harp in heaven."

This is not the kind of information a person on the other end of a computer could know. I had not discussed my recent visit to the cemetery with anyone.

I was now smack in the middle of my spiritual awakening. I had no more doubts — absolutely none — that the messages the mediums gave me came from Kim. I truly understood that love is the reason such other-worldly connections are made — our love for them and their love for us.

Kim was not about to stop working her miracles. She knew I needed to meet yet another person to aid me along my continuing journey, so she led me to him. Of that I have no doubt.

Lou Baccash is an especially gifted spiritual medium who lives in the New York City area. Lou helped me discover that Kim was one of my guides and, more significantly, that she and I would work together to bring healing and comfort to others.

Meeting Lou was not mere coincidence — if there is such a thing. As I entered one of my regular chatrooms, I discovered it was empty. I was about to leave when Lou entered the room. We had never met before, so we did the usual introductions then settled down to chat. We were in one of the chatrooms that did not permit readings. Nonetheless, it wasn't long before I heard those familiar words: "Someone on the other side has messages for you."

I did not know at the time that Lou was a medium, but by then I wasn't surprised to hear from Kim. He asked if I would telephone him and, for some reason, I felt the urge to call this stranger I had just met. Crazy as it seemed, I placed a call to New York.

I listened anxiously for some validation to come through to prove Kim was actually communicating through Lou. By the time the reading concluded, I had no doubts. Lou was very detailed and accurate. I soon came to believe that Lou entered my life to aid me in my understanding of the "other side" and our connections to it.

Here is the reading Lou gave me, taken from my documented sheets.

> Lou: "I have messages for you from a young lady. She has asked me to explain to you what I do and has stepped back while I do that."
>
> Sandy: "Okay. I am listening."
>
> Lou: "When I lost my partner, Scott, I immediately began getting messages from him. Scott is now my guide, and I work with Scott to bring messages to others from their loved ones on the

other side. Your daughter wants you to know that you will be working with her like I work with Scott. She is showing me a key to open a door to your learning. She says she is guiding you and leading you to the books you need to read and the people you need to meet. She wants you to read more about meditation and breathing."

Sandy: "Well, that is all very nice, but I need some verification that you are really talking to my daughter."

Lou: "Okay. Just a sec, I will ask her for some." *The idea that Lou could just ask Kim like that surprised me. What shocked me even more was what he came back with!*

Lou: "She is saying 'anniversary party.' Is there one coming up this summer? A big one! She wants you to know that she will be there, too. Wouldn't miss it for the world."

Sandy: "Yes, her grandparents' 50th. Wow, Kim."

Lou: "Will it be held outdoors?"

Sandy: "I think so." *It was to be a backyard party but, as I was not doing the planning, I was unaware of this at the time.*

Lou: "'Try to enjoy it, Mom.' Now she is talking about school. I see white flowers and a hat, like a graduation hat."

Sandy: "Yes. Her school is giving her the diploma she worked so hard for. We will receive it for her. We just found out."

Lou: "Well, she is okay with it. She is showing me that she will have a graduation where she is now. 'So don't be sad, Mom.'"

Sandy: "I will try, but she should be here."

Lou: "'I will be, Mom.' Now she is showing me a white cat that is with her in spirit."

Sandy: "I don't know."

Lou: "'Yes, you do, Mom!'"

Sandy: "We had a white cat when she was a little girl."

Lou: "That's it then. Now she is showing me another cat that has significance, too, and now I see a bed with white eyelet on it."

Sandy: "Yes! I know what she means." *I remember a picture that makes this message significant. Kim is lying on the bed with a cat; the bed has a white bedspread on it. It looks like eyelet. I did not explain the significance of this picture. I just confirmed the information.*

Lou: "Says you are drinking too much."

Sandy: "Maybe." *I didn't want to admit this to Lou. I had been drinking too much wine. It helped to ease the heartache.*

Lou: "Kim says the name 'Bonnie,' and that she guided you to her, too. Just a second! I need to listen to her. Okay, she told me that you would have an out-of-body experience with her. Kim will take you by the hand, and you will travel together. She wants you to ask Bonnie to help you understand what this is." *I was surprised again. Bonnie and I had just been talking about astral travel. I had asked her to explain more about this.*

Sandy: "Wow, Lou! That is fantastic. Thanks."

Lou: "Now something about a silver bracelet. Mean anything?"

Sandy: "Yes! All three girls had matching silver bracelets."

Lou: "She is saying to take hers. Now she is showing me a gift box with a pink bow. Look for it. It will come. It will be from Kim."

Sandy: "Okay, I will." *And it did come a few months later!*

Lou: "Now I hear the name 'Ron,' and 'Tell him, too, that I am okay.' Now she is saying the name 'Tim.' She goes to Tim right now, too. He knows."

Sandy: "She has an Uncle Ron and a friend named Tim who is in Saudi Arabia right now and is probably very lonely."

Lou: "'Look for signs, Mom. There will be lots.' She says she was insecure about her religious beliefs before but knows God now. Big smile."

Sandy: "Yes, makes sense, as we aren't very religious."

Lou: "Now I don't know if I should give you this because it seems so silly, but she is telling me to. She is saying, 'Dirt and lots of it. Dad likes it.' She is laughing. Do you understand?"

Sandy: "Yes, definitely." *We had dug up our whole backyard the second year we were in our house. Then mounds of dirt had been dumped to fill in a ditch in the back. We had been the talk of the neighborhood.*

Lou: "She is saying that Dad did this."

Sandy: "Yes, he did."

Lou: "She tells you to talk to your grandmother about all this and about your learning." *My grandmother was the only one who had always held these spiritual beliefs and had told me that Kim had appeared to her at the end of her bed.*

Lou: "Now she is showing me a plant — a factory — and saying she goes there, too. Does this make sense?"

Sandy: "Yes." *All the girls had worked at the Chrysler plant during their summer holidays.*

Lou: "She talks about a sister who goes there. Does she have a sore ankle?"

Sandy: "Yes. She hurt it recently, I think."

Lou: "There is something else about her ankle. She is pointing to her ankle and smiling."

Sandy: "She has a tattoo around her ankle. I was so angry when she got it."

Lou: "She says that her sister is tough and will tell anyone off if she needs to."

Sandy: "Yes, that's right." *Laughing.*

Lou: "Now she is stepping back and there are two men here. One she is calling 'Grandpa.' The other may be a great grandfather."

Sandy: "Okay. What are they saying?"

Lou: "Name of John mean anything?"

Sandy: "Yes, that is her grandfather's name."

Lou: "He comes to tell you to put her rings back on soon. Do you understand?"

Sandy: "Oh, yes! Definitely."

Lou: "He is showing himself taking both her hands and helping her. This must be his wife."

Sandy: "Yes. That is his wife. She has been sick and lost so much weight that she had to take her rings off."

Lou: "Now she is excited, talking about a party with her friends. This was very recent; she went there, too. She wouldn't miss all the fun, she is saying."

Sandy: "Yes. I know what she means." *Kim's friends, both from her hometown and from her university, went away just the weekend before. This was a tradition Kim had started so that all her friends would get to know each other. They had decided to go again this year, to honor what she had started. Now I knew Kim had been present at the party, too.*

Lou: "She loves all of you and will guide you in this work. She is excited because she knows you can learn very quickly. Says you will work together. 'Look forward not back,' she is reminding you. You will have a new relationship together."

Before I hung up, I told Lou that the spirit who came through him was my daughter named Kim. Not one doubt troubled my mind, for I knew with certainty that Kim had given these messages to Lou. I now accepted that Kim had her hand in our meeting and that Lou and I were destined to meet each other that day. Through this reading I also received validation that Kim had guided me to Bonnie as well.

I spent a sleepless night mulling over all the messages I had received that evening. I was in total awe of those who were able to bring through

*Would we, Kim and I, really work together as Lou had predicted?*

these comforting messages from the other side. I was a mere beginner, but because of the success of my automatic writing, I thought I must possess a certain amount of ability. I was now being told that I would "do this type of work!" Would we, Kim and I, really work together as Lou had predicted?

My mind briefly reviewed all the spiritual occurrences since Kim's passing, and I somehow knew in my heart that Lou's prediction would come true.

It wasn't long before I opened another door and walked through.

❋ ❋ ❋

**June 1999.** At this point I was firmly dedicated to my mission to learn as much as possible about the other side. On June 23, I went with my sister-in-law Ruth to hear a speaker talk on the subject, "Your Guides and Angels and How to Meet Them," at a nearby bookstore. Ruth had become involved in my journey in a big way because she was so often with me when a new door opened during my search for understanding. Ruth was the one who suggested we go to the bookstore that evening.

While listening to the speaker talk about guides and angels, I met two women who were to become my friends: Joanne Rankin and Jeanne Lightheart. I discovered that they both also did automatic writing. I had never seen anyone else do automatic writing, but as I watched them, I recognized what they were doing. It was through their automatic writing that the name "Holly" was confirmed — again — as one of my spirit guides.

Joanne, Jeanne, and I quickly became friends. As we got to know each other, we noticed many parallels in our lives. The fact that the three of us attempted automatic writing and had begun to open spiritually at about the same time were just two of the parallels. We discovered many more: all three of us were in the teaching profession, and our husbands were all electricians. Joanne and I drove identical cars, right down to the color and the model year. When I walked into her home, I was startled to discover we had decorated with the same pink-striped wallpaper. We also had chosen the same hallway lights and large ceiling chandelier.

We had a hard time believing these were mere coincidences.

We talked about our automatic writing and how to progress. We decided to form a learning circle. Not knowing anyone at that time who could lead us, we began getting together once a week, eager to help one another. During our third learning circle, I was suddenly struck by the realization that I did know someone who could help us — Bonnie.

Actually, Kim had reminded me of Bonnie during one of our automatic writing sessions. When I approached Bonnie, she quickly agreed, although she was somewhat nervous about teaching. It later became apparent that I played a part in helping her open the next door on her own journey to enlightenment.

The four of us got together for six more weeks and, with Bonnie as our leader, expanded our knowledge. Together we learned such things as grounding, centering, cleansing, and the importance of protection. Our vocabularies had to expand to include all these new words and the unfamiliar concepts they represented. Together we experienced wondrous growth.

Our learning circle also practiced visualization techniques to help us manifest what we wanted into our lives. With the help of several books, I began to create my own meditation and visualization tapes, which I happily shared with the others. By this point, I was meditating more often and hearing messages clearly from those on the other side. My writings became more detailed as my spiritual knowledge unfolded.

I began to scan bookstores for books that might expand my own abilities. I started purchasing volumes that taught meditation techniques, chakra clearing, astral travel, and how to develop my own psychic powers. I wished to learn it all, to forge a solid link to my daughter on the other side.

No one could make me stray from this new awakening, but I had to learn how to balance this spiritual exploration and development with the everyday world around me. I knew that come September I would have to go back to teaching part-time. Even though I was absolutely determined to keep this new link to Kim, it was imperative to step back into mainstream living.

Meanwhile, I was still getting readings over the Internet but not spending as many hours at it. I always expected Kim to arrive during these readings and was not often disappointed. I did, in addition, receive nice surprises from two very important people on the other side. On June 12, my Aunt Rita stepped forward to talk, after giving me definite proof it was she. I have a copy of this reading in my files, but the messages are forever in my heart.

Here is the free mini-reading I received:

Online Medium: "Okay, Holly is next."

Sandy: "Thanks."

Online Medium: "Holly, who do you want to contact tonight?"

Sandy: "My daughter or my aunt or both."

Online Medium: "Okay, Holly, was your aunt slightly plump, not too tall with black, wavy hair with streaks of grey?"

Sandy: "Sounds just like her."

Online Medium: "Does the name Rena mean anything to you?"

Sandy: "No, but it's close to her name."

Online Medium: "Okay, thanks. Heard an R for sure. Let me listen again. She sounds like she is saying Aunt Rita now. Is that her name?"

Sandy: "Yes."

Online Medium: "Seems to be a jolly person?"

Sandy: "Yes." *My Aunt Rita was known for being a happy person, funny, and always smiling.*

Online Medium: "Passed over fairly young. Has been there a long time because she is saying it has been awhile."

Sandy: "Yes, she died 23 years ago."

Online Medium: "Was she in her 40s when she passed?"

Sandy: "Yes."

Online Medium: "She is showing me a sewing machine. Mean anything to you?"

Sandy: "Yes."

Online Medium: "Who sews, you or her?"

Sandy: "Me."

Online Medium: "Now she is showing me curtains and saying they are really nice. Boy, she is sending you lots of love. Were you very close?"

Sandy: "Yes."

Online Medium: "Well, she is making me feel so much love for you. Wow! She sure loved you a lot."

Sandy: "I loved her, too."

Online Medium: "She is showing me some curtains now. Green, poofy things with green flowers. Make sense?"

Sandy: "Oh, wow! They are in my house now. I made them."

Online Medium: "Well, she is proud of you. You do nice work."

Sandy: "Say thank you to her."

Online Medium: "You can do that yourself."

Sandy: "Okay." *The fact that my Aunt Rita had described the curtains I had made three years earlier gave me the verification I needed to believe the messages. There was no other way for the medium to know anything about my curtains. Aunt Rita was giving the messages loudly and clearly. The physical description at the beginning of the reading was also accurate. While I was growing up, my Aunt Rita was like a second mom to me. We were very close. I really missed her. Aunt Rita was my dad's sister, who passed from cancer in 1976, the year Kim was born.*

Online Medium: "Now she is showing me apples. Do you make a connection?"

Sandy: "Don't know." *It would have been easy, at this point, for her to drop this subject, but this is what she was hearing and she was pursuing it.*

Online Medium: "Did she like making apple pies?"

Sandy: "Maybe. Don't know."

Online Medium: "Oh, no! She is saying an apple for the teacher. Does this make sense?"

Sandy: "Yes." *I am a teacher.*

Online Medium: "She is such a lovely spirit."

Sandy: "Yes, she always was a lovely person."

Online Medium: "Big smile and is sending you lots of love. She is glad you asked for her. She is fading now. Glad I could get her for you. She is really lovely and jolly."

Sandy: "Thank you so very much." *I felt happy and comforted with the knowledge that Aunt Rita had come to pay me a visit. It had been such a long time. It felt so nice.*

The second unexpected reading came on June 24, when my father-in-law John showed up. It was a pleasure to hear from other loved ones who had crossed over. I was so happy that John came through, as we had been quite close.

John arrived with three verifications to let me know it was really him. He had always been bald when I knew him. He had difficulty using one arm because of polio but had still enjoyed carpentry work. All three of these facts were brought out during the reading. I had no doubt it was John doing the talking. I was sent a copy of my reading to place into my files.

This is the reading I received:

Online Medium: "Holly, you will be next on the list. You ready?"

Sandy: "Yes."

Online Medium: "Who would you like to contact tonight?"

Sandy: "My daughter."

Online Medium: "Okay, let me focus."

Sandy: "Okay."

Online Medium: "Not getting anyone like a daughter. Seeing an older man though. He is about 70."

Sandy: "Okay. This could be my father-in-law."

Online Medium: "Let's see what I can get. Says he is worried about your driving. Make sense."

Sandy: "Could. Don't know."

Online Medium: "Okay. Let me focus. He is saying you are not paying attention. Be careful."

Sandy: "Okay. Can you tell me more about this man?" *I had not admitted to anyone that I was having a hard time keeping my mind on my driving, but I was. A few months later I would have a minor mishap when I hit a median in the center of the road.*

Online Medium: "Name of John or James mean anything?"

Sandy: "Yes, John."

Online Medium: "Is that his name?"

Sandy: "Yes."

Online Medium: "He is rubbing his head and saying, 'I can have hair now.' Funny man."

Sandy: "Yes, makes sense."

Online Medium: "He is sending you lots of love."

Online Medium: "He is waving his arm around now. Not really a wave. Was there something about his arm?"

Sandy: "Yes. He had polio."

Online Medium: "Oh, okay. He is waving it around and saying, 'I can use it now.'"

Sandy: "Oh! This is great. I am glad he has finally come."

Online Medium: "Shows me he is a carpenter type. Like he has tools around him. Make sense?"

Sandy: "Yes."

Online Medium: "He is fine and sends his love to all."

Sandy: "Thanks. Does he have a message for his son?"

Online Medium: "He is smiling. Clean out the garage(s) he says, and he will be there, too."

Sandy: "Oh, that is so right."

Online Medium: "Wants him to get his knife, like a pocket knife. He wants him to have it."

Sandy: "Okay. I will tell him."

Online Medium: "Green handle. I think in a work room 'He knows,' he says."

Sandy: "Okay. I will try to find out."

Online Medium: "He is saying again that he wants him to have it. Tell him to look for it in a work room."

Sandy: "Okay. I will."

Online Medium: "He is going now. But love to all of you."

Sandy: "Thanks so much." *I was thinking that the reading was over, but spirits can always surprise you. This is what I was told next.*

Online Medium: "You're welcome, but there is a young girl that is standing behind him."

Sandy: "Oh, really! Maybe my daughter?"

Online Medium: "She is shy and won't come out from behind."

Sandy: "Oh, that won't be my daughter. Can you tell her age?"

Online Medium: "Looks about 14 or 15. She is very shy. Looks like she has not done this before and doesn't know how."

Sandy: "Oh! I wonder who she is?"

Online Medium: "Well, she is standing behind John so is probably connected to him."

Sandy: "Oh! Gosh, I know who that might be! Wow!"

Online Medium: "Okay, but she won't come out and it is fading. I am asking her to come back again. They are both gone now."

Sandy: "Thanks so much. You were right on." *I do feel I know who this young girl was, but she has not yet come back during a reading. Someday I hope she will. I had a very strong sense she was a cousin of Doug's who passed away suddenly some years before. After this reading, I did receive a message from this young girl who, I believe, was with John. She came through in my automatic writing.*

For the next few days, each time I doubted the contact I received from my loved ones who had crossed over into the other realm of existence, I would remind myself of all the verification I had received. Everything — from my old belief system to the way I spent my days — had changed in such a short span of time.

I had read, over and over again, that we are spiritual beings having a human experience. I often pondered that statement. It was becoming evident to me how thin the veil actually was between the two worlds. I understood that the "people" on the other side just wanted to let us know that they were okay. I learned we all have guides who are ready to assist us when we ask them to, but we must ask. I was hearing about and investigating ideas I had never before contemplated.

*I learned we all have guides who are ready to assist us when we ask them to, but we must ask.*

I became more and more interested in the topic of astral travel — or out-of-body experiences — and considered this might be possible for me. If I could really leave my body and travel to the other side, it would give me another way to reach my daughter.

I had discovered books written about near-death experiences and read about people who experienced spontaneous astral travel. I knew from reading John Edward's book, *One Last Time*, that he had done spontaneous astral travel since he was a child.

Could one induce an out-of-body experience? I had to find out.

I wanted to try but wondered if it was dangerous. I needed more information and went in search of a book on the subject. I found many, finally selecting one by Rick Stack called *Out-of-Body Adventures*. This book provided, according to the author, a simple, effective approach for learning how to consciously leave your body. According to the author, out-of-body experiences could be incredibly exciting, spiritually enlightening, and easy to do.

I was ready to try.

I had also read about the effective use of affirmations. Affirmations are positive statements one repeats over and over, such as, "I am happy, healthy, wise, and wealthy." Effective affirmations are written in present — not future — tense as if you have already achieved your goal. I learned we do have the power to bring what we want into our lives, and affirmations are one way to accomplish this.

I started to repeat affirmations in order to make astral travel happen for me. Following are some examples of the affirmations I used:

"I have out-of-body experiences easily and with great clarity."

"When I leave my body, I am completely safe."

"I use my personal power of thought to lift myself out of my physical body."

If saying these affirmations was going to help me be successful, then I was determined to repeat them. Because I wanted it so much, I tried to convince myself I wasn't afraid. Not wanting to admit that I had some reservations about trying to induce an out-of-body experience, I asked Kim and my guides to help me.

I blocked out the magnitude of what I was attempting but I was unable, at this time, to leave my body. I decided I would have to read more information about this phenomenon and then try again.

I did try a few more times, but I was still unsuccessful and decided to leave that idea alone for awhile. However, after my reading with Lou, I knew I must try again. When I had studied the procedures and gained more confidence in my ability to accomplish this, I was sure all I needed was more time to learn and understand the process.

I began reading about Edgar Cayce, renowned as one of America's greatest psychics. He believed in the power of the mind to create our own reality and once wrote, "The thoughts we entertain in our mind become real in the circumstances in our lives." Henry Reed's book, *Mysteries of the Mind*, explores Cayce's explanation of this process and provides scientific and philosophical viewpoints on this subject. I reasoned that if "ideas create physical realities," then through visualizations, I would be able to create an out-of-body experience.

I discovered a book called, *Edgar Cayce on Channeling Your Higher Self*, also written by Henry Reed. This book was dedicated to the subject of channelling and the superconscious mind and how it can affect our lives. "For as he thinketh in his heart, so is he." Proverbs 23:7. If this statement were true, then our thoughts were more powerful than I had previously understood. Could this be why the art of visualization was so important to psychic development?

Creative visualization is a process by which we hold an image, idea, or thought firmly in our mind and expect it to materialize. I wanted to astral travel, I needed to astral travel, and I was prepared to visualize this becoming a reality. I needed to believe the statement, "Ideas create physical reality."

I practiced my visualization techniques and repeated affirmations to create the experience of astral travel for myself.

Chapter 4

# My Spiritual Transformation

*It is only with the heart that one can see rightly;*

*What is essential is invisible to the eye.*

—Antoine de Saint-Exupery, *The Little Prince*

**July 1999.** This month had been both difficult and enlightening. Fascinated by the information that had come through during my automatic writing sessions, I began to feel unusual sensations around me when I sat down to write. Although the words now flowed smoothly from my hand onto the paper, I felt pressure bearing down on my hand. I didn't fully comprehend what was happening to me, but I did believe I was making contact with my guides, as well as Kim and other loved ones who had passed on.

I immersed myself in books detailing how to strengthen my connection to the other side. I knew I had made an important connection through my automatic writing but was coming to understand that there were other avenues to pursue, as well. Meditation was the common thread woven through many of the books I had read, so I began to set aside more time for meditation.

I had prayed for protection prior to each automatic writing session, despite the fact I had never included prayer in my life before Kim's unexpected passing. I had recently read about the power of prayer in an article that advised, "Pray for what you want and trust it will happen for you." I decided to look for more reading material on the subject of prayer.

Finding just the right book was a hard task, but I settled on one by Marianne Williamson, *Illuminata, A Return to Prayer*. As I scanned through this book, I liked what I read. I was especially drawn to her words: "Both prayer and meditation open us to the wisdom that is within us and around us. They are the stepping stones to what we call miracles. As we pray and meditate, attuning our hearts and minds to God, we become universal channels for the power of good."

I found these words compelling enough to make a conscious decision to include more meditation and prayer in my life.

During the few months since Kim's passing, my spiritual path had opened quickly, but I realized I needed to re-focus on other elements of my life that used to be important to me. It continued to be a struggle to maintain a balance between my spiritual journey and the everyday tasks of living and being a part of this busy world.

*My spiritual journey was my way to reach Kim and ease my aching heart.*

My spiritual journey was my way to reach Kim and ease my aching heart. It seemed more comforting for me to remain connected to the other side.

Grieving is stressful and complicated. Despite all my efforts and certainty that Kim was very much alive on the other side, I continued to experience panic attacks. When they hit, they were intense and unexpected, causing my emotions to erupt. I still spent far too much time in the safety of my home. When I ventured out into stores, I had to work hard to keep my emotions in check.

I was, however, feeling a greater sense of peace as I went about my daily routines. This was the direct result of the spiritual transformation that was taking place within me. I desperately wanted to reconnect with my family members still in this world. I loved them all so very much but at the same time I yearned to understand why Kim had to die. Kim's passing had shattered my old world. I had to strive daily to live with my grief while I forged my new world.

Overwhelmed by the rapid progression of my spiritual enlightenment, I sometimes felt as if I were spiralling out of control. It was so like me to be fearful of new things. I was never one to take chances. I had always liked to play it safe, but now I had opened a door into a mysterious world. I do know that my love for Kim was the driving force, and remembering that Kim had always been an adventurer emboldened me.

I was driven to continue my spiritual journey even though I realized I needed to slow down the pace. I shared these feelings during a discussion with Sharlette, the medium who had opened me to the other side with my first reading. She casually informed me that I could just ask "them" to slow it down if it was frightening me. This had never crossed my mind, and I appreciated the insight. That is exactly what I did! I asked my guides for balance and guidance in my journey.

All went silent for a nerve-wracking three weeks. It was as if I had pulled the proverbial plug.

What had I done? I sat down, prepared myself to write, but nothing happened. I tried to force the process and even strained to make up the words, but it didn't feel at all right. I worried that I had lost my ability to hear those on the other side and perhaps would not be able to receive further messages from Kim.

When my writings abruptly stopped I blamed myself. I prayed to be allowed to hear the messages again. Then, at last without warning, I began to hear messages from the spirit world once more. It was like a faucet had been turned on, the connection restored, and communication flowed again.

I was so relieved that I was now willing and ready to learn everything they wished to teach me. During the three weeks of silence, I focused on improving my meditation techniques and engaged in one-sided conversations with Kim. Not receiving responses from her was frustrating for me.

I believe this whole episode of silence was a lesson from my spirit world teachers. I was learning patience, that's for sure. I have no doubt that this frustrating break from my writings was exactly what I needed in order to put my life back in balance. I had focused so desperately on my new relationship with Kim that I was not dealing with my earthly family or my grief. Now I vowed to spend more time with Kerry, Kristy, and Doug.

Taking this hiatus from my spiritual journey was necessary at that time. I now realize I was in dire need of emotional healing. My spiritual teachers had warned me that I needed to work on "clearing my chakras" in order to balance my energy. They maintained it was critical for me to balance myself emotionally, physically, spiritually, and mentally. Now I was beginning to understand. I was off kilter.

It was time for me to learn more about the energy centers called chakras and how to begin to clear them. Reading three books on the subject taught me important information.

Chakras are energy centers located at various places on the body. There are seven major chakras through which our life energies flow. For thousands of years, people of the Hindu and Buddhist faiths have applied their knowledge of the chakra energy centers in their meditation and yoga practices.

The word chakra literally means "wheel" in Sanskrit and, like wheels, they spin. The seven primary chakras are located down the center of the body from the crown of the head to the pelvis. Each corresponds to a major nerve center. Each chakra vibrates with a different color and spins in a clockwise direction. Several minor chakras are located in various places throughout the body, including the hands and feet.

When these energy centers are open and balanced, they allow the free flow of subtle energies throughout the body. When one or more are blocked, so is the body's energy flow. Learning to clear, open, and balance these energy points is essential to spiritual growth, physical healing, and becoming a clear channel to the other side.

My studies made me recognize I had many blocked chakras that needed to be cleared. This break from my automatic writing gave me the time to focus on my chakras and healing. Bonnie introduced me to a meditation and visualization tape on how to open and balance these charkas. I spent some time each day working to clear these energy centers. This work led the way to my greater understanding of energy.

I was also awakening to the fact that almost anything spiritual one wished to learn is available on tapes, CDs, and videos. I was grateful for these wonderful learning tools and used them frequently.

During this temporary three-week break from my spiritual journey, I was healing within. Through meditation I discovered a greater sense of peace. I had a better understanding of the statement, "Everything we need to know can be found in silence by going within." I discovered firsthand that we can and will find inner peace when we go within.

I couldn't assign a surrogate to go through the process for me. No one could do this but me; practice was the key. Through silence, visualization tapes, the use of music, and many books, I learned to meditate and find that peaceful place within my soul.

I loved getting readings from mediums but realized I could not constantly rely on my connection with them to hear from Kim. I knew I would eventually have to rely on myself to connect with her. I realized I had to meditate in order to do that.

It was important to be patient with myself since meditation is an art that must be developed through practice. I found a method that worked best for me, then I practiced, practiced, practiced. I had so much to gain from meditation that it was well worth the time I invested.

I read that meditation is simply a method to quiet the mind. A quiet mind allows access to subtle energies. It helped me feel a connection to those on the other side and brought clarity as well as insights into my daily life. Each time I meditated, I was aligning myself with higher vibrations and opening myself to healing that comes from within. I read about researchers who discovered that physical and psychological benefits are gained by meditating. Some of these benefits are better sleep and reduction of the intensity of pain. Meditation has been proven to help asthmatics by allowing them to relax. It lowers blood pressure and cholesterol levels and has a calming effect in times of trouble or grief. This last application was the most pertinent for me.

*I have overheard people say they are in too much pain or too much grief to meditate, but it is precisely because of these feelings that we should.*

I have overheard people say they are in too much pain or too much grief to meditate, but it is precisely *because* of these feelings that we should. I learned to set my grief aside, to visualize it in a bag that I set outside my room and to pick it up again at the end of my meditation session. I needed to assure myself I could pick up my grief at the end of my meditation time. This method aided me on my journey into meditation and helped me find a more serene place within myself.

One evening while I was sitting in meditation, as mysteriously as the messages from the other side halted, they began again. A flood of relief washed over me as I realized I was still able to make the connection to spirits on the other side.

❊ ❊ ❊

**August 1999.** I was feeling more relaxed about my spiritual transformation and definitely more balanced. Sometimes my mind would wander back to the subject of astral travel. I had done a considerable amount of reading on the subject, but I was still afraid to attempt astral travel on my own. I trusted that somehow I would find a way to experience this — at the right time.

Was this really something that could be done? Could I consciously will myself to leave my body? The books I had read definitely confirmed the fact that many people had been successful in their own attempts, but I still had my doubts.

On August 3, I received the first sign that I was going to be successful in my attempt at astral travel and that it would happen very soon. I had been absent from Internet sites for about six weeks now and missed receiving Kim's messages through others. I decided to check out a new site that someone mentioned to me. It was at this site I got confirmation about my future out-of-body adventure. It came in the form of a mini-reading.

The information that follows is taken from the notes I recorded during this short session. Unfortunately, I did not receive an email copy afterwards. My notes are not as detailed as some of the others because I jotted down only the highlights of the session.

The medium described Kim, her ponytail, and her red car. Then she told me she was saying "Starbucks Coffee." Wow! This was a great confirmation for me as I had been there the night before with Joanne. I was asked if I understood the message. I replied that Starbucks had significance for me.

The medium stated that Kim was saying the name "Mandy" and connected her to a poem. She asked, "Did this Mandy write a poem for her?" This was such a big verification, and I told her so. *Mandy had written a poem in memory of Kim, placed a laminated copy of it at the cemetery, and delivered a second copy to us. We framed and hung it on the wall in Kim's bedroom.*

"Kim likes it and says to tell her," the medium said.

The session continued as she noted that Kim was a very bright spirit and was saying I would be traveling soon. She asked me if I was planning a trip. She stated that Kim would be traveling with me.

I knew Kim was talking about astral travel because I had asked for her help when I meditated earlier in the day. I was not planning any other type of trip.

This lady ended the session with, "She sends her love to all, and she is gone."

Saying goodbye after a session has always been a sad experience for me because it signaled a disconnection from Kim. By now, I had the confidence to know she was often with me, in fact, with all of us when we needed her to be. Now I had received much-needed validation from Kim about my "upcoming trip." If Kim said this was possible, I believed it.

Then, through a series of circumstances, I ran into Hazel, the housekeeper/medium I had talked to when my brother-in-law Murray connected us back in April. I had not called her after that initial telephone conversation but had thought about her often. I felt when I needed to see her, I would.

On the afternoon of Thursday, August 7, I dropped in on Murray. Hazel came to his house only on Mondays, yet there she was, just packing up to leave. This was the first in-person contact I had with Hazel, so I introduced myself. I walked out to the car with her so we could talk privately. Because I knew she was a spiritual person herself, I realized I could share some of the remarkable — almost unbelievable — events that had taken place in my life since we had first chatted.

I asked her if we could go for coffee someday to talk about our journeys. As we discussed when to meet, I disclosed my hope to try an out-of-body experience. I will never forget her response.

"This is why we had to meet today. I can take you there."

"Take me where?" I whispered.

Hazel held my eyes with hers. "To your daughter."

I went weak in the knees and leaned against the house for support.

Hazel continued, as I grappled with my emotions. "We need to do this soon because Kim is saying that she is ready and so are you." Hazel told me she'd have to go home to check her appointment book but would get me in as soon as possible.

On the drive home, I again marveled at the synchronistic circumstances surrounding my meeting Hazel that afternoon. On August 10, just three days after my meeting with Hazel, I received my second confirmation regarding my soon-to-happen astral travel. This time the information came from my friend and medium, Sharlette. I had more faith in the fact that these events were not happening just by chance! "Spirit," Hazel told me, "never ceases to amaze us."

Hazel and Sharlette do not know each other and, in fact, do not even know about each other. Hazel lives near my hometown in Ontario, and Sharlette lives thousands of miles away in Arkansas, yet both these ladies were to give me separate confirmations about my plans for astral travel.

I "met" with Sharlette online in the chatroom on Tuesday, August 10. There were about four or five others with us that evening, having a pleasant discussion. I began silently asking Kim to show up and tell Sharlette about my plans for astral travel. I know that sounds a bit crazy, but I was aware of how well Sharlette heard Kim. I kept telepathically telling Kim to please give the information to Sharlette.

Kim is really amazing. She always was and still is. Within minutes Sharlette came back with. "Sandy, I am getting all these messages in my head for you, and I don't know why, but this information is coming from one of your guides. Kim is here, also, but she is standing behind your guide. He is the one that is talking, which is strange because Kim always talks to me directly. Oh, she is saying he can do this better than she can! Your guide is big, powerful, and full of light. He is saying that he will take you in his hands and help you. He says you will be traveling soon, this week, in fact."

She concluded with this statement: "I really don't know why I am getting all this."

I excitedly told her. "I know! I've been asking Kim to tell you about my plans to attempt astral travel. I asked her to tell you because I hadn't shared this with you yet."

"Wow! That is some verification," Sharlette replied. "Let me know if it happens."

I told her I would and informed her I had arranged to try it the next day with a woman named Hazel. I told my husband that I was going to attempt astral travel and explained to him what that entailed. He naturally expressed concerns. I told him I would be careful but *had* to try.

On Wednesday, August 11, I met Hazel at her home. She led me to her reading room upstairs. As I sat down in the chair, Hazel asked if I had brought any pictures with me and told me that she already had messages to give me from Kim.

I explained I didn't need a reading, but she emphasized I needed to trust her first before we began our attempt at astral travel. She revealed she would tape the initial part of our session. However, the astral travel part could not be effectively taped since most of it would be spent in silence.

I handed her the tiny book of photographs I had brought with me. As she slowly turned the pages, she relayed information to me about the people in the pictures — things about their lives and their personalities that she had no way of knowing. Some of the pictures were of family members. Some were of Kim's friends. Everything she told me was accurate. She explained that her guides and Kim were channeling the information through her.

I was mesmerized. The messages were entirely accurate.

Finally, she asked me if I was ready to astral travel to my daughter. I felt safe and comfortable with her, so I nodded, and we began.

This experience was emotional for me and therefore is extremely difficult to put into words. Hazel instructed me to relax and breathe deeply. She then led me through a visualization technique to relax me and induce an out-of-body experience. When she asked me if I felt myself lifting out of my body, I said I didn't think so. She softly reminded me just to relax.

As she talked me through another visualization, I still did not feel I was "going" anywhere. I sensed doubt seeping in when, suddenly, I felt myself slowly "swoosh" up. I recall thinking; "I *am* somewhere! I *am* somewhere!"

I'm not sure if I verbalized these words. Hazel's voice seemed far away as she reminded me to relax.

Then in one incredible moment, I felt an all-encompassing love. No earthly words can describe the feeling, and I will never forget this experience. For a few seconds I forgot I came to be with Kim. I was surrounded by the most magnificent warm, white light. I was crying because so much love enveloped me.

Then I began hearing words. I discerned Kim's voice. I never believed I would hear Kim's voice again! What joy!

We talked telepathically, mind to mind. I had planned to ask her so many questions if I did see her, but I think the emotions of the moment made my mind go blank.

Here is my conversation with my daughter, Kim:

Kim: "Mom, I am here. Feel me."

Sandy: "Kim, are you okay?"

Kim: "Yes, Mom. Better than okay. See how beautiful it is here?"

Sandy: "But I need you with me, Kim."

Kim: "I am with you, Mom. Feel me. I am here. God is here."

Sandy: "I miss you."

Kim: "I know, but you are doing great. You are progressing. This is your destiny."

Sandy: "Why, Kim? Tell me why?"

Before she could answer, I started to return to my body. I had no control over it. I gradually realized I could see my body sitting on the chair. I slowly "swooshed" back down into it. I felt myself align my invisible body with my physical body. I was to find out later that this invisible body was my astral double.

Words are inadequate to describe what I experienced and all the emotions that followed. No words known on this earth can do it justice.

Hazel left the room for a while so I could collect myself and be alone with my thoughts and tears. When I was ready to describe my experience, I told Hazel that, initially, I didn't think I had "gone" anywhere.

"No, they knew that you needed help," she said, smiling at me. "I saw your guide take you in his hands and help you."

*I had been transported to and surrounded by a Love and Light that was not of this earth.*

These were the very same words Sharlette had said to me the night before!

I was forever changed that day. When I was "gone" from my body, I still felt like me. I wondered if this is what it is like to die.

How does one truly understand what all this means?

This experience awakened within me the longing to do what Sharlette, Lou, and Hazel were able to do. The three of them had given me so much comfort with their messages from Kim. They helped to lift me out of the depths of despair and bring me to the realization that Kim was indeed very much alive and could still reach into our world — and that I could reach into hers. Over the last few months, Sharlette and Lou had relayed many loving messages from Kim. Now, with Hazel's help, I had been transported to and surrounded by a Love and Light that was not of this earth.

Hazel informed me that when I was ready I could astral travel on my own. I was too emotional to think about anything but the present moment I was in, but I knew I would later process that possibility.

Reflecting on the experience over the following week, I felt a wide range of emotions. I was disappointed with the fact that I did not "see" Kim as I thought I would. She was part of the Light. To describe this is nearly impossible with the words we have available on this plane. I had wanted to actually see Kim in the form she'd had on earth, but I did not physically see her. I did, however, feel her presence.

I didn't know what I really thought would happen. I only knew what I *wanted* to happen. Of course I had wanted to spend time with Kim. I was elated that I had, without a doubt, accomplished that.

I didn't feel the need to try astral travel again for a while, and I got the feeling this was something I shouldn't do on a regular basis. Nonetheless, it was something I needed to do at that time. Thanks to this experience I understand so much more.

I did feel somewhat envious of people who spontaneously left their bodies. However, I had read that we all astral travel in our sleep but most of us just don't remember the trip. Well, I had definitely had an experience *while I was wide awake* that I would never forget!

While I was with Hazel, a friend waited out in the car. She had agreed to come with me in case I was too emotional to drive home. When we first arrived, I asked Hazel if my friend could come in and find a quiet place to read. Hazel explained that if my friend were in the house during my reading, her energy might interfere with the clarity of my reading.

This was another new piece of information for me to process — subtle energy. I had so much to learn.

Before I left Hazel's home after my successful astral travel experience, Hazel informed me that my guides were telling her I would be doing a similar type of work. She suggested I read *Opening to Channel, How to Connect with Your Guide*, by Sanaya Roman and Duane Packer. I was utterly startled because I had just bought this very book. In fact, it was in a bag in the car. Nothing much surprised me anymore.

Hazel and I walked together to my car. I leaned into the car, lifted the bag sitting on the floor, and yanked out the book. "Yes," Hazel said with a smile, "that is the book!"

As much as I wanted to read this book immediately, I was so completely exhausted I went directly home to bed. I kept advising myself to keep my logical mind out of what had transpired that afternoon. In fact, I knew I had to guard against my logical thinking interfering with my unfolding spiritual journey. I knew, if I wasn't careful, I could "talk myself out of" this wonderful series of experiences.

The next afternoon, wondering what I was to learn, I began to read. This book, crammed with valuable information, explained the process of "channeling," which manifests in various forms but basically is a process where a person brings through communication from the other side. After finishing the first two chapters, I learned we are all capable of channeling if we put the effort into making the connection.

By the time I had completed this book, I had a better understanding of the process. I liked what I read and found comfort in some of the concepts presented:

1. We can make a connection by working with a high-level spirit guide on the other side who helps us to access the higher realms. These high-level guides are able to step down or slow down their higher vibrations to make it easier for us to connect with them since earth plane vibrations are slower

due to the density of energy.

2. Channeling involves consciously shifting one's awareness to be able to form a bridge from our world to theirs. To achieve this shift in awareness, you need to learn to concentrate and get your own thoughts out of the way.

3. Our guides assist us with making this connection, but we must learn to become clear channels. To achieve this, we must take the time to quiet our chattering minds.

I had just found a compelling reason to improve my meditation techniques! For the remainder of August, I worked on meditation plus clearing and balancing my chakras. I spent very little time on the computer now, as I had so much to learn. More of each day was now spent in meditation.

My friends and I set aside one evening a week to participate in our learning circle. One week Bonnie brought a beautiful healing meditation tape for us to try. I enjoyed following the suggestions made by the soothing voice. It felt comfortable and right. During the discussion that followed the meditation, I shared how I thoroughly enjoyed it. Someone else, however, felt it was too confining, suggesting that soothing music without a voice-over was a more enjoyable way for her to meditate. Each of us had our preferences; no one was right or wrong.

I came to understand how much we could learn from one another, how important it was to practice meditation, and the great value of discussing spiritual concepts with others. We were all receiving messages as individual as we were. It became apparent that I "felt" much more than I could "see" or "hear."

These weekly gatherings were over all too soon. Bonnie had to continue with her own learning, a circumstance that necessitated our finding a new teacher. Our last meeting with Bonnie was on August 27, 1999. "Trust the process as it unfolds," Bonnie had often affirmed as our weekly gatherings were ending.

I now had to trust that a new teacher, someone as yet unknown, would present himself or herself when the time was right.

❋ ❋ ❋

**September 1999.** On August 28, I received a phone call telling me that my 89-year-old grandmother, Gladys Gallant, had crossed over into the next life.

Early in the evening of September 4, I was sitting alone in my room, quietly reflecting on the passing of my grandmother. Scores of memories of happy times in her company flooded my mind. I certainly would miss her, but she had lived a good, long life, and I was comforted by the fact she no longer had to struggle.

I felt a bit guilty that I wasn't grieving for her, but I truly understood she was okay. My grandmother openly believed in life after death so I began to talk to her. I told her I wanted to maintain our closeness and asked her to give me a sign when she felt ready.

In the morning I decided to meditate and have a session of automatic writing before I got on with my day, which would include a family gathering to celebrate my grandmother's life. It was also the day that I received my first message from her through automatic writing.

Kim delivered the message: *"Grandma wants lots of laughter and lots of stories. She always loved talking. She is learning lessons here and is asking for forgiveness for all her wrongdoings to others, but she says this is not to be talked about today. She is saying, 'Happy day!' She is dancing a jig with the other old folk because she is free. She is saying, 'Not old. Not old now.' She is a riot. We love you and send you our strength today. Love always, Kim and Grandma."*

What a miraculous journey I was on! I could not prove to anyone that this was a true communication from Kim, but the feeling in my heart was all the proof I needed. I enjoyed a feeling of contentment that only this message could bring.

As we approached the middle of September and drew nearer to the first anniversary of Kim's death, I was in a downward spiral of emotions. The reality of our profound loss had me in its grip, and I felt panic. The full force of my heartrending pain engulfed me.

My growing belief in the other side did help to get me up every day, but as the anniversary date loomed, I wanted to retreat to the safety and security of my bedroom.

Also fast approaching was the sentencing date for the man who caused the accident. We not only had to cope with the first anniversary of Kim's crossing, but we had to write our victim impact statements as well. How could I put into words what Kim meant to me? How could I adequately explain what a special young woman Kim had been?

The task overwhelmed me. As a way to ease my sorrow, I immersed myself even deeper into my new spirituality.

As far as our spiritual study group was concerned, my friends and I found a new teacher named Marlene and set a time to meet. We began our Tuesday evening classes eager to learn. We worked on improving our meditation, practiced new visualization techniques, had discussions about angels and spirit guides, and did further work on our chakras.

Marlene was a stress therapist among other things. With her at the helm, our band of "spiritual travelers" focused on ways to make more positive things happen in our lives. Because I was going through such a stressful time, I was particularly thankful for the love and support my friends gave me. They encouraged me to come to the classes even when I felt I was not strong enough to go. Here I had an opportunity to deal with my loss and my grief. Nonetheless, I would constantly attempt to keep my emotions in check. I would feel tears well up behind my eyes and swallow hard to keep them from spilling over.

It was during these classes that I woke up to the fact that I must express these feelings openly and shed my tears. We were all on our healing journeys, and my friends were ready to listen. We ended each evening session with a healing circle. I was often on the receiving end of their healing energy and was grateful to have it directed at me.

Outside of this class I immersed myself in learning. I read a new book approximately every three days, and my library of spiritual books was mushrooming. I sometimes would borrow a book someone suggested and end up buying it later.

Not every concept I read about I believed to be true. I was awakening to the fact that I could proceed on my own journey of developing my own beliefs without absorbing all the beliefs of others. This was empowering and affirmed my belief in myself. Affirming my own powers allowed me to seek my guidance from within. I knew I would be led to take the right path for my own enlightenment and healing.

Some days I would sit in silent meditation without asking for anything in particular. I would just open to the possibility of inner healing. I had focused most often on Kim and getting messages from her because that was why I was walking this path in the first place. Now, I also felt the value of listening in silence as I allowed my next step to unfold as it was destined. It was toward the end of September that I got re-acquainted with Lou. Lou was the medium from New York who had given me such accurate information during my reading over the telephone when I met him earlier in the year. He had told me Kim was going to work with me. He had reached out to give me what I so much needed back in May: a message from Kim.

We met for the second time as a result of another strange set of circumstances. I believe Divine Order was at work once again. On September 21, I decided to see if I could get a reading through the Internet. I had gone to a "reading room" and was put on the waiting list. The wait seemed endless, so, more than once, I almost left.

I sat for more than two hours watching other people have their readings and wondered when it would be my turn. By this time it was extremely late. The woman who was doing the readings suddenly stated that she was exhausted and would be leaving for the evening. She reassured us she would continue readings for the rest of us on her list at the same time next week.

Disappointment and sadness flooded over me, especially since I knew I was close to being next. I sat in the privacy of my computer room, reflecting on the evening, while I remained online. Within minutes, and before I had a chance to leave, we were told that Lou had just entered his reading room and that he would be happy to continue the readings.

When I saw his name, I thought about the last time we had talked. We all moved into his room. What follows is the reading I received. This was recorded, sent to me by email, and is filed away for reference. This was an extremely long reading but, because of the importance of all the information, I have included most of it here.

I remind you that I still used Holly as my pseudonym.

Sandy: "Hey, Lou. I am on the list. Second, I think."

Lou: "No, Holly, you are first. Ready?"

Sandy: "Yes."

Lou: "Everyone, I have read for Holly once, a long time ago."

Sandy: "Yes, last May."

Lou: "Let me focus. Okay, Kim is here and, boy, is she ready. She is saying, 'Mom you are wonderful. You are doing more than I could ever imagine.' Boy, is she ever strong and fluent and so fast. Slow down, Kim."

Sandy: "That is so her!" *Smiling.*

Lou: "She is showing me a cat. Light brownish and white. Shows me her holding this cat. Understand?"

Sandy: "Think so."

Lou: "Says you would understand."

Sandy: "Yes, I do." *This picture of Kim hangs in our family room. Copies of it had been made and given to friends and family.*

Lou: "Good. She is saying it is something special. 'You know, Mom,' she says. Now she is saying 'Jane.'"

Sandy: "Yes."

Lou: "Her friend?"

Sandy: "No, mine."

Lou: "Oh! Okay. Says you talk to her about all this."

Sandy: "Yes." *I began sharing my experiences with Jane very early after Kim's passing.*

Lou: "That is your confirmation that she is here and that she is around you, but you already know that."

Sandy: "Yes."

Lou: "Gosh, she is a highly evolved spirit. She talks so fast. I can't keep up. I am trying, Kim." *This made me smile. This was so typically Kim. Not many of us could keep up with her. Staying silent, I was busy reading the words as Lou typed them.*

Lou: "This is wonderful! She is saying she is one of your guides. Beautiful soul and funny. Big smile. She is saying I can get the messages so she can go fast. LOL." [online abbreviation for Laugh Out Loud.] *Smiling.*

Lou: "Okay, now she is showing me a boy with dark hair. She says, 'Tell his mom he has a new job. She will understand. Tell his mom.' She is repeating this. Do you understand? Will she be open to this?"

Sandy: "Oh, yes. She sure will. Wow, Kim!" *This was a big verification for my friend Judy Piers. A few weeks prior to this reading, Judy had asked Kim to help her son, Mike, in his search for a job. Judy had recently called to tell me of his new job, and we discussed the fact that she had enlisted Kim's help. Whether Kim was able to help with this we will never know, but we were now sure she heard Judy and me discussing it.*

Lou: "This lady is your friend. Kim is smiling. 'Her friend, too.'"

Sandy: "Yes, exactly."

Lou: "She is saying 'thanks' to her. Do you understand?"

Sandy: "Sure do! Great!" *I too thank Judy from the bottom of my heart for being my lifeline. I am so thankful that Kim has been able to thank her, too.*

Lou: "Work. She is saying something about work."

Sandy: "I wonder what?"

Lou: "Do you travel in your job? She is showing me suitcases, so I think travel?"

Sandy: "No."

Lou: "Okay, don't know, then." *This is yet another big verification from Kim in regard to my astral travel. This topic is picked up later in the reading.*

Lou: "She says she loves you very much. Now something about a teddy bear and a halo? Okay, like an angel bear, I think."

Sandy: "Thinking."

Lou: "Seeing the number three."

Sandy: "Oh! Yes. I know what she means; a bear with a halo. Yes to three of them. Wow, Kim."

Lou: "She is great, Holly." *These three angel bears were very important. Someone had given a gift of an angel bear to each of my daughters and placed Kim's with her at the funeral. The medium's reference to them was more verification that Kim was able to see us. Although I had advanced far enough on my spiritual path that I didn't need much validation anymore, others around me still did. I could hardly wait to pass along this message to my family.*

Lou: "Now she is showing me candles and cake. A birthday soon?"

Sandy: "Maybe? Her father and sister?"

Lou: "Soooooooo funny. She is singing happy birthday." *I thought Kim was talking about my husband's birthday only a few weeks away. During the emotions of a reading, it is hard to think quickly about the information that is being relayed. Often it was only after the reading that I had time to reflect on the information and realize the truths that I was unable to recognize.*

Validation came months later as I was showing this account of the reading to my two sisters-in-law, Norma and Carolyn. Norma quietly asked me, "Don't you know what day that was?" As I looked at her, puzzled, she said,

"It was Carolyn's birthday. She was 52 on the day of the reading."

At that moment, we realized this was a birthday wish from Kim to her Aunt Carolyn. Not only had the reading occurred on the actual day of her birthday, but the number 52 that Kim relayed to me as "important" in the section of numbers below was also acknowledgment of her. These were also two more verifications for me.

I could see the tear in the corner of Carolyn's eye when she realized Kim had wished her a happy birthday from the other side. I feel confident Norma was correct in her belief that the message was meant for Carolyn.

> Lou: "Gives me 8 and 10 or 10 and 8. More numbers now and FAST. Slow down, girl. 2 and 4, 25 and 52."
>
> Sandy: "Thinking... Dad's birthday is 10 and 8. Thinking... sister's day of birth is 25. Don't know 52 or 2 and 4."
>
> Lou: "Okay. Oh, sorry. She is correcting me 2 and 14."
>
> Sandy: "Don't know."
>
> Lou: "She is showing me a calendar, so it is a date. Maybe February 14th? Yes, she is saying. Oh, she is saying I am so smart. Neat! Going to be a special day for Mom she says."
>
> Sandy: "Okay, don't know."
>
> Lou: "Are you wearing your hair differently? Says she likes what you did! Very becoming."
>
> Sandy: "No, I haven't changed it. Ohhhhhh! But my friend has. Wow! We stripped and dyed her hair and laughed a lot."
>
> Lou: "Well, apparently she was there. SMART COOKIE, she is. What's with 'the BUDDY system?' Says, 'He is okay.'"
>
> Sandy: "Oh, that is our dog."
>
> Lou: "She is wonderful, Holly."
>
> Sandy: "Yes. She sure is. Buddy fell down the stairs this week. We thought he broke a leg."
>
> Lou: "She is saying he will be okay. She has a gift for you from her."

Sandy: "Oh, wow."

Lou: "Something with perfume."

Sandy: "I know."

Lou: "Did you get a catalog with perfume scent inside? It is from Kim. She says, 'Go for it, Mom. You deserve it!'" *Crying.*

Lou: "You know what to do with the perfume. Buy it. Apparently, you felt it was too expensive, right?"

Sandy: "Yes."

Lou: "She is more than encouraging you to get it for yourself. Actually, it is a gift from her."

Sandy: "Oh!" *Crying.*

Lou: "'I found it for you, Mom.' She's sent you a sign in the form of a butterfly."

Sandy: "Yes! Yes! This is more important than you could ever know." *What a wonderful confirmation of the little white butterfly that followed me while I was cutting the lawn back in April. Kim has definitely proved to me that she was still around me and could hear me when I talked to her.*

Lou was able to hear Kim so accurately and clearly. Once I had received numerous messages through him that were both personal and accurate, it was easier to accept the validity of unknown information as it came through. I was learning that when information comes that one cannot prove — even if I did not understand it — I could accept it because of the earlier validations.

This is how I felt about the next section of this reading. It cannot be proven, but I absolutely believe it to be true.

Lou: "All these bright, vivid colors. That means she's in a VERY high place in heaven. She says that she works with kids. She says she brings them over. Oh! Now I know why you are supposed to travel in your work — with astral travel. WOW, this is neat. She is really excited. You know what she does?"

Sandy: "What?"

Lou: "She assists kids who astral travel to heaven."

Sandy: "Really! This is amazing."

Lou: "Abused kids who need to come home, but for a short time. She also helps children who pass, but she is very active in transporting kids to heaven who are abused and need the love in order to go on. WOW! This is wonderful stuff. These kids have no love here on earth. They would otherwise spread negativity here. Kim and others like her take them *there* while they are sleeping to assure them that there is some love for them. The kids come back refreshed, new persons. They will lead good lives, thanks to the good work that Kim does. You and she will continue to play a major role in this."

Sandy: "How?"

Lou: "She says, 'Don't be afraid, Mom.' She will guide you. Your daughter is an angel, VERY strong. 'Just rely on me, Mom. I'll take care of it.'"

Sandy: "I believe she will."

Lou: "I personally have never heard of all this before. This is wonderful and amazing." *This information filled my heart with wonderment. The following section is just as amazing!*

Lou: "Pumpkin now. Mean anything? Did she love Halloween? Oh, is it the ghosts?"

Sandy: "Her funeral was on Halloween."

Lou: "Wow, she is pulling our leg. The funeral? Ghosts. She is making a joke of it. P.S. I am not being disrespectful. It's her joking, truly."

Sandy: "Not really funny to us, Kim. I know, Lou, it is just like her to do that."

Lou: "You know I wouldn't do that to you, to anyone. She is soooo fast."

Sandy: "She was known for her quick wit."

Lou: "I can understand why! What is this about Christmas now? Tree, turkey, decorating the tree. 'All the fixin's,' she says. Were you going to downscale Christmas this year? Don't, she says. 'Do it for me, Mom.'"

Sandy: "She probably knows I don't want it without her. She loved Christmas. She was just like a little kid."

Lou: "'Please, Mom. Do it for me. Here's why.'"

Sandy: "Okay, I better listen."

Lou: "She's telling me that you are needed to spread joy, happiness, and fun. Ripple effect, she shows me. Understand? She is showing me the ripple effect in a lake. You, Holly, are the pebble tossed into the lake. Gosh! She is so smart! 'Without you, there would be no ripples. When you spread joy, happiness, and laughter to others, they will spread it, too.' She goes so fast. Darn!"

Lou: "Do you decorate a tree?"

Sandy: "Yes."

Lou: "I see one outside with lights on it, too."

Sandy: "Yes."

Lou: "She's informed me that this is a sign to others that love is emanating from her, you, and the house. It's really important to her."

Sandy: "Okay."

Lou: "Did you see or buy an ornament recently? It's a sign from her, a sign about this reading. This is incredible! She is telling me that you will keep this out all year as a reminder." *I didn't know then that in December we would receive a Christmas ornament from our Coping Group as a tribute to Kim. This ornament was engraved with her name, and I do keep it out all year. I forgot about this specific information until I was going over this reading to include it in this book. It is yet another fact that came true, but then Kim and others on the other side know what we don't.*

Lou: "There is more, Holly."

Sandy: "Okay."

Lou: "What about a pink rose?"

Lou: "'Remember about the rose, Mom. The picture frame?' You understand?"

Sandy: "Yes! Oh, yes!"

Lou: "She says, 'Is there any question about it now, Mom?'"

Sandy: "I received it for Mother's Day from the girls and put a picture of the three of them in it." *I sighed and sat back, overcome by emotion. Of all the details I'd heard that day, this was one of the most amazing. As I mentioned before, I do a lot of talking to Kim in my day-to-day existence. For Mother's Day, my other daughters gave me a picture frame decorated with pink roses. It was too painful for me to think that it came only from two daughters and not three. I needed it to be from all three. As I set it out, with a picture of our three daughters in it, I said to myself: I know that it is from you too, Kim. It has to be. I can't stand it if it isn't.*

Lou: "'Hugs again, Mom. Too bad Dad isn't here.'"

Sandy: "Tell her to talk about him."

Lou: "She's not a puppet for me to command. Sorry." *Another enlightening fact about spirit for me to digest.*

Lou: "But she is doing great the way she's going. Good thing I can type fast. She will love you for all ETERNITY. By the way, is the perfume *Eternity*?"

Sandy: "Yes."

Lou: "There you go! It's a confirmation of what she just told me. She will love you for ALL OF ETERNITY! Wow! You're crying?"

Sandy: "Yes. May I ask her a question?"

Lou: "She says not now, she is on a roll. Dice? Gambling? Casino? Bingo? Is there a casino near you? She is telling me that Mom likes it."

Sandy: "Yes, I like it. Just went and lost."

Lou: "She is telling me slots."

Sandy: "Yes."

Lou: "She was with you. There was something unusual about this trip."

Sandy: "Special, yes. Oh, no! She watched me lose all that money."

Lou: "What is $500? Is that how much you lost?"

Sandy: "Yes, between my husband and me." *I was too ashamed to admit I had lost that amount all by myself. Kim wouldn't let me get away with this lie.*

Lou: "'Come on, Mom, 'fess up.' She is so funny. I love her. This reading is why I had to be here tonight."

Sandy: "Yes."

Lou: "She says you needed this."

Sandy: "Yes." *Our 25th anniversary had just passed and Kim was not with us to celebrate. Before Kim's passing, the family had looked forward to the Silver Anniversary celebration our girls would plan for us, but now I just couldn't bring myself to celebrate in that way. I just wanted to hide from the world. I know I disappointed both my husband and our daughters. I regret that now, but at that time, I just could not face all the people who would have come to a party. We spent the day with our daughters, my brother-in-law Dave, and his family at Marineland in Niagara Falls, and the evening in the casino.*

Lou: "'Always, Mom. You are never alone. Not with me around.'"

Sandy: "I know, Kim. Always."

Lou: "She says, 'I am around you like this.' She says, 'Do you feel something around you now?' It's her and the hug."

Sandy: "Okay." *Crying.*

Lou: "She says you are doing great. She is proud of you. Wow, she says she has something for me!"

Sandy: "What?"

Lou: "Don't know. She says I will know when I get it. You will help." *Then she proceeded to give a message to her grandpa, my father, which I will keep just for him. I plan to show it to him when he is ready to see it.*

Lou: "Please understand that Kim is there with you and with me at the same time. She wants you to know that."

Sandy: "I understand, sort of."

Lou: "That means that she is at a VERY high level of heaven. Has integrated herself into God to a very high degree. She is truly wonderful!

Lou: "What's this about a box?"

Sandy: "Don't know. Thinking."

Lou: "'You know, Mom.' She says 'PINK.'"

Sandy: "Yes! Amazing!" *She was reminding me about the box with the pink bow on it. In my first reading with Lou, she'd told me I would receive it. The pink bow was actually part of the decoration of the box. She was acknowledging that I had received it — just as she had told me I would — and that it was a gift from her. Someone had given me this box with a little statue in it. It was a "Precious Moments" figurine of a little girl holding a sign that read, "I will always love you."*

Lou: "Kim is leaving, now."

Sandy: "There are no words to thank you."

I was speechless! I cried for a good ten minutes and anxiously waited for my email copy of this incredible reading to arrive so I could read and savor it.

Having a copy of the reading is so very valuable because it is proof of what transpired. As time went by it would have been easy to believe that what I remembered as fact might not really have been said, initiating disbelief. When the transcript of the session arrived, I meticulously read through it, filled with the wonderment of it all.

I mulled over the part of the reading where Kim told Lou she had a gift for him, and he would know when he got it. I wondered what gift Lou would receive from Kim. Of course, I also questioned what part I would play in it.

This present came shortly after, in the form of a message in my automatic writing. It was from Lou's partner and guide, Scott.

This was the first time someone not connected to me arrived to give a message. Unprepared, I was completely taken by surprise. My reading with Lou took place on the 21st day of September; just two days later I got the message for Lou through my automatic writing. I was surprised to hear from Scott but was glad I could relay his message to Lou who had done so much for me. I believe the message was a "thank you" to Lou from Kim.

I was extremely nervous about sharing Scott's information with Lou. I knew, however, that I must email him with this personal message. What would he think? He heard Scott so clearly. Did he really need this message from me? Still, I knew I had to send it.

His reply to this message came quickly: "Thank you so much for the beautiful note from Scott! I did not know that you did automatic writing, but the message means so much to me."

The following day I received a second response from Lou. "I am so happy that you decided to convey the information from Scott to me. As you know, it's wonderful and special to receive information, signs, and love from our loved ones in spirit. You will gain more confidence about conveying the information as you see the wonderful reactions and feedback from loved ones. It will come."

On September 28, I received yet another response. It stated: "I just reread your message tonight. I wanted to mention to you that there is a personal message to me from Scott in your writing. I just recognized it tonight. Thank you. Love to you and Kim from Scott and me."

This is how we sign all our correspondence now. I believe that the loving energy we send out to others always comes back. Lou reached out to me and, in return, received his own message.

I made great strides in my spiritual transformation this month. I would need this faith in the next few difficult months that were to follow.

❊ ❊ ❊

**October 1999.** I was in the process of reshaping my faith and trying to understand why seemingly bad things do happen to good people. My heart felt broken. It would soon be a year since Kim was taken from us and, on the human level, I felt excruciating pain. On the spiritual level, I continued to search for an understanding of why this had happened. Maybe this question could not be adequately answered while we remain in this earthly plane of existence, but I was making a conscious choice to further delve into spirituality. My heart ached to understand.

Through therapy I was coming to understand that the death of a loved one, especially that of a child, often makes us question our faith and propels us on a search for answers. I was no exception. My inconsolable grief over the loss of Kim had triggered my journey.

During this very difficult month, my emotions would swing back and forth with great intensity. I wrestled with the difficult decision to get back into the work force and return to teaching. My loved ones were worried about me, telling me I "should" step back into "normal" routines. I promised them that when November arrived, I would make contact with my teaching friends who were anxiously waiting to hear from me.

Now I questioned that decision. I was nervous. Was I emotionally strong enough to handle the stresses my job would involve? As a substitute teacher, I took on a job that was difficult at the best of times. Now with the grief that encompassed me, I doubted my ability to cope with the little ones. I had always liked my job as a substitute, priding myself on doing a good job. Since Kim's passing, I couldn't maintain even an interest, let alone a passion for it.

With the year anniversary of Kim's passing almost upon us, it definitely wasn't the right time for me to make such a big decision. I set it aside until the next month.

My priorities had changed and so had I. Although I understood I would never again be the person I was before Kim passed, I vowed to allow my future to unfold as it was destined. If teaching was not what I was to do at this time in my life, I trusted that the new path would be shown to me.

It was a difficult month for all of us. Even though nearly a year had gone by, some days I still expected Kim to come bouncing through the door with that beautiful big smile on her face. Then, reminded that I had to write my victim impact statement by November, I would be catapulted back to reality.

I thought if I could focus on this new spiritual journey, I would remain strong. I believed that Kim was around me and felt comforted by this fact. Sometimes, however, my grief was still like a knife that stuck in my heart and lodged there. This pain, when it hit, was — and is — unbearable. There is no greater loss than the death of one's child. It causes utter devastation within a family. We were no exception. Each of us had to deal with our grief in our own individual way.

I wanted to talk about Kim — about her life, about our loss and about my new awareness of spirit. My husband Doug would listen to my experiences, but I never really knew what he was thinking. My sister-in-law Ruth, having been involved in so much of my journey, believed I *was* making contact with Kim and with others on the other side. I am thankful for her faith. For a long time, we had not been close. It was nice to have her and her family in our lives again.

I began drawing in the other members of my husband's family to share what I was doing. They were — and this surprised me — inquisitive about all I had done and learned. They were open to the possibility of "the other side." They wanted to know more, and I was glad to share. They understood it was giving me some comfort.

Everyone missed Kim so much, and, as we shared our memories during that first year, we wondered if Kim was listening. It was comforting to know they were open to the possibility she may very well be hearing our words.

Regardless of all this, I felt myself being pulled back into pain. Was I just masking this pain with my quest for answers?  Was my mind, addled by grief, just making all of it up? I spent many hours reduced to tears, again hiding in the safety of my house. By now, however, I had wonderful friends and a small circle of family members who would not allow me to den up like a wounded animal. Knowing what a difficult month it was, these comforting supporters would call me. Any time I didn't answer the telephone, they would hop in their cars and come for a spontaneous visit. These loving people allowed me to lean on them for emotional support.

*I felt myself being pulled back into pain. Was I just masking this pain with my quest for answers? Was my mind, addled by grief, just making all of it up?*

It dawned on me that it was time to find an "inspirational seminar" to attend. I was reminded time and time again that I needed to "go within" to find healing for my broken heart. How would I be able to meditate when my heart was so full of grief and I could unexpectedly break into tears at any moment?

There is an old saying: "When the student is ready, the teacher will appear." One morning, turning on the television, I happened to catch Dr. Wayne Dyer speaking on the topic: "Staying on Your Path." How appropriate, I thought! Yet another synchronicity.

He was being introduced as one of the foremost inspirational speakers of our time in the field of spiritual growth and personal development. He possessed both wisdom and warmth, expressing his perceptions with humor. At the conclusion of the televised hour, I felt uplifted and stronger.

Names of his books and tapes available for purchase were listed at the conclusion of the program. I had found my "inspirational seminar" right in the privacy of my own home.

In the last few weeks, I had neglected meditation and my automatic writing. I was now inspired to "put my mind and body in a peaceful place," as Dr. Dyer advised, and have faith that I would receive what was right and perfect for me. I made the conscious decision to return to my daily meditations and my automatic writing.

I was open and sharing the messages I had received in my automatic writing with my circle of friends. During a discussion one evening at our learning circle, someone asked if I could do this automatic writing for others who would like to receive information from their guides or loved ones.

I had never before thought about this possibility. Immediately, I felt moved to describe my experience when I had received a message for Lou through my automatic writing. "This was an unplanned, spontaneous experience," I told them. I wasn't confident yet that this was a possible avenue to pursue as my continuing journey unfolded. I needed to do my own inner work, but perhaps, some day, I would be ready to channel information for others.

*I needed to do my own inner work, but perhaps, some day, I would be ready to channel information for others.*

I understood I had to trust that I had all the answers within me and, through meditation, would discern these answers. I felt a strong desire to try astral travel again; it was time for my second attempt. I made another appointment with Hazel, eager for the day to come. My mother-in-law Mabel lived in the same town, so I arranged to spend some time with her before I met with Hazel.

Mabel wanted to buy a new outfit for a special event that was coming up so I happily agreed to help her shop. The morning, however, did not go as planned. As Mabel stepped out of the passenger side of the car, she fell, breaking her arm. I spent the rest of the afternoon with her in the hospital emergency room.

Naturally, I had to telephone Hazel and cancel our appointment. As I explained the reason, I couldn't contain my disappointment and broke into tears.

Hearing the distress in my voice, Hazel comforted me. "Sandy, there is a reason for this delay. Trust in that fact." As she went to get her appointment book, I wondered if that was true despite my extreme frustration and disappointment.

When Hazel returned to the telephone, she informed me she had only one opening in October — on the 27th — the exact day of Kim's passing one year ago. Stunned, I tearfully mumbled something about being too emotional that day.

Hazel responded, "Divine Order! You will be okay. This is why you were not to come here today. Wednesday, October 27, it is then."

I telephoned my husband to tell him about his mom, assuring him I would stay with her until she was safely back to her seniors' complex. When I did arrive home late in the evening, I finally let go of my disappointment as I sat huddled in my room having a good cry.

After I had a cup of tea with Doug, he went off to bed. Although I was exhausted, both physically and emotionally, I wanted to go onto the Internet in search of Sharlette. I wondered if she would still be online so late in the evening.

Clicking on to her website, I saw her name and knew she was there. She was just saying goodbye to someone else. As soon as she acknowledged me, I related the happenings of my day and my extreme disappointment at not being able to keep my appointment with Hazel. Sharlette said, "I think it will happen on Wednesday. Kim is saying it will happen on Wednesday."

I marveled at how Sharlette could have such a direct link to Kim. I envied her connection with my daughter — after all, I knew how hard I strived to create one of my own. "That is exactly the day I re-booked my appointment for!" I said in amazement, humbled by the confirmation.

I wondered if Sharlette understood the peace that her messages provided to others. I am so grateful Sharlette came into my life; she became an important lifeline for me. I once told her I didn't want her to think I only wanted to get messages from her. She replied, "If I am offering the information, it is because I wish to." Someday I hoped I would be able to return the same kind of loving energy she offered so generously.

*When the first anniversary of Kim's passing arrived, I woke up thinking I didn't really want this spiritual enlightenment. I wanted to return it all! I wanted to exchange all my knowledge, all my new awareness if I could only have Kim back.*

We chatted for a moment, then she was off to bed. I wondered why she could hear Kim so clearly. Perhaps, I reasoned, we enjoyed a special connection. A thought crossed my mind that maybe we were together in a past life. I smiled. Someday I would pursue that avenue, too.

When the first anniversary of Kim's passing arrived, I woke up thinking I didn't really want this spiritual enlightenment. I wanted to return it all! I wanted to exchange all my knowledge, all my new awareness if I could only have Kim back. I wanted Kim here with us. As I dressed, my mind dwelt on the fact that I planned to astral travel today.

I spent the morning of October 27, the first anniversary of Kim's passing, visiting the cemetery and sitting on the grass talking to Kim. Many others had already visited and had left cards and flowers as tributes to Kim. A small book, *Girlfriends, Enduring Bonds,* was wrapped carefully in plastic and left behind. A bookmark flagged a page in the book that one of Kim's friends had intended for others to read.

I asked for Kim's help and the help of my guides. "Guide me to success later today in my second attempt at astral travel." I tried not to have my own preconceptions of what I wanted to happen. "Help me remain focused and calm. Kim, I ask for your help to accept that I will have the experience I need for my own spiritual growth."

When I went home, I meditated and repeated some affirmations. I trusted that these positive thoughts would help put me in the proper state of mind for my journey. I wanted this so much, especially today, when I missed Kim so terribly. Part of me wanted to stamp my foot — it was not fair that I had to go to such lengths to have a connection to Kim.

I decided to take a quiet walk outside. I had read that being in nature, enjoying the smells and peacefulness of its surroundings, would bring in powerful earth energy to ground and center me. The walk felt good, and I returned home feeling more peaceful.

Then I headed for Hazel's. I wanted the security and safety of being with Hazel while I attempted to leave my body for the second time. When I arrived, she said we would get right to the reason we were together. She spoke slowly and quietly as she took me through a visualization technique.

I felt that "swooshing" sensation and was immediately out of my body. There, in front of me, stood Kim. I believe I actually felt her touch.

It is hard to put into words and even more difficult to explain the sensations I experienced. After seeing Kim, I was drawn into the Love and Light again, but it was a feeling very different from the first time. Kim said, "See the little twinkling lights? They are the children that I am here to help."

She would not take me closer to these lights. Instead, she told me telepathically that I had somewhere else I needed to go. I found myself traveling in a downward motion. We arrived in a place full of books. I could sense these books around me. Kim stood in front of me holding a book. She called it my "book of records."

I was not allowed to see the writing on the pages of my book, but Kim told me a little about them. "See all the pages left in your lifetime? You have much left to do. I will help you along your journey and share it with you. That is our new path together. This will help to open another door on your spiritual journey. Do not dwell on how it *was* but how it *is*," Kim advised.

She told me how much she loved me, but I needed to be aware that she would not be around me as much any more and that I was to work more with my guides now. She said she had much to do and was eager to do it. Then in a flash, I sensed that Kim had once more become part of the Light even though I still felt her presence!

Suddenly my astral travel was over, and I swooshed back into the chair. Emotionally drained, with tears streaming down my face, I sat quietly for a short time. Hearing Hazel's voice brought me back to my earthly surroundings.

After I had time to compose myself we talked about all I had seen and heard during my experience. Hazel reminded me how important it was for me to let go of Kim. Hazel helped me to understand that, because of Kim's concern for me, she was "going back and forth too much." Trying to function in two worlds held her back from her own progress and learning.

"Kim told you that the two of you would work together," Hazel gently reminded me, "so she is definitely coming back. Kim is itching to be busy." Although Hazel spoke those words, they sounded exactly like Kim. That cemented my belief in the accuracy of that prediction.

Kim was the same on earth *and* the other side. We couldn't hold her back from meeting the many goals she always set for herself when she was alive. I now understood that I mustn't hold her back from the tasks — whatever they were — she had to do on the other side.

As we discussed my experience, I learned the room of books I saw was called the "Akashic Records," where each soul's past, present, and future information was stored. I had just found another topic to study and went in search of information on the Akashic Records.

*I knew I would be forever changed. My original goal was to get to my daughter. In the process, however, I had eliminated my own fear of death.*

By the end of October I had come to a comfortable place of spiritual awakening and was completely open to all that was taking place. I spent less time on the Internet. I stopped searching for free readings, no longer needing them. I had my contacts and could get messages from Kim whenever we chatted. By this time, I was also getting my own messages.

I was on the road to increasing my "gifts." I attended classes and spent some time each day by myself, meditating and learning. With the new understanding I gained from my astral travel, I knew that our spirits survive without a body, that our soul does live on. During my out-of-body experiences, I had the same consciousness apart from my physical body as I had when I was within it. I *saw* myself return to my body just like I return to my car after shopping.

You can't experience this phenomenon without its having a profound effect. I knew I would be forever changed. My original goal was to find and connect with my daughter. In the process, however, I had eliminated my own fear of death.

In one year's time, my whole belief system had changed. From no awareness of even the basic concept of guides, I was now asking for my guides on a regular basis. Holly was still around me, as I believe she will always be, but now I was introduced to a more powerful guide named Raphael. This guide was full of Light. He had access to more wisdom and, once I started to ask him for information, what was given to me in my automatic writing took me to a greater depth of understanding. I could feel when Raphael was with me. Now I received more talk about God and God's plan for all of us. I began to feel God's energy. Using my automatic writing, at the end of this month I began to bring through messages for others.

Sue, my friend from the health club, let me have time to grieve and get through this most difficult month, but she was waiting anxiously until after the 27th to ask me to do a writing for her.

Sue had been intrigued with the information I received through my automatic writing. Just a few weeks earlier, Sue had received her own "miracle," an awakening that happened as quickly and as suddenly as my own. For her, it took the form of spontaneous, unplanned poetry that appeared in her head and lasted for two days.

Sitting in a meeting one afternoon, Sue began hearing words inside her head. She was extremely perplexed. But the words wouldn't stop, so Sue opened her computer and started to write the words that were flowing through her mind.

Sue hoped this "craziness" would end, but still the words — these lyrical phrases — did not stop. At the end of this first startling day, Sue attempted to go to sleep. Giving up on that, and with her husband sleeping beside her, she reached for a paper and pen. In the dark, she continued to write. The next morning, when she gazed at the words she had written the night before without benefit of a light, she was stunned to discover she was able to read them all.

In a quandary, Sue called me to detail the events of the night before. As soon as I entered her health club to continue our conversation, Sue handed me pages of short poems. I slowly read through the pages and felt an awareness come over me that these were special words. She had written verse after verse until her mind had gone silent. Stunned and exhausted, Sue reviewed the beautiful verses of love she had written. They brought us both to tears.

My friend insisted the words in these poems were not *her* words and that she herself had not written them. She wondered who on the other side had given them to her. Sue continued to share with me how out of control she had felt. She had been unable to stop the words or block them out.

I understood exactly how she felt. It was the same feeling I experienced during my automatic writing events.

Now immersed in her own spiritual awakening, Sue approached me with the idea of trying to get some answers for herself. She hoped to use my ability to connect with the other side in order to discover the name of, or information about, her own guide. I understood that by agreeing to do this, I would open myself to others in the spirit realm. I wanted to be sure I would be safe. I had no desire to connect with earth-bound spirits or spirits who had not gone to the Light.

On October 29, 1999, I prepared myself to write. First, I requested the protection of my guide, Raphael, as well as Kim. Almost immediately, my hand flowed with information. When the writing stopped, I eagerly looked at what had come through. With some trepidation, I gave this information to Sue.

The information I was able to access through Raphael was from Sue's guide. He introduced himself and gave her his name and some insight as to her own journey. She was relieved that she now had a name to call her guide. I prayed the name was accurate. I was aware that from this day forward, she would refer to this guide by the name given in this writing.

Was this really the name of her guide? I trusted the messages that came for myself and could only hope I had obtained accurate information for her as well. Sue felt certain I had, but my inexperience affected my confidence. As I continued to grow along my path, I trusted my doubts would give way to greater clarity and confidence,

It was only a few days before the annual psychic fair at the International Center in Mississauga. Sue was quick to inform me she planned to attend. It was here that Sue had a reading by a spiritual reader named Kate, who told Sue her guide's name. The name she gave Sue was the same name I had received.

How exciting — for both of us — to receive this verification! I now knew I had heard the messages accurately. Later in the year, more information from Kate's reading would be confirmed through my writings and by Sharlette.

I was once again taking a new, unexplored path and knew I was gently, but intentionally, being guided to open another door on my journey into the Light. This writing for Sue awakened within me a desire to reach out to others in need of receiving healing messages.

Chapter 5

# Embracing The Light

*We are all visitors to this time, this place. We are just passing through. Our purpose here is to observe, to learn, to grow, to LOVE. . . and then we return home.*

—Aborigine Philosophy

**November 1999.** Kim had been gone for over a year, a long, hard year filled with heart-numbing pain and much spiritual growth. My life had gradually taken on a powerful new light. Kim's body was no longer with us, but her spirit — her soul — definitely lived on and remained connected to us.

It seemed to me that love was the major component required to make the connection between this physical world and the spirit world. As much as it was necessary for me to have communication with Kim, I now knew she also desired contact with me. Kim had taken every opportunity to let me know that she was still "alive" on another plane of existence. My new spiritual beliefs had not only awakened in me a thirst to understand more but had also brought me some relief from the torment of grief.

With the realization that Kim was safe and well on the other side, I was ready to accept the belief that there was more around us than we could see with our physical eyes. Was our physical realm just one dimension of many? I was being shown it was.

I was struck by the enormity of it all and recognized this was not something to delve into carelessly. As my psychic abilities became stronger, I was driven to develop them further. In order to strengthen my connection to the other side, I would open myself up to many concepts — and, perhaps, entities — I was too naive to fully understand. I would have to strip away my old thought patterns and learn to reach beyond the normal five senses. The development of my psychic abilities, whatever that encompassed, needed to be undertaken seriously and with great respect. This new journey of discovery, unfortunately, did not diminish my extreme feelings of loneliness for Kim.

A continuous, unbearable ache burdened my heart. I missed Kim's being part of my everyday life. It was still painful to think about the future because to do that meant I had to think about a future without Kim in it. The past, filled with memories of Kim, was easier to talk about and reflect on.

I let my friends and family know it was always okay for them to talk about Kim; in fact, I needed them to. I did not want Kim to be forgotten. She existed. She was important.

Remaining focused on my "miracles" of the last nine months brought me renewed hope. What I considered miracles were really my new awareness of those on the other side intertwining themselves into my life and into my soul in meaningful ways.

I now embraced the belief that each one of us has a purpose here on earth to fulfill. We are here to learn the lessons needed to advance our souls. If I could just remain open and listening, my spirit guides and loved ones on the other side would continue to help me move through my grief, keep me focused on my healing journey, and teach me the lessons I was here to learn.

It was becoming more obvious to me, as the months went on, that although I was the one who initiated the journey, I was now being gently guided along my path. The messages in my automatic writing made it clear I was to use my gift to help others. How, I had no idea, but I was starting to believe I would be shown the way. Would my new awareness enable me to bring messages of comfort to other grieving parents? I sincerely hoped so.

My automatic writing had been a focal point in my spiritual journey up to this time. It provided my connection to Kim, as well as to my guides. I could hear "them" when I was focused and writing.

I spent even more time now in meditation, both alone and with my friends. I enjoyed the sense of calmness meditation gave me. My group of spiritual friends, each one on her own spiritual journey, was expanding. We continued to attend classes with our latest teacher, Marlene, twice a month. I found strength from being among these like-minded people.

Each week for the duration of this course, we practiced meditation exercises and held a healing circle. This course initiated my first real experience of sending out spiritual healing to others. I, myself, had received a spiritual healing months before I truly understood what it meant. I had come a long way and now was learning how to send that healing energy to others.

"It is important to keep our minds, bodies, and souls in balance," someone explained to me. That same person suggested I do some reading on the subject of auras. The aura is a multi-layered field of energy that surrounds each person's body. It vibrates constantly and radiates light and color. It was easy to find a book on the subject. I even found a chart explaining what each of the colors of an aura represents. As I wandered through a local new-age bookstore, I discovered a laminated copy of a similar chart and bought it. This gave me a quick reference if anyone should ask me to explain each color's characteristics.

Most of us cannot see an aura with the naked eye. James Van Praagh, in the book I mentioned earlier, *Reaching to Heaven*, discusses auras in great detail. He has had the ability to see auras since his early twenties. What he sees, he explains, is a vast array of colors and lights that surround each person.

His well-written book is full of the worthwhile knowledge he gained through his own personal experiences. One of the most valuable pieces of information I gleaned from his work is that our spiritual energies may become blocked by negative emotions — such as guilt, worry, anger, or fear. This hit a responsive cord with me. I was all too aware I had more work to do to release my negative emotions. My biggest challenge was forgiveness, especially toward those closest to me who failed, in the early months of my grief, to support and comfort me.

As I began to work on releasing these negative emotions, I became aware of the extreme difficulty of this task. It is never easy to face your own demons! Opening this door and looking inward at oneself demands both strength and willpower. My intense grief over the loss of Kim made working with my emotions a supremely challenging task.

A wise teacher explained, "Your friends and loved ones only disappointed you because they did not live up to what *you* expected of *them*. It was your expectation of them that let you down. This was a lesson you had to experience for your own spiritual growth. They have their own lessons to learn, too."

Digesting that thought was hard on my heart, but I realized that holding onto these negative feelings would block my spiritual progress.

Some weeks I didn't want to go to our spiritual learning group because of anxiety I would collapse into tears. My friends encouraged and supported me, gently reminding me that Kim was still very much around me. Because of their persistence, I would attend our group meetings. At the end of each evening, I gratefully accepted the healing energy each person sent me with love.

Even though I was opening to the miracles of spirit, nothing took away all the pain of losing my child. It was up to me to cope with my loss and move forward with my life.

One afternoon I paid a visit to my friend Judy Hunt. She had been a constant source of strength for me as I learned to cope with Kim's loss from the earth plane and expand my understanding of the spirit world. She never doubted any of the unusual experiences I shared with her.

This particular morning had been emotionally draining. I had attempted to complete the victim impact statement I would have to read at the trial. I was finding it impossible to put into words the person Kim was and the loss I felt. What kind of daughter was she? I could have written a book about the person she was — and would have been. Reality stared me in the face. What did all this spiritual enlightenment really mean anyway since Kim wasn't here in this world?

Sitting and talking with Judy always had a calming effect on me, so I ended up on her doorstep. She listened silently to my ramblings and supplied me with tissues for my tears. When I calmed down, Judy and I discussed our spiritual journeys. I did inherently understand how significant my newly formed beliefs were. I had just lost sight of them for the moment.

*"You are going to write a book. . . about your journey, all about your loss and your awakening."*

Judy suggested we do a meditation. She headed upstairs and returned with one called, "The Healing Waterfall." Perfect! I thought. We each comfortably settled in and spent the next 30 minutes in meditation. When it ended, I felt calmer, more at peace.

Unexpectedly, Judy said she had a message for me. "You are going to write a book. This book will be about your journey, all about your loss and your awakening. That is the message that came through loud and clear."

"I have been told that before," I said, "but I just can't see that happening." We lingered over a cup of tea, talked about Kim and the progress of our spiritual journeys. Before I drifted off to sleep that night, I prayed for guidance and trusted that if a book were to be written, I would be shown when and how.

It was a few days later that Judy asked for my assistance. She wanted to know the name of her guide. She had heard a name in her meditations and wondered if I could verify the name for her. This would be my second attempt at bringing through messages for someone other than myself via automatic writing. Because my first attempt for Sue a few weeks earlier had been successful, I mustered the confidence to try again.

I decided I would attempt to bring through messages for Judy by typing on the computer. I had some previous experience with typing the messages but always preferred to have Kim and my guides work through my hand using pen on paper. After all, I reminded myself, the renowned Ruth Montgomery had transitioned from pen and paper to automatic writing using her computer. I felt it was time to give the keyboard another chance.

My guide Raphael came through first and imparted his messages for Judy. Raphael advised, *"I will channel for Judy's guide and tell you about him. He is from another earth life that they spent together. He is waiting to be talked to. He is waiting for the bridge to be formed from her level to his. She was a healer in a past life with him. They were strong energy and still are. She knows. Her earlier sickness was a sign for her to atone for inner beliefs and open to us. She did then begin to listen to the voices around her. This was needed for her advancement. It was a knock on the head, so to speak. It began the advancement of her soul."* I had forgotten that Judy had cancer 12 years earlier. She had been clear for many years.

Next Kim arrived to acknowledge Judy and bring through some information for her. Kim, as well, came through with this astonishing statement: *"I have been going to her for some time now. She has started on her life's journey. She hears the angels, intuitions that are heavenly words to her. Her angel of devotion is called Sunshine. Yes, Mom. You know the word. Interesting how we are all connected. Does anything surprise you anymore?"* Interesting, indeed, I thought. I had been using "sunshine" as my computer password.

I was not surprised that Kim had shown up to deliver a personal message to Judy. That was Kim's way to acknowledge all the help Judy had given me over the last year. We did not, however, receive the name of her guide in this particular writing.

As Judy read the message from Kim, she recalled how often she had sung the song, "You Are My Sunshine" to her children when they were little. It had been her favorite song. We wondered if that meant anything. Had Judy felt a connection with her angel all those years ago?

While driving to work the next morning, Judy listened to a radio talk show. The host was having a contest for his listeners. He would hum a few bars of a song then request people to phone in and guess the name of the song. She immediately thought to herself, if all of this is true, then make this contestant guess the song, "You Are My Sunshine."

When those exact words exploded over the radio, Judy almost lost control of her car. When she finally arrived at work, I received a very excited phone call. This sign — this miracle — became her next stepping stone toward the pursuit of her own life's purpose.

These automatic writing messages for Judy provoked much thought and discussion. Is it true that our darkest times ultimately awaken our soul to the Light? What about the information that Judy had a past life as a healer? This was not the first time I had received information about past life connections.

I prayed I accurately heard the messages for Judy. We could not verify the information the same way we received validation about the name Sunshine. Nor could we do so in the way Sue and I received validation about the name of her guide. We would just have to trust the messages.

Over the course of two weeks, I had relayed messages to both Sue and Judy through my automatic writing. I felt I would gain more confidence with practice. Kim had said, "Practice, Mom. Practice makes perfect."

Ready to practice, I put out some calls to my friends.

Bonnie — more than willing to receive messages this way — was the next person for whom I did an automatic writing session. I was aware she received her own guidance and did not need me to bring her messages, but I was on a mission to practice. The date was November 4. I prepared to write, tuning into the energy around me. I was surprised to receive the information in hand-lettered print, not in my usual cursive handwriting.

Bonnie's guide delivered private messages for her as well as more general, enlightening information such as, *"Miracles are not really miracles;*

*they are truths. They are what we believe, and with love and compassion and an open heart, they happen."*

Bonnie and I met for lunch and discussed the information. She would just smile reassuringly when I expressed how important it was for me to "prove" my messages were really coming through from her guide. "You don't need to prove anything to me. I already know." Bonnie said.

It was I, not she, who needed to have more faith!

Judy Hunt requested a second writing. She desired answers about where her spiritual journey would lead her. More feelings, sensations, and words had appeared to her during meditation. She was eager to have a more personal relationship with her guides.

Without one moment of hesitation, I agreed to try. I invited her guides to communicate during one of my automatic writing sessions. When I had completed this writing, I read what came through. I was surprised to discover I had received a message for Judy's husband as well as for Judy.

I excitedly dialed their phone number. Judy answered the telephone and announced they had just arrived home from the psychic fair at the International Centre in Mississauga. Judy chuckled when she told me she had dragged her husband to the fair, too. They had both received psychic readings that afternoon. They weren't too sure about all the information they were given during their readings but said it was "interesting."

I proceeded to read the words that had come through for Judy. Then I relayed the information designated for Gary. There was silence on the other end of the phone. "Are you guys okay?" I asked.

"We are just so shocked at this information," Judy said, "because Gary was given a message in his reading today very similar to the one you just gave him." Judy explained that both messages concerned a man named Ron. Gary had worked with him until he had crossed over within the last year. Now, the messages said, Ron was around him, helping him in his work. No wonder they were stunned to silence!

I had not been aware of the death of his co-worker, so, for me, this became solid validation. I was pleased I had stepped out of my comfort zone and had begun to relay messages for others. I had also delivered messages for three of my friends, two of whom had attended the same psychic fair Judy and Gary had attended, where they also received verification of some fact revealed in my writing. The synchronicity of the timing of these two events — the fair and my writings — did not escape me.

Was this how I was to help others? Was I to bring messages of comfort and healing through my automatic writing? I had been told I would work with Kim and, I assumed, also with my guides. I was intrigued and awestruck. "This is BIG," my mind told me. Now I had validations to prove I could really receive messages for others through the automatic writing technique.

*Was this how I was to help others? Was I to bring messages of comfort and healing. . . I had been told I would work with Kim. . . Now I had validations to prove I could really receive messages for others through the automatic writing technique.*

I was not to write again for about two weeks. This was a time of intense stress and sadness, as we went to court to confront the reality of Kim's passing. We read our victim impact statements. I did not feel justice was served, but the court proceedings were now behind us.

In meditation and prayer during these weeks away from my writings, I prayed for the four of us, and I prayed for Kim. I prayed for the strength to embrace this spiritual journey and continue on my path.

On November 14, I again picked up my pen. I had an urge to write all day and decided it was time to continue on the path to enlightenment. Without question, I was being guided along. Just getting ready to write always brought a sense of peace to me as I settled my mind and brought in the love of God. I called in my angels that day, too.

Kim and my grandmother were the two who showed up, encouraging me to continue toward my spiritual destiny. It was an emotional and very healing half-hour spent connected to their energy. Words of encouragement, support and incredible love spilled onto the paper. Tears streamed down my cheeks as I marveled at the fact that we shared this time together — and we still could.

As my circle of new spiritually-oriented acquaintances continued to grow and we related our personal stories, we began to understand that we were destined to meet. We had all chosen this new journey together, to learn from one another. We were finding the support in each other that we needed to grow spiritually.

Toward the end of November I returned to substitute teaching. I contacted two schools in my area where I had friends to let them know I was ready to come back. I knew those friends would support me if I needed their help throughout the day. It was time to give it a try. For the next three weeks, I became a regular at one of the schools.

I was quick to realize that my heart wasn't in it, but it was nice to see my teaching friends again. Two of my closest friends, Jane and Patty, had kept in touch over the past year. Both worked at the school. I felt stronger when I was around them.

Thanks to phone calls and visits, Jane had comforted me during the past year. I felt safe to express my sadness and show my tears to her. She would often whisk me away to a quiet room over lunch so we could talk. I told her how much I needed to continue my spiritual journey and that teaching was taking me away from it.

My close friend Patty and I had taught together over the years. I was grateful for her support, too. On my first difficult day back, in fact, I substituted for Patty herself. I knew I would be a stranger to her first grade students. Patty thoughtfully phoned to welcome me back and to set my mind at ease.

"The lesson plans are there," Patty reassured me, "so please don't worry about anything."

I was glad for those lesson plans. I did not have to think about what to do. I just followed the instructions. I was grateful that Patty had made the day as simple for me as possible. I was just going through the motions. When the bell rang to signal the end of school that day, I left as quickly as I could and cried all the way home.

Each day I taught became a little easier for me. I knew in my heart that I was not the same caring teacher I used to be and felt guilty about that. My passion for teaching had disappeared. It had never been difficult for me in the past, but now it was. One truth kept intruding: directing my time and energy toward teaching slowed down progress on my spiritual path.

One morning after I arrived at school, Patty met me in the staff room and asked if I would like to go out for lunch with her. "I would enjoy that," I responded without hesitation.

While at lunch together, an opportunity opened to describe my amazing spiritual experiences of the past nine months. I cautiously formulated my words, not sure how much detail I would share. Would Patty think I had lost my mind? I had no intentions of discussing my automatic writing with anyone outside my "special circle of friends," but when I started talking, it was like a dam bursting. I couldn't stop!

As I poured out my heart to Patty, she listened patiently. When I finished, she began her own revelations. She admitted she believed in heaven, the afterlife, and contact with those on the other side. She confessed she had often felt her deceased sister-in-law, Jackie, around her at various times.

"You really believe in all this?" I asked her excitedly.

"Yes, of course, I always have," she confirmed.

Patty's support, encouragement — and reassurance that I was not crazy — were just what I needed to hear, sending me off with a new sense of confidence to continue on my spiritual journey. Within 24 hours, Patty had phoned to inquire if I would do automatic writing for her.

Similar requests began to pour in. Well, I had asked for it!

Over the course of a week, I brought through messages for Patty and two more of my friends. Then a woman at the exercise club overheard me talking one afternoon and asked if I would try one for her, too. I successfully received information and inspirational messages from their guides. All marveled at the wisdom of the messages and told me so.

Now I was busy balancing part-time teaching with my spiritual journey. Everywhere I went, I was awakened to the fact that this spiritual pilgrimage now intermingled with the other aspects of my life. Teachers at the schools where I substituted — many, I found, open to and firm believers in the afterlife — asked questions and discussed their personal beliefs with me. I relaxed around the teachers and opened my heart to them as I talked freely about my journey.

❊ ❊ ❊

**December 1999**. Our second Christmas without Kim was fast approaching, bringing with it immeasurable sadness. I struggled to focus on my spiritual learning. I felt myself falling into depression. I was unable to concentrate during my meditation time and pulled away from my friends. When I was called to teach, I declined. I couldn't face all the Christmas events at the schools. I just could not put on a happy face. I didn't know how I would get through the holiday season. I dreaded going into stores with all their decorations and Christmas songs playing everywhere — too much happiness for me to tolerate.

It struck me that only two years ago I had been one of those happy people going about my life oblivious to the pain of others. I had to lose Kim to understand the anguish that holidays brought to a family who had lost a loved one. I realized that people couldn't understand the depth of our pain unless they had experienced their own. Being aware of this fact, however, didn't help when I tried to go shopping. I withdrew more and more into the safety of my home, hiding from everything and everybody as I had done in the first weeks after losing Kim.

I wondered how I could best get through the Christmas season. Doug and I discussed taking a family holiday somewhere warm. The more I thought about this idea, the more I liked it. I checked out a trip to Mexico, discovered an available, all-inclusive, one-week holiday, talked to Doug, and booked it. It all fell into place. Doug, Kerry, Kristy, and I were to leave a few days before Christmas.

We needed to spend time together as a family. This was the perfect answer. I didn't feel I was running away. Of course, now I understand that I was, but it's what I needed to do at the time.

Preparations for the trip kept me busy. With my focus taken away from the holiday season, I was better able to deal with the Christmas activities around me.

I remembered and reflected on the message Kim had given to me, through Lou, on September 21. She wanted us to enjoy Christmas and decorate the tree outside for her. To please Kim, Doug and I did this together. I even managed to put up a few decorations inside the house.

My heart was heavy, but I knew how important it was for my husband and daughters to see me stronger. Just as important was for them to feel some happiness during this holiday season. I knew in my heart that I had done the right thing when Kristy's face beamed as she arrived home from school and found the house decorated for Christmas.

I certainly was happier when both the girls arrived home for the Christmas break. I worried about them constantly. If I could have taken their pain away, I would gladly have done that. I hated that they had to suffer. I hated that Doug had to suffer. I knew our family would never be the same. We would have to create a "new normal" as our Coping Group called it. Our new normal would be one without Kim in it.

Anyone who has not experienced this kind of profound loss, I believed, could not understand the depth of our pain. Truthfully, we could not even understand the depths of each other's pain, and we were a close family.

I phoned relatives to tell them we would be away for Christmas. Then I planned what I would buy to fill the girls' stockings. Venturing into the basement where the Christmas things were stored, I searched for the girls' stockings to take with us to Mexico.

What I found, of course, were three stockings, not just two. I picked up the stocking Kim's aunt had made for her when she was just a baby. Each of the girls had one. They were all unique and decorated especially for them. Each had a girl's name written across the top in sparkles.

Grief overwhelmed me. I crumpled onto the floor hugging Kim's stocking to me. I lovingly ran my fingers across the letters in her name. All I could think was that Kim would never be here again to share Christmas with us. An immense wave of despair swept over me as this horrific reality gripped me like a vise.

I allowed the pain to engulf me and didn't resist it. After some time and many tears, I carried all three stockings to the first floor. I carefully wrapped Kim's to protect it and returned it to the box where I found it. I took Kerry and Kristy's stockings upstairs and placed them on the dresser to pack in my suitcase.

As usual, after a good cry, I felt stronger. I made a detailed list of items I needed to buy for our trip, including stocking stuffers. I had to make lists and organize myself before I could shop during the holiday season.

With both of the girls home temporarily for the holidays, I had stepped away from my spiritual pursuits and focused on being a mom. I could feel a sense of panic creep in as I lessened the intensity of my spiritual work. I stayed connected to my spiritual self by continuing to read spiritual books. This was the one thing I could do with the girls at home and their friends around.

I purchased a new book, *The Lightworker's Way*, by Doreen Virtue, Ph.D., and spent any spare time immersed in it. I finished it one day before our trip to Mexico.

I pondered the concepts presented by the author. I inherently understood that if I had read this book earlier in my journey, I would not have been ready to acknowledge or understand her precepts. The time was right for me; therefore, I was particularly struck with the truth of her statement: "Everywhere on the planet right now, lightworkers are awakening to faint memories of why they came to earth. They hear an inner calling that can't be ignored."

This is exactly what had happened to me. This seemed to be what had been happening to so many of the people I met along my journey into the Light. We were all opening to the Light, each for his or her own individual reasons.

Doreen Virtue's chapter on spiritual healing helped me grasp the concepts I encountered during my first healing session back in February. She reaffirmed the idea that through the power of our thoughts, we can create what we need in our lives.

I found great comfort and knowledge within the pages of her book. It is her belief that when we believe, miracles do happen. It was her statement and my need to believe in the statement, "Nothing is lost in the eyes of God," that was responsible for another miracle to take place in my life a few months later.

I completed my shopping only hours before it was time to leave for our Christmas vacation in Cancun. To all outsiders, we looked like a typical happy family of four enjoying the balmy weather. We needed to have this time and feel the joy of being together. In our own ways, we were creating our "new normal." As I lay by the pool and watched the girls laughing and enjoying themselves, I hoped they felt the immense love I was sending them. I prayed for them to know how much I loved them.

Christmas Eve arrived. It was the night the hotel celebrated Christmas with their guests and the big meal was served. An archway of colored balloons created a festive lobby entrance. A gentleman offered to take our picture. Of course, he had no idea of the mixture of the emotions I felt as he snapped the picture and returned our camera to us. I was happy to be with my girls and my husband, but I was acutely aware that Kim was missing from the picture. "We should be five!" my heart screamed.

Even in Mexico we continued our family tradition Christmas morning as the girls ran into our room, waking us up by jumping on our bed. Happily, we shook gifts out of our stockings. The girls informed us they had another gift to give us and handed us a flat, square package. Doug and I opened it together. It was a calendar with laminated pages. It contained twelve beautiful pictures of our girls, all three of them. Each picture for each month held a special memory. They spanned the years — some pictures of the girls when they were little, others when they were older. I couldn't have held back the happy tears even if I tried.

It was obvious lots of planning had gone into creating this wonderful gift. Most important was the love that was obviously the main ingredient. We had two wonderful, special daughters, and we knew how blessed we were.

We spent Christmas morning together by the pool, missing Kim in our own individual ways. By the time we returned home, I felt more peaceful and relaxed. Remaining this way was difficult, however, because everywhere I went I overheard people talking about how they were going to celebrate the new millennium. Radio and television announcers blasted the airwaves with activities being held all over the world in honor of this momentous day. Would the computers crash? That was the big question on most people's minds.

For me, it was another year without Kim to share in the wonder of it all. Sadness enveloped me. Again, I was receding into my protective shell. I was hiding, as my husband called it. I called it immense, all-encompassing pain — the kind that, when it hit, totally debilitated me.

❊ ❊ ❊

**January 2000.** The new millennium arrived and, despite the dire predictions, computers did not crash. Celebrations were finally over. I survived another milestone. By the middle of the afternoon on the first day of January, I felt a sense of calmness engulf me. We took down the decorations, cleaned the house, and enjoyed a quiet day. I spent a few hours curled up on the couch writing about my feelings, both happy and sad. I recorded the pleasurable memories of our trip and the holiday season. I gave thanks for my family.

Learning to be thankful for what I had was something I now spent more time doing. I made a conscious decision to do this. I had come to an understanding, through my spiritual studies, that we all have choices. I could remain in my grief, hurting both my family and myself, or I could cope with my grief in a healthier way. Expressing my feelings on paper, even if only for myself, helped me to clarify things in my own head. It became a technique that I would use often and benefit from.

After I completed my journal, I slipped away to the computer room. I wondered if there would be someone to talk to in one of my regular chatrooms. Once again I became "Holly" and spent an hour or so chatting with my online friends.

Later that same evening, after a meditation session, I felt someone was trying to give me a message. Automatic writing was the only way I felt confident that the messages I received were accurate. This time I felt compelled to write using the computer. Take logic out of this, I reminded myself. I can't adequately describe how I knew I was directed to the computer, but my spiritual lessons had taught me to trust my instincts.

I settled myself at the keyboard, booted-up the computer, and prepared to write by saying my now-familiar prayer of protection. As I positioned my hands on the keys, I became aware that the screen in front of me was flashing, as if someone was adjusting the light/dark level of the screen. It went from light-to-dark-to-light for about ten seconds. This same phenomenon had occurred a couple of times before, a few months back, and both times chill bumps peppered my arms. This time I not only sprouted the chill bumps, I also felt a distinct warmth around my shoulders.

I understood, thanks to the books I had read, that those on the other side could manipulate electronic devices to get our attention. My mind toyed with the question whether it was Kim or my guides who were responsible for this today. I asked for some sign to let me know if it was "them." It was at exactly this moment I felt a pressure on my fingers, which started to move without my conscious participation.

> Kim began to type. *"Mom, I am here right now. I am at your shoulder. I love you too, always. Today was hard, I know, but I still have a life, you know, just a different one than we had planned there. I love Dad. Tell him I know. I miss talking to him, too. Tell him to talk to me.*
>
> *"I knew you would know it was me. I like to let you know I am here when you are on the computer. We do flash the screen to get*

*your attention.*

*"Boy, Mom, this is so neat that you can hear me so well. You are learning quickly. You are hearing us so clearly now. I love being able to get your attention. See, you have not really lost me, Mom. I am right here.*

*"I understand why you must do this. Accept this new relationship, and I will be happy. There really is no death. I know this is hard for you to handle because I am your baby; but I go on, Mom and Dad, I go on. Remember that, please. Love you both always and forever. Your loving daughter, Kim. Gotta go now, bye!"*

With tears streaming down my cheeks, I digested the words that jumped back at me. She still had a life! I didn't always like the messages I received, and I certainly didn't understand or like this one. I felt anger with Kim for leaving us and being happy; nonetheless, I wanted her to be happy. I re-read the words and tried to embrace the message. It made me sad yet filled my heart with her love — all at the same time.

*The most consistent message brought through from loved ones on the other side is that they want to reassure us they still love us and they are fine... We are too quick to ignore or discount the signs they give us because we cannot see them.*

I have no physical proof that this information really came from Kim. I can only tell you that I am sure it did. All the spiritual events since her passing had made me a believer. I had faith in the fact that I could clearly hear Kim as well as others from the spirit realm. It is the way the information flows through my mind as I am writing that removes my skepticism of the process. I vividly remember that two-week period where nothing came through; even when I tried to force it, no words came forward. When I'm in genuine contact, the words flow effortlessly without my conscious awareness during the process.

The most consistent message brought through from loved ones on the other side is that they want to reassure us they still love us and they are fine. From my perspective, they seem to be standing on the other side of a thin veil. We are too quick to ignore or discount the signs they give us because we cannot see them. Since the incident with the flashing computer screen, I have talked to many people who have had signs from their loved ones on the other side through computers, radios, lights, and televisions. The accepted terminology for this kind of communication from the other side — E.V.P. or Electronic Voice Phenomenon — is recognized as the process the "so-called dead" use to communicate with the living through electronic devices. Often, they project images and sound.

I yearned for a greater understanding. I was finally ready and strong enough to sign up for a class with Shawna Ross, the healer I had met at the beginning of my journey, the one who had given me my first spiritual healing. It had been 11 months since I had gone for a healing session. Now I was ready to learn more about energy work and spiritual healing.

For eight weeks our spiritual support group studied how to open ourselves to hear, feel, and sense energy fields. We gained more understanding of our guides and angels and practiced receiving and relating messages for each other. Our confidence grew as we gave our messages and had them acknowledged by others.

Each new mentor had something unique to offer and introduced us to new ideas, which I often explored further on my own. Our study group reinforced the importance of continuing meditations on a regular basis. I became increasingly convinced meditation was essential to facilitate our connection to the spirit world. I discovered the better I became at meditation, the clearer I heard those on the other side.

By this point I began working diligently on building a stronger connection without the use of automatic writing. For the next few weeks, I set my pen down and purposely didn't write as often. Instead, I went in search of new meditation tapes and worked to improve my meditation skills.

While in a local bookstore, I was drawn to a picture of the Dalai Lama staring at me from the cover of a book. I settled into a chair to see if this was a book I wanted to add to my growing collection. I was still new to the concept of meditation so found the information enlightening.

Meditation has been a Buddhist practice for 2,500 years. Buddhists understand the importance of dedicating themselves to long periods of meditative silence. Buddhist monks were known to spend almost an entire lifetime devoted to periods of intense training, including hours and days in seclusion, silence, and prayer to free themselves from their negative feelings.

The Dalai Lama was quoted in this book as saying, "All human beings have an innate desire to overcome suffering, to find happiness. Training the mind to think differently, through meditation, is one important way to avoid suffering and be happy."

I was intrigued. It was obvious the western world has been much slower to accept this practice. Most people in western society have a difficult time understanding the wisdom of dedicating themselves to long periods of meditative silence. I was definitely one of those people — until Kim's death set me onto this path of enlightenment.

I discovered there was no prescription for the amount of time one should spend in meditation. Instead, I noticed the duration I required varied depending on my personal needs at the time. But regardless of time spent, I learned the practice was essential to gain clarity and a sense of peace.

❊ ❊ ❊

**February 2000.** I was diligently trying to balance my spiritual life with my physical one. Called often to do occasional teaching, some days I went and some days I declined. I continued to feel uneasy about teaching and became more impatient with the children. The sad reality dawned on me that I wasn't being fair to them.

I reflected on all the joy I had experienced over the years thanks to my teaching career and the sense of pride it brought me. I knew I had been a good teacher, but now I had changed. I had lost my passion for it, and I simply could not deny that reality.

The days I remained at home, I pursued my spiritual study. Meditation now occupied a huge chunk of my day. I searched for spiritual teachers and enlightening classes offered in and around my hometown. I was continually amazed by the numerous people in my area actively pursuing their own journeys and by the number of teachers available to help us on our way. I truly had one foot in each world, as was predicted so many months earlier. Now I understood what that meant.

I began to devote more time to both my immediate and extended families. I enjoyed spending time with Kerry and Kristy and worked hard to be a "normal mom" and do everyday things with them. I also spent more time with Doug.

Snow had fallen and snowmobile trails were opened. Over the years, we had been avid snowmobilers. We each had our own machine. I had not driven my snowmobile since Kim had passed for fear I would run it into a tree. I now felt I could concentrate enough on my driving that it would be safe for me to maneuver my machine through the twists and turns of the trails.

The local snowmobile club had planned an event for the first Saturday in February that included a chicken barbecue at the end of the day. We decided to go. The fresh air felt stimulating on my face, and we enjoyed the ride. We parked our machines and went to see which of our friends had already arrived. The smell of roasting chicken filled the air. Finding a place to sit at one of the long rows of tables, we removed our helmets and gloves and got in line to pick up our food.

It was during dinner that I noticed my naked finger, unadorned by my beloved family ring. Panic set in. Gone was the ring that represented our family of five. I picked up my gloves and looked inside each one for my ring. I frantically shook them as my mind raced. Had I taken it off? No! I never took it off. Dread threatened to overtake me as I went out to my snowmobile and scrutinized the surrounding snow.

Doug followed me, wondering what was going on. My mind replayed a long series of snapshots of the numerous times I had taken my gloves off enroute. Obviously, the ring could have fallen off anywhere along the winding trail. I became conscious of the falling snow, which dashed the already remote chance to recover my ring.

When Doug asked me what was wrong, I couldn't even stammer an answer. I didn't want to say the words and make it real. My ring couldn't be missing! My heart would break. That ring represented my intact family of five — Kim, Kerry, Kristy, Doug, and me.

In my frenzied state, I remembered the words from Doreen Virtue's book, *The Lightworker's Way*, that nothing is lost in the eyes of God. God knew where my ring was, and Kim would know where my ring was. I just had to find it.

Thoughts swirled around in my head, but still I could not tell Doug. Instead, I insisted we head home. Silently I began repeating these words. "Nothing is lost in the eyes of God. God knows where my ring is. Kim knows where my ring is. My ring is safe at home on my dresser." Over and over, under my breath, I mumbled this phrase.

Everything outside my mind was a blur. I knew Doug was asking me a question, but he seemed far away. Still, I said nothing. I knew he was becoming angry with me. Finally, I said, "I just need to get home."

I was busy repeating my "nothing is lost" mantra, wanting to believe that my ring would be at home when I got there. Of course, I never took this ring off my finger, so logic told me it could not be at home. Still, I trusted that I would find it in my bedroom.

Doubt crept in the minute I opened the door. I ran to check by the hand cream in the downstairs bathroom. Maybe I had taken it off there. I silently repeated the phrase: "Nothing is lost in the eyes of God. God knows where my ring is." It was not in the downstairs bathroom. I raced upstairs. There, on my night table, lay my ring.

I rushed over and picked it up. As I did, I noticed a puddle of water on my night table, exactly where my ring had been sitting. Amazing! My night table was made of wood; yet there was absolutely no water stain on it, even though we had been away all day. Then I saw that the band of my ring somehow looked different, slightly out of shape. Could a snowmobile have run over it?

I understood the significance of the water I had found where the ring had lain. It was my proof that I hadn't left it there. I knew "they" put it there. I had my miracle, a miracle created by our love. To this day, my ring is still slightly out of shape as a way of reminding me of the miracle I received that evening. Now my ring means more to me than ever.

As extraordinary as this event was, I discovered that teleporting objects is a kind of paranormal transportation event in which an object is moved from one location to another, often through solid objects such as walls. I wasn't the first to experience it and certainly won't be the last.

That experience fully transformed me from a person in awe of all that was happening to one who had seen the Light, without a doubt. This was my final stepping stone! I was ready to embrace the Light.

I felt Doug would never be able to set aside his logical mind long enough to understand this miracle. I was certain he would find some way to discredit what had happened. How could I blame him? It made absolutely no sense. It was totally beyond reason in the physical world.

But none of what had taken place in my life since Kim's passing was logical. I now understood and embraced it, but would Doug? I couldn't tell him yet.

I phoned two of my friends and described my incredible experience. Then I wished desperately to share my miracle with Sharlette. I went on the Internet but was unable to find her. Next I located Doreen Virtue's book and headed for bed. I reread the chapter pertaining to my miracle and reflected on my day. I said a prayer of thanks and finally fell soundly asleep.

The next morning I went in search of Sharlette. She responded to my instant message almost immediately. Before I shared the events of the day, I put out a request. I asked Sharlette if she could ask Kim to be with us, because I had a question to ask her. Sharlette said, "Kim is always around when we talk, so why don't you just ask her the question that's on your mind."

I typed this sentence to Sharlette. "Ask Kim if she helped find and return what I lost recently." Her typed response was: "She is showing me a ring. Kim is saying of course she found it. You needed it." I never doubted the miracle, but hearing Kim say it brought an inner peace I cannot describe.

*Receiving this miracle gave me the strength I needed to share my new beliefs with other people who had suffered the loss of a loved one. I needed to reassure them that their loved ones were around them . . .*

Receiving this miracle gave me the strength I needed to share my new beliefs with other people who had suffered the loss of a loved one. I needed to reassure them that their loved ones were around them and were fine on the other side.

My mind now bubbled in a constant state of awe. One of my friends suggested that I read about Florence Nightingale and Joan of Arc, as both claimed they were aided in their work by messages from the other side. Even though I remembered studying about these famous historical luminaries when I was young, I did not recall the spiritual aspects of their lives. Now I had to find out, so I went to the library.

Florence Nightingale, the founder of the nursing movement, acknowledged she had received assistance from the spirit world during her pioneering work in the health field. Joan of Arc, at the age of 15, knowing nothing of warfare, claimed to be guided by visions of saints directing her into battle to drive the English out of France. Many people of the time felt such visions amounted to sorcery. It was only after her death many came to believe that, indeed, she had been divinely guided, and she attained sainthood in the Catholic Church.

Many famous people in history have claimed similar visions and voices. Perhaps, I realized, it is simply the limitations of our human senses that block us from receiving our own messages. I began to believe that those on the other side were waiting for us to expand our awareness of them.

I became more conscious of various energies around me. I could not see them but definitely felt their presence. I was now cognizant of the fact that it wasn't only Kim who hovered nearby. I had guides and angels waiting for me to pay attention to them. I felt my guide Raphael around me often. It was amazing enough for me to feel his energy, but I was dumbfounded that he could actually get my attention. Sometimes, when I sat quietly, I received little pushes at my head.

It would have been easy to think I was letting my imagination run away with me. The biggest obstacle for me was my logical mind. Following a close second was my fear. Of what, I wasn't certain.

This journey was moving forward so quickly. Could I stop its rapid progression if I wanted to? Did I want to? If I opened the next door, what would await me around the corner?

It was time to pick up my pen for an automatic writing session. Raphael delivered this message to me:

> *"Raphael here, my dear. You are trying to ignore us, but we are here all the same. You feel us touch your face and know that it is us. Don't worry about what you are to do with all this knowledge, just know that there is a purpose and that all will be shown to you, as it is supposed to be.*
>
> *"Do not doubt the information you receive — just give it, my dear. God's love surrounds you, and you need to be more accepting of it. Really try to focus on the pictures, as this is your next victory, all through God's love. Open to it, and you will feel the strength that is within you. God is working on you as I am. Believe in the messages, and ye shall be strong. Open your chakras! Work on your heart, third eye, and focus on the colors. Absorb the colors. You are progressing, but meditation is to be done. That is your path to us. Love, Raphael."*
>
> I felt Kim's energy take over my hand as she delivered this message for me: *"Hey, Mom, you know you cannot ignore me. I will get your attention. I am on your left side and touching your forehead. You feel it! I need you to be stronger. You are, you know. How do you think I became strong?*

*"I love you, Mom, and I am guiding you, so please continue to grow. Don't slow down. You are growing. Learn and practice. Practice makes perfect. I am not there anymore so don't focus on this. Focus here and around you. I am right here, ready to work with you. I am waiting, and you know I am not very patient. This is our plan, you and I, and I am ready to help you all I can. You must continue to do your part. Forever together, Mom."*

I knew immediately that I was finished. The words ended and the energy felt different. I was becoming very accustomed to these feelings. I reflected on the messages. Raphael told me to focus on the pictures. What pictures? Does he mean the pictures I see in my mind's eye?

Emotions of sadness and wonderment filled me as I reread Kim's personal message. When I felt calmer, I remembered my friend Patty had asked if I would see if I could find out anything about her guide. I refocused and asked silently, "I would like some information for Patty. Please talk to her guide, as she has asked for more information."

I felt Raphael's energetic presence around me, and I heard words as they crept before my mind's eye. I began to write. Then the words stopped abruptly, the energy shifted, and I was once again connected to Kim, who wrote, *"Well done, Mom. You need to focus on the words you hear and don't ignore me. I will make myself felt. You wanted me around you, and I am around you, always. Hugs, Kim."*

When I read the messages that had come through for my friend, Patty, I realized some very specific information had been given. I was especially intrigued by the references to Scotland. Her guide, who gave me his name as Samuel, spoke of her love of bagpipe music and Scotland. I was not aware of any connection Patty had to this country, so I was anxious to share the information with her to see if it had significance.

After arriving at Patty's house the next evening, I handed her the written message. Her first comment was, "I always liked the name Holly and had decided to call my daughter that, but when she was born I looked at her and knew she had to be called Samantha." Patty confirmed her obsession with

Scotland and how she had never understood why she felt such an attraction for a country she had never visited. She emphasized that the information felt right to her. She was excited to know the name of her guide so she could begin her own personal relationship with him.

*I know many people assume they lack psychic abilities because they were not "born with them." . . . I came to comprehend that the greater the energy I exerted to expand my learning, the more my gifts awakened.*

I was beginning to understand the magnitude of what I had inaugurated and did not want to stop the rapid growth period I was going through. Did I really have the strength and determination to continue my journey into the Light and discover my spiritual destiny?

Yes! This path was the only path to my soul's contentment! But with this new awareness came that familiar emotion: fear. If I advanced to another level of awareness, would I never be able to turn back? How would my husband be with this journey of mine? Would he accept it? What might happen to us if he didn't?

I was also very aware that my journey would be open for public discussion as more people around me became aware of what I was doing. I knew this would affect every member of my family. What would I put them through?

Without question, I would have to draw strength from within. I needed — as much as I needed food and water — to continue to grow in my understanding of the spirit realm and spirit interaction in our lives.

As I forged ahead, to study and open to the energies around me, my abilities expanded, and I began experiencing new sensations. I know many people assume they lack psychic abilities because they were not "born with them." However, I have learned through my own personal experiences that psychic abilities can be developed. I came to comprehend that the greater the energy I exerted to expand my learning, the more my gifts awakened.

❊ ❊ ❊

**March 2000.** With the arrival of March came the reality, for the second time, that Kim would not be here to celebrate her birthday. I was comforted by my knowledge that she was around us and decided it was time to attempt another out-of-body experience. What better way to find comfort than to spend time with Kim!

I decided to attempt it on my own. I was confident that Kim and my guide Raphael would keep me safe. I had done a significant amount of reading about inducing your own out-of-body experience and had prepared for this since January. Kim's birthday, March 15, seemed to be the perfect day to try.

Until that day arrived, I kept myself busy with my family, my spiritual lessons, and teaching. I worked hard to repair my once-close relationship with my husband and daughters. I also labored to forgive myself for not being there for them when they needed me the most. I prayed they, too, would be able to forgive me.

I didn't think my heart could break any more than it already had, but when I felt the strain between my earthly daughters and myself now, I knew it could. The pain of their emotional distance from me seared like a knife. Now that the numbness of grief had waned, I could again feel pain acutely on a human level. I had not experienced anything so intense since Kim passed. The floodgates opened, drowning me in pain once again.

How could I have been so selfish? I hadn't meant to be, but grief had encompassed every part of my being. I had been capable of nothing but grieving and breathing.

I credit my spiritual journey for giving me strength to want to live and love again. It had taken me almost a year-and-a-half to step back into life and be engaged in living again. I loved my husband and daughters. I realized it was important that I show them I did. My spirituality was now an integral part of me. It was definitely time to re-integrate my important roles of wife and mother.

I began each day in silent meditation then joined in family activities during the times Doug or the girls were home. One evening while the four of us sat at the dinner table together, we spontaneously shared stories of happy past experiences including our weekends at the trailer. We had recently sold the trailer and were feeling a bit sad about that.

That evening we recalled lots of happy memories, and I heard laughter ring in my ears and felt love in my heart for the family I still had. We all acknowledged that we missed Kim and how right it felt to acknowledge that together, too.

March 15 arrived. The day was bittersweet since it was not only Kim's birthday, but Kerry's as well. I could only imagine the sadness Kerry must feel not being able to celebrate with Kim.

I began the day in meditation, praying for all of us, with an extra prayer for Kerry. I asked for help and guidance when I would attempt to astral travel later that evening. After breakfast I spent some time with Doug then wrapped Kerry's presents. She would be home for supper, after which she wanted to spend the evening with her friends. Kristy was away at school and couldn't be with us. We planned an early dinner and a quiet celebration at home.

I took the meat for dinner out of the freezer then headed to the cemetery to spend time alone with Kim. I understood that I did not have to be at her grave in order to be with Kim; yet I wanted to be there. I noticed that some of her friends had already visited that day. I carefully examined the personal items left at the gravesite. Some of the cards were sealed in envelopes as if only Kim were to see them.

I had a good cry and knew Kim would understand. I missed her so much. As I stood up to leave, I asked her to join me on my "trip" I was planning for that evening.

It was getting late when I arrived home to prepare supper. Really wanting to make it a happy day for Kerry, I spent the next few hours being Mom. Then Doug left for work at 6:30 p.m., and Kerry headed out for the evening with her friends.

Finally the time had come for me to prepare for my astral travel adventure. I planned to meditate then listen to a soothing visualization tape. I was putting the tape into the machine when I heard the telephone ring. Should I answer it? I didn't want the outside world to interfere with my thoughts or plans.

But what if it was Kerry or Kristy? I ran to the phone and heard the voice of one of Kim's friends asking if she could come to our house for a visit. I knew how difficult Kim's passing had been for her and how much she missed Kim. I couldn't refuse her, so I welcomed her visit. By the time she left, I was too emotionally and physically exhausted to continue with my astral travel plans.

I recognized it must not have been the right time for my astral trip or it would have happened. I let go of my disappointment and was confident that when the time was right, I would have my visit with Kim.

I was not expecting it to happen so soon, however, and without any preparation. The next morning, while sitting in my car at the cemetery, I had my first, and to this day, only spontaneous out-of-body experience. I had been sitting on the grass talking to Kim, sharing some quiet, reflective time with her. When I returned to my car preparing to leave, I heard one of our special songs by Celine Dion playing on the radio.

While I listened, a sense of peace swiftly and unexpectedly washed over me. I placed my head on the steering wheel and quietly told Kim I would be okay now. Then I was "swooshed" away. I instantly found myself hovering above what I thought was a car, looking down at my friend Bonnie. I knew, without knowing how I knew, that Kim was beside me. This was amazing!

I was told to take note of all I was seeing, then I was traveling once again. I found myself with Kim floating near the ceiling of the exercise club owned by my friend Sue. I could see her working at her desk. Kim was telling me to thank Sue for the roses and the poem she had sent me the day before. Sue was wearing black stretch pants and a dark, oversized sweatshirt. My beloved Kim was with me the entire time I was out of my body. I felt her presence and her love.

As quickly as it began, it was over. I was back in my car with my head resting on the steering wheel. I didn't immediately feel I belonged in my body. I did not fit. Then a shift or adjustment occurred, and I did.

When I got my breath back, I reflected on what had just happened. During my previous two astral travel adventures, I had traveled to other realms. This time I stayed on the earth plane. I remembered the feeling of floating and then moving at a fast pace, but I didn't have a sense of traveling across and over things. During this trip, I was looking down at Bonnie; then I was aware that I was seeing Sue.

I got myself together, found a pen, and wrote down all I had seen, just as instructed. Next I headed for Bonnie's place of employment. She should have been at work at that time in the morning, so I couldn't understand why I had seen her sitting in a moving car. When I arrived at her office, I found it was closed for renovations.

I had to wait a few days for confirmation. When I did catch up with Bonnie, I found out that, sure enough, she had been taking a trip with her husband and daughter that day. As close as she could remember, she had been in the car at the same time I saw her during my astral trip.

I had more immediate verification from Sue. When I walked into her exercise club, she had on the exact clothes I had seen her wearing during my "visit." I handed her my written notes and asked if she had felt anything different around the time of my observation. She admitted that she hadn't felt anything but, looking at my notes, she offered congratulations on my successful journey and said she was honored Kim had chosen to visit her.

My first spontaneous journey out-of-body was so very healing. It caused a profound change within me and, most importantly, gave me a new understanding of the true nature of "soul." I was, however, left with a sense of sadness that this adventure was over. I wondered about the sanity of what I had done. Was it sane to want to astral travel on a regular basis? This would take some pondering.

The next evening as I sat down to prepare myself for an automatic writing session, I wondered what insights I would be shown this time. I didn't have to wait long for my mind to be filled with words.

*"Don't be so hard on yourself, Mom. It will be okay. How can you doubt this now? You must stay strong in your belief and trust God to heal and strengthen you.*

*"I am really okay and I am here. I am here to guide you. This is your destiny. We are to work together and, with Raphael's help, you will be shown your path. You have already begun. Continue to learn, to work with your energy, and you will help many to understand that there really is no death.*

*"I know it is a very hard lesson for you — losing me — but have you lost me? Who are you talking to right now? I am just away doing what I need to be doing.*

*"We are forever together. Remember that always. We are connected, heart to heart.*

*"Don't cry, Mom. We will all be okay, because our only true lesson is one of love. Open your heart once again and don't be afraid to love."*

*"Don't cry, Mom. We will all be okay, because our only true lesson is one of love. Open your heart once again and don't be afraid to love. We are here to help you. Remember: Love yourself enough to spread your love to others. That is God's plan for eternity. Take time to listen to the silence. I love you, Kim."*

It was now time for me to directly focus on my own personal healing journey. I had closed my heart to feelings for the sake of my own self-preservation. Opening it would bring on a flood of emotions. I hoped I would be strong enough to handle it. The next day, I borrowed a book titled, *One Day My Soul Just Opened Up*, by Iyanla Vanzant. It was a book my friend Joanne had suggested I read. I was now ready.

The first words that jumped out at me were, "This journey requires boldness of heart, strength of mind, and power of spirit." Well, I prayed I had these qualities and the determination to work through my issues.

This book was designed to take 40 days and nights to complete. It advised that each morning my focus be put on the inspirational thought for the day and the last few minutes of the evening be spent in quiet reflection.

The author advised that if I spent time honoring the things that really matter in life, I would take crucial steps in my personal growth and gather spiritual strength.

Iyanla reminded me to be patient with myself, be gentle with myself, and know that all things are working in my favor. "If you take one step toward the Light of Spirit, Spirit will take five steps on your behalf," she promised.

By the time I had completed my 40 days and nights, I had done much soul searching. I included Iyanla's book in the list at the back of this book in the hope it will help you to grow, heal, and change.

❋ ❋ ❋

**April 2000.** One morning I sat at the kitchen table having a cup of coffee. As I looked out through our large kitchen window at the openness behind our home, movement in a tree caught my eye. As I focused, I saw a robin perched on a branch. This sighting prompted me to recognize it was a perfect day to spend time outside and bask in nature. I decided I would drive to a lovely nearby spot where a small waterfall trickled over some rocks. Doug had shown me this site only a few weeks before.

It was still chilly but the day was sunny. I parked the car and decided to take a short walk down a path I spotted. A friend of mine had told me we should hug a tree every day and feel the positive energy the tree radiates. I smiled at the thought. I was conscious of the fact that if someone saw me hug a tree, I would be discounted as a kook.

Returning to the waterfall, I found a smooth rock and sat down. I had a strong desire to talk with my guides. I had not brought a pen and paper with me. I hoped to "hear or know the answer" to the questions that were deeply baffling me.

I stated my questions out loud, to make my intentions clear. "How am I, by continuing to open to the Light, to use my new awareness to aid others grieving the loss of a loved one? How am I to share with others that their loved ones, although gone from us, are safe on the other side?"

I began a light meditation, silently asking for guidance, wisdom, and answers to my questions. After taking a few deep breaths, I felt my body relax. I must remember to just let my mind flow naturally, I thought. When I finally opened my eyes, I had "sensed" two different things. The first was that I was sitting with someone. We faced each other. I did the talking as she listened. There was a candle burning beside us.

The second awareness came in the form of words: "When you are ready, you will know and understand your purpose. Have patience."

"Just great!" I mumbled to myself. Driving home, I understood the advice to have patience. I wasn't ready yet to hear the answer.

I began my second psychic development class with Shawna Ross, eager to move forward with my spiritual growth so I could understand where this journey was taking me. It was exciting to embrace my new spirituality. Whatever my lessons were for this lifetime, I longed to discover them.

The classes were inspiring and thought provoking as our group studied energy and healing techniques. Our studies renewed my interest in spiritual healing and taught me to be more open to the invisible energy that is around our human bodies. Up until this time, receiving messages from the other side had been my primary focus. Now it was becoming increasingly apparent that to become an effective spiritual communicator, I must open my mind to other avenues of learning. I now had an intense desire to understand the many facets of the unseen world.

During one of my meditation classes we were told we would learn to feel our auras. I had never attempted this before. I was surprised how easily I could feel an aura! We each paired up with a partner. We were instructed to hold our hands about two feet over the top of our partner's head as she sat in a chair. As we took turns, we were to slowly lower our hands until we felt we had made contact with our partner's aura. I felt it immediately. It was as if I had encountered a wall I couldn't see. I felt a tingling sensation in my hands.

My partner was able to feel my aura, too. She said she felt warmth when she made contact with my aura.

Next we formed two lines on opposite sides of the room. Putting our hands in front of us, palms facing out, we were directed to walk slowly toward each other and to stop when we felt our partner's energy field. Again, I was quickly able to feel this invisible energy.

Following these exercises, we discussed our experiences as a group. It became clear that each person felt and sensed things in her own unique way. All of us were successful in feeling each other's energy fields.

I went home that evening with a heightened sense of awareness about the energy field surrounding my own body. I recalled my first healing session when I was told my energy field was depleted. I decided it was time to do some more reading on the subject. I had done a little, a few months back, but was not really interested in the topic at that time. The class had now spurred my interest.

What I learned was that when our body is distressed, as mine was because of my extreme grief, this energy field is affected. Instead of radiating a strong, uniform glow, the energy field shrinks and grows weak from stress. I hoped that all my spiritual work not only helped me emotionally and physically but had repaired my aura as well.

Over the course of these classes, I was learning how individual each journey is. As far as I was concerned, I could "feel" colors — not see them — in my meditations. Some of my friends in the class saw specific colors in their mind's eye. Instead, I "felt" the warmth and vibration of the color. I would have a sense of things but could not see or hear them, which, I was to learn, meant I was clairsentient.

I got frustrated in the beginning wondering why I couldn't "see" colors until I learned that psychics receive information in different ways. One who *sees* an image is *clairvoyant*; one who *feels* the emotions or information is *clairsentient*, and one who *hears* information is *clairaudient*. Some combine all three.

More to read, more to learn, more to understand. I continued to do automatic writing but not to the extent I had in the early days of my journey. I was writing maybe once a week for myself now. Occasionally I would do automatic writing for a friend. Judy Hunt constantly reminded me that I needed to practice bringing messages through. "Don't forget," she said, "you can practice on me."

On April 8, I prepared myself to write. I was unaware, however, that this session of automatic writing was to be a turning point on my journey. It was during this writing that I had my first experience with a spirit "stepping forward." I was not only shocked but also intrigued by an older gentleman who stepped forward. Raphael told me to focus on what I sensed, saw, and felt. Here is the entire experience.

> *"We like Judy for her charge-ahead attitude. She has never been one to drag her feet. Verifications she will receive. Remind her to strengthen her connection as much and as often as possible. It is only with practice that she will flower and bloom to her potential. This is Raphael, my dear.*
>
> *"An older man is stepping forward. He wishes to be acknowledged. He is very excited to be making this connection. He is stuttering because he is so excited, and I will connect with him and see what messages he wishes to impart.*
>
> *"This is his message for Judy: He is your mother's guide, he states, but he loves you and guides you as well. He likes your husband. Good choice for you, although there have been many struggles. They have made you stronger."*
>
> I silently asked Raphael to describe this man and give me more details about him. *"Tall man for his era; not very proper, he laughs. He would rather have fun. Responsibility was not his strong characteristic. Proud of his hair and his birthmark. What a great smile! He wants you to sense him without writing. I say, my dear, this is what you must practice, so the time is perfect. Write all that you sense."*

At that moment, I was aware that I sensed this gentleman within my third eye. Startled, I began to write what I sensed:

*Shadow on face, right side*

*Yellow teeth, looks like they need work*

*Long thin nose; stepping into water, salt water, I sense*

*Pocketwatch, not originally his, maybe dad's or granddad's; he is proud of it*

*Smelling a pipe*

*He says lots of family with him*

*Says he will make you smile with one of his off-color jokes; you would appreciate it more than some*

*Poppa, I think — over and over, Oh! Pepper; he likes it*

Suddenly he was gone. Chill bumps broke out all over me when I asked him if he was Judy's mom's grandfather. He just smiled. I didn't sense he was the father. I felt very safe and sensed a happy person. It was a nice feeling for me.

The following morning I called Judy to share the messages received for her. Judy admitted she didn't know who this man was, but her mother probably would. Since Judy's mother lived miles away from us in Eastern Canada, I believed Judy would not be able to verify this information right away.

"When do you think you'll be talking to your mom?" I asked.

I could hear Judy's laugh over the telephone. "Would you believe Mom arrived unexpectedly for the weekend? I'll see what verification she can give me."

I marveled at the synchronicity of her mother's visit. No coincidences. No, never again would I think in those terms. All happens according to plan.

Judy's mother, Pat, verified some of the information immediately. This man was not her father, but she remembered her grandfather having been from Wales; therefore, the feeling of salt water made sense. He was not a tall man by today's standards, she recalled, but was definitely tall for his era. Pat said she would try to find out more.

Within a few days Judy had a photograph of this gentleman to show me.

Pat had remembered she had given Judy some old pictures a few years earlier, so they went in search of them. Among the black-and-white photographs was a picture of Pat's grandfather.

Judy phoned me. "You have to come right over. I have something important to show you." She hung up. Meeting me at the door half an hour later, she quickly ushered me into her kitchen, where I saw a picture lying on the table. The man in the photograph was the man who had stepped forward in my recent session.

"Look closely at his face," Judy urged. This man had a very distinctive nose — long and thin. Judy couldn't wait for me to notice something else about his face. She pointed to a large shadow across the right side of his face!

Two obvious verifications stared back at me from the photograph: exactly what I had seen. I had no doubt this was the man I had talked to.

"This is the only picture we have of my mother's grandfather."

As I continued to learn and expand my beliefs, I felt my abilities shift and increase. I was continually amazed by the clarity, depth, and accuracy of the information I received.

We all have these abilities if we choose to discover them. I trust the statement, "As we travel this journey, believe in your heart, be open to all possibilities and miracles will surround you." This has become my new philosophy and my reality.

*Despite the fact that thousands upon thousands of recently bereaved people say they have felt the presence of or received signs from their deceased loved ones, I, like so many others, completely dismissed the possibility that eternal life was a reality. Those of us who now believe. . . receive a measure of comfort as we travel through our grief journey.*

Each one of us must face death, be it our own or someone's we love. Yet society treats death as an "untouchable" subject. Fear of death is pervasive, despite the fact that all the major religions profess belief in eternal life.

Even though thousands upon thousands of recently bereaved people say they have felt the presence of or received signs from their deceased loved ones, I, like so many others, completely dismissed the possibility that eternal life was a reality. Those of us who now believe, or at least stay open to the belief, that so-called death is but a transition to another plane of existence, receive a measure of comfort as we travel through our grief journey.

All the signs, messages, and miracles in my life since Kim's passing had finally brought me to this insight. I did not *like* the fact that Kim now lived on the other side, but I did believe it. I knew that no matter what anyone said to dispute the events that had occurred, their words would never be successful in dissuading me.

My personal journey allowed me to know the truth.

Chapter 6

# Discovering My Purpose

*The intuitive mind is a sacred gift, the rational mind is a faithful servant; we have created a society that honors the servant and has forgotten the gift.*

—Albert Einstein

**May 2000.** I was now getting expansive glimpses of the other world and, because of this, fully believed in the existence of an afterlife. I was certain more of my life's purpose would soon unfold for me.

I had never spent any thought pondering my purpose for being here on earth. I was just busy living my everyday life as a wife, mom, daughter, sister, aunt, teacher, and member of my community. Then Kim passed.

Now, thanks to my newly developed deep faith, I had the strength to face any skeptic I encountered. I was ready to talk freely about spirituality and the beliefs I now held. I had begun to put my ideas together for the writing of this book. My life was extremely busy as I balanced my spiritual work with my physical existence. Although no longer spending hours in chatrooms, I felt a debt of gratitude to all those online people who helped to lighten my burdens during the darkest moments of my life.

I stayed in contact with Sharlette as our comfortable friendship blossomed. Lou and I chatted often and on occasion he would relay messages from Kim. I received additional messages from Scott, Lou's partner on the other side, and was glad to be able to bring through some much appreciated words for Lou. The process helped me understand that, even though Lou was a medium himself, it still warmed his heart to receive personal messages through someone else.

Since Kim's passing, my family and my spirituality were the two most important elements in my life. It was only because of my spirituality that I could still have my whole family. My search for Kim opened my eyes to the discovery of my reason for being on this physical plane. I was now willing to do whatever it took to strengthen my connection between the physical world and the spiritual world. It was time to relinquish my ego and be willing to allow my spiritual journey to unfold as it was pre-ordained. I let go of my fear of the outcome, able to trust that all would unfold for my greater good. That knowledge relieved much of my worry.

I asked for Divine help to release the feelings of anger and lack of forgiveness toward those who had disappointed me since Kim's passing. I worked diligently to focus on the positive attributes in the people I encountered, which was not always an easy task. If my human emotions crept in, I would ask for help and guidance from the other side to release them. I also wanted someday to find a way to forgive the man who caused Kim's death. I was now working on these feelings I silently continued to struggle with.

I had read that what we give out comes back to us ten-fold. I pondered that wisdom. As I tendered more loving thoughts toward others, more love flooded into my life. I felt a sense of contentment unknown since that awful day in October 1998 when Kim left this physical realm.

A wide range of emotions assailed me! Eager to see what I would be shown next, I was always conscious of the fact that Kim had to die in order for me to be on this journey in the first place. Some days I just wanted to grieve. On those days, this journey to stay connected to Kim felt like a burden. Then something magical would occur, and I would marvel at my spiritual awakening.

*I was always conscious of the fact that Kim had to die in order for me to be on this journey in the first place. Some days I just wanted to grieve.. . . Then something magical would occur, and I would marvel at my spiritual awakening.*

The Friday before Mother's Day was one of those magical days for me. I could feel the sadness growing as Mother's Day approached. Though happy I still had two daughters with whom to share this day, I grieved for the daughter no longer here to celebrate with us.

Sitting at the computer that Friday evening, I opened up my email. I scanned down the list of new messages, noting one from a bereaved mom I had met on the Internet. Because we each lost a daughter, we spent time and shed many tears trying to comfort each other. This evening she had sent me a poem. It was titled, "Surviving Mother's Day after Losing a Child." Reading her love-filled poem reminded me how grateful I was for her friendship.

I noticed this poem had been received then forwarded from, I assumed, one bereaved mother to another. The bottom of the page showed an attached memorial link, one I assumed was made in memory of someone's child, since it was attached to the Mother's Day poem.

I opened the memorial, unprepared for what I found. It was a picture of Kandi Willis Webb with a story of her life and an account of her passing. This was the young lady I had read about months earlier, who had been born on March 15 and passed away on October 27, dates identical to Kim's. I had thought about Kandi often since the day I had opened that first memorial and been struck by the synchronicity of the dates.

Where was that memorial I had printed out? My memory had been so bad back then, but I recalled putting it away for safekeeping. I fumbled around the drawer in the computer desk but couldn't find it. Then I remembered: it was in the desk drawer in my bedroom. With the retrieved memorial in my hand, I rushed back to my computer to compare. My memory had not failed: it definitely was the same girl.

The memorial just received was more detailed and included a beautiful picture of Kandi. I stared at her picture for a few moments, wondering if I would see a resemblance to Kim. Kandi was slim, her beautiful smile framed by shoulder-length brown hair. Kim was also a slim young woman with shoulder-length brown hair and a beautiful smile. Although such similarities were striking, there were also differences. Kandi wore a cowboy hat. I could never imagine Kim in a cowboy hat, as she was most certainly not a country girl.

Mesmerized, I tried to read the words but had a hard time keeping my focus. Then I read how Kandi had passed. She too had been killed in a car accident. This was uncanny.

The memorial told me that the writer, Sharon, had not only lost her daughter in the accident but her grandson, Jeremy, too. He was four years old. In 1971, she had previously lost another daughter, Pennie, who had lived for only 24 hours.

Then I saw the email address for Kandi's mom, a woman I had longed to write for months. Within minutes I was typing a letter to Kandi's mother, Sharon. Apparently this was the ideal time for contact.

How should I introduce myself? What should I say? I didn't hesitate long. I told her about Kim, when she was born, how she passed, and the date of her passing. I added, as an afterthought, the fact that both girls had the same initials. Now she, too, would see the three startling parallels to her Kandi. I took a deep breath and sent it. I nervously wondered how long it would take to receive a reply.

Sharon responded swiftly. Not surprisingly, we both had many questions. Sharon definitely wanted to talk as much I did, so we arranged to hook up to an instant message service through the computer where we could talk privately and without cost.

The first discussion was, of course, about our daughters. They had followed different paths in their lives. While Kim had focused on education and a quest for adventure and travel, Kandi had married at the age of 16 and had two children by the age of 19. When it was time to say good night, we promised to meet online the next evening.

As we continued to get to know each other, more parallels in our lives emerged. We spent our second evening comparing facts about our families and discovered other similarities. Sharon had also given birth to three daughters. Sadly, she had lost two of them. Her husband drove a truck for a living, just as my husband had done for ten years before he changed careers.

But one of the most startling similarities was the date of birth of our youngest daughters. They were born on exactly the same day. Wendy, her youngest and only surviving daughter, had the same birthdate as my youngest daughter, Kristy.

I shook my head in disbelief! What was the significance of all these similarities? Our lives — Sharon's and mine — paralleled each other in so many ways. Could we have a soul connection of some kind? Could our daughters in spirit have brought us together?

We discussed both of these possibilities in an attempt to understand what it all meant. Since that day Sharon and I have continued to share a bond far beyond friendship.

I wondered if Sharon had ever received a reading from a medium. Would she be open to it? I hoped she would be willing to meet with Sharlette. If Kim and Kandi were somehow connected on the other side, then Sharon must be introduced to Sharlette. I was confident Sharlette would be able to bring through information from Kandi since she always heard Kim so clearly.

I broached the subject with her the next time we chatted online. She said she had not known such a thing was possible when Kandi first passed but had developed some belief in it now. I told her about Sharlette and the reading I had received from her. I cautiously asked her if she would like to meet Sharlette. Sharon said she would.

Now I had to figure out a way to get them together. Both Sharon and Sharlette used the instant message system to talk to me when we connected by computer. I could easily link to both of them the same way. Sharon and

I agreed to meet at a specific time the following evening. I planned to see if I could have Sharlette there, too.

Nothing astonished me any more, so when I registered that evening on the IM, I was not surprised to see both their names on the list of active users. Putting them together was easy. Sharlette had her own chatroom; Sharon, Sharlette, and I met there.

The three of us chatted for a short time; then I saw Sharon say she would be interested in having a reading. That very evening a spontaneous reading took place in the chatroom. Although Sharlette knew nothing about the special connection I had with Sharon, I was invited to stay and watch Sharlette do what she does so well.

When the reading was over, Sharon felt confident she had been conversing with her daughter. Sharlette was able to confirm many details about Kandi and her life. I was surprised to discover, during the course of the reading, that Kandi was also pregnant with her third child at the time of the accident. This fact, brought out by Sharlette, was confirmed by Sharon. Sharlette also confirmed a little boy was standing with Kandi. This was undoubtedly her four-year-old son, Jeremy.

Pleased for Sharon, I felt honored to be a part of the evening.

I thought the channelling was finished when Sharlette suddenly addressed me. "Kim was standing in the background during the reading and is now stepping forward." Sharlette continued: "Kim is saying you need to understand more about past life connections."

I understood the significance of the message, again awestruck by this miraculous journey. Sharlette, not having previous knowledge of how Sharon and I met nor of the parallels of our lives, was intrigued. We shared with Sharlette why we felt our girls were together on the other side. She had just proved our intuitions right: they were together.

Some attachment greater than I could comprehend was going on between Sharon and me. Although we will never truly understand the significance of some events until we ourselves cross over to the other side, it was clear to both of us that we were meant to find each other at this time in our lives.

As our friendship grew, I confided in her that I did automatic writing. I hoped Kandi would come through with messages for her mom. To find validation of whatever messages I received, I needed to do this soon, before Sharon gave me more details about their lives. With Sharon in agreement, I sat down to connect with Kandi.

I connected with both Kim and Kandi that evening and felt an incredible amount of peace from this contact. I did not understand all the information Kandi relayed to me, but I realized it was not for me to understand since the messages were for Sharon and her family. After I relayed the information by email, Sharon confirmed that, in addition to some personal information, Kandi's personality had definitely come through, that Kandi would have spoken to her in "just that way."

I understood what she meant. During my readings with various mediums, Kim's personality had shone through, too.

I explained to Sharon that she could have this same direct connection with Kandi if she wanted to. I requested her address so I could send her some information about automatic writing. In the package, I also included a picture of Kim for Sharon and her family. I wistfully noted how far from each other we were; Sharon lived near the U.S west coast while I lived in Ontario.

For the next few days I thought about the events leading up to our meeting. Sharlette and Sharon had now connected and that fact brought happiness to my heart. It then dawned on me that all our names began with the letter "S." I smiled to myself. It was a little thing, but I decided I would start to pay more attention to such "coincidences."

I talked to more and more people about my automatic writing and, because of my openness, was asked more frequently to bring through information for others. At the exercise club I met a woman eager to receive messages from her guides and loved ones on the other side. This was the first time I would channel information for a total stranger.

I nervously settled in to a session of automatic writing. Upon completion, I viewed what I had written: some very detailed information including a man's name had been channeled through. She read the page, grew pale, then gasped with astonishment, overcome by the accuracy of details and the fact I had written her brother's name.

The writing also introduced her to one of her guides. Excited now, she asked me a lot of questions. I told her I felt she was ready to open to more understanding of the other side and suggested attending classes to awaken to her own abilities.

On May 29, 2000, I completed my level-two psychic development class. On the final evening some people in our class asked Shawna Ross if she could and would give them information about their guides. She agreed. As I already had a personal relationship with my guides, Raphael, Holly and Kim, I was not as enthusiastic about this as others in the class. We did a light group meditation before she began.

Asking the first woman to stand, Shawna told her she had a Native American guide and described what he looked like. How strange, I thought; before she told the woman, I *knew* she was going to say the guide was Native American. I didn't know what he looked like, but I had sensed a native connection. I didn't say anything.

The next woman stood up. I sensed a little girl hanging onto her leg but smiled at how silly it was for me to get such an image. Seconds later, I heard the teacher say, "You have a little girl hanging onto your leg, and she is happy to finally be acknowledged."

I started to pay more attention. As each person was introduced to a guide, I focused on what I felt, saw, and heard. Along with our teacher, I had also accurately sensed each of their guides. Fascinating!

When it was my turn, I was expecting one of my known guides or Kim to step forward. Of course, I hoped it would be Kim. I was informed that I had two new guides around me. "They arrived recently," our teacher explained, "to teach you new things and take you to a higher spiritual level."

She relayed the following message from these guides: "You are ready to advance. Take your next step with confidence, as you are ready. We are here to teach you more of your life's work."

Whatever they wanted to teach, I was eager to learn.

This evening had already been a learning experience for me. I could not see or hear the guides. I just sensed them. I could hear messages but not in the traditional way. I didn't use my physical ears. I just had a "knowing" of what was being said. It was as if they stepped forward inside my mind to give me an awareness of their presence.

Why could I sense other people's guides yet be unaware that I now had two *new* guides?

I drove home that evening with more questions and a deep knowing that something new had just opened for me. I could now sense guides.

I didn't have to wait for the opportunity to confirm my recently acquired ability to sense other people's guides. On May 30, I was invited by a friend to meet a woman who did healing through a technique called "Therapeutic Touch." Three of us went that evening. It was my first experience with this form of healing. As the evening wore on, I agreed to be a recipient of this healing technique.

What happened while I was on the healing table was totally unexpected. While receiving treatment, I went into a relaxed state. I don't know how long it took before I became aware of the presence of two guides around me. Their appearance startled me, but I quietly made mental notes of all that I sensed.

One of the guides stood behind Jill, who was working at my feet. I could sense a beautiful female guide who, I knew, was Egyptian. Then I focused on Liz, the woman at my head, and sensed the powerful presence of a uniformed soldier standing at her left shoulder.

Despite my excitement, I tried to remain calm to allow the healing energy to work. It was my first meeting with these women, so I did not know how much, if anything, they knew about their guides. I was about to find out.

I started with Jill and related to her all I had sensed. Her response was immediate. "Oh! That is so right. I am obsessed with Egyptian artifacts. If you could see my house, you would understand what I mean."

Next I went to Liz, asked her about this man in uniform and received immediate confirmation. Liz replied she was glad he was back because she hadn't sensed him for a while. She continued to tell me that he always stood by her left shoulder just where I sensed him.

The other ladies in attendance that evening gathered around. They began to fire questions at me including how long I had been doing this work. Laughing, I said, "This was just the second time. Both experiences occurred spontaneously, unbidden." I detailed what had taken place on the last evening of my learning class, only a few days earlier. They asked if I would try to focus on their guides, too, but I told them I was nervous and tired.

The women's attention returned to the reason they had come: to experience and understand more about Therapeutic Touch. Next, it was my friend Sue's turn for a healing. I was exhausted and ready to leave. I peeked into the healing room to see that Sue was already lying down. I headed off to the kitchen where a few of the ladies were pouring cups of tea. I knew Sue would be a while, so I poured myself one.

A few moments later, one of the ladies sat beside me and quietly told me that her daughter was sick. She had come here tonight so her daughter could receive a healing. "Would you please focus on a guide for my daughter?" she asked. I noticed a young girl of about 14 enter the room and approach us. The woman introduced her daughter to me.

I explained again that I was not experienced at sensing other people's guides. Both asked me to try. It would be okay if nothing happened, they reassured me.

As I considered my decision, the daughter approached me. "In my room at night, sometimes I feel the presence of someone helping me. That's why we are asking for your help."

I promised to try. I began to focus the attention of my third eye on this young girl. Then I began to talk, to tell all that I sensed. I heard her guide as he spoke directly to me by making words appear in my mind. Another first.

I described the two "energies" around her. One, I sensed, was a Native American, a man, and very protective. Her mother said, "She has been told that before."

I told them the other energy was a young girl, also Native American, who said she was the one around her at night. She hoped she would share her "special teddy bear" with her. The young girl energy explained she was around her so she wouldn't feel alone, while the older Native American was more of a protector.

The 14-year-old girl told me she had felt the presence of a little girl around her at night and that she wanted to find out who it was and why she was there. "The special teddy bear," she said, "was a gift from a friend when I first got sick." A few other messages came, then the guides were gone.

Some of the women who had overheard the session asked if I had business cards with me so they could telephone to make an appointment for a reading. "What business cards? I don't give readings."

"But you should!" came a chorus. The evening came to an end and we headed home. I was grateful Sue was driving, as I sat exhausted, reflecting on the evening's events.

I worried about the lack of time for my automatic writing. I was often too tired to focus on writing and had reduced the amount of time I spent on this communication technique from every day to three or four times a week, then to only once a week. I had much to learn, and many new doors were opening simultaneously.

I was becoming increasingly interested in Reiki healing. Although this meant additional study for me, I felt drawn to learn more about this ancient healing technique. My friend Joanne and I signed up for a level-one Reiki class on June 3.

A series of unexpected circumstances arose, however, that would ultimately delay the Reiki class. A family function had been planned for the June 3 weekend, one I felt I should attend. I had tried to call Carol Baltkalns, who was to teach the course, to see when she would hold another first-level class. I had decided if I didn't have to wait too long, I would reschedule with Carol and be with my family.

Joanne phoned to tell me she could not attend the class the June 3 weekend. "I hope you can wait and attend a later Reiki class with me."

"I've been trying to reach Carol to cancel, too. Why am I not surprised we both want to postpone?" Because of our hectic schedules, the only Saturday we both had free for a while was June 17. We didn't figure Carol would offer another class so soon after June 3, but I said I would call and find out.

When I returned home, I found a message on my answering machine from Carol canceling the previously arranged class and rescheduling the workshop on the 17th.

Synchronicities like this no longer struck me as odd. In my new life, I expected them. Do things like this just happen at random? No. Is there really such a thing as a "coincidence?" Not in my new understanding. I had become an adamant believer in Iylana Vanzant's suggestion: "Remain open. There is something bigger than you know going on here."

❋ ❋ ❋

**June 2000.** On June 6, I sat down to meditate and do some automatic writing. Kim came through that evening.

> *"Don't doubt the Light that is surrounding you. You are protected and are ready to advance to the next stage. I am so proud of you. We will work together to share the Light and spread it to others. This is our Divine plan, Mom. The world must wake up to the goodness within.*
>
> *"Nature is the natural energy that is around you. Use this powerful energy and you will feel its power. I am here, and so many are waiting to show you the power you possess, that everyone possesses if they would just open to the possibility.*
>
> *"Now I will explain, as you are finally ready to hear. You are to be a spiritual teacher. Your clear words will 'turn on a light*

*bulb,' so to speak, in the minds of people who are ready to open to the Light of our world. You will speak and they will understand. You will put them on their own path. With this new understanding these people will begin to walk a new path, one of greater love and understanding. They, in turn, will send others to you and you will empower more.*

*"You have a great many around you now to encourage you and support you. You must support each other. Mom, you can't enlighten everyone, so please don't try. The ones who are ready will come. The others can't be forced to, so step back and know that when the time is right they, too, will be enlightened. Everyone's journey must be in his or her own time.*

*"You have two new teachers now. Together we will open many to the Light that we all possess. You are thinking: why am I not your teacher? Well, we need many teachers, in both planes of existence, to complete our growth. They are but two more for you. Don't doubt that you are ready. I am so excited about this new adventure. We share it, and together we will help others."*

*. . . This was the day I knew I would complete my book. . . so others who struggled with the loss of a loved one might. . . . find some comfort and hope.*

This was the day I knew I would complete my book. I felt compelled to share my personal story so that others who struggled with the loss of a loved one might connect with their loved ones on the other side and thus find some comfort and hope.

I was now receiving messages for others on a more constant basis. Messages were beginning to come through me in the form of thoughts. Previously, I needed to meditate and get into a state of relaxation to connect to those on the other side. But now, I received spontaneous and unexpected messages — always for others.

The first time it happened was when I ran into a casual friend while walking in the mall. We were just exchanging pleasantries when out of my mouth popped a name and information I didn't know I was going to say. The information, as close as I can describe it, seemed to fill my head; then I heard my voice say the thoughts. I was as surprised as my friend was.

She turned pale. "Are you okay?" I asked. "I'd better sit down. This has really stunned me." We headed to the food court to find a seat.

She explained that I had uttered the name of her paternal grandfather and the report that he was "looking over" her father. "My dad just had open-heart surgery, you see. He returned home from the hospital only a week ago."

Totally unbidden, this information came to me as a sensation not of hearing words but of "knowing." In spite of Kim's confirmation that my life's purpose was now to do spiritual work, I drove home marveling at how accurately I had sensed the information.

When I was out in public around people, my head was bombarded with messages, draining my energy. Over the course of my spiritual journey, I had opened a door to the other side that I now did not know how to close.

Fear prickled my neck. What had I done? In my attempt to find and connect to Kim I had, apparently, opened up to many other spirits on the other side. For the next two months I continued to be bombarded with these messages. I wondered if I would ever be normal again.

On June 17, Joanne and I took our level-one Reiki Class. We knew that four other women would also take the course. As we introduced ourselves, I was drawn to one lady named Yvonne. As I sat quietly, minding my own business, a sensation of knowing came to me that I would relay a message to her from someone on the other side.

I moved closer to give her the message. "A man wants to say hello. He told me he had passed in a car accident. He gave me a girl's name." I told Yvonne the name. Although startled, she understood who the man was.

For some years, Yvonne had worked with healing through Therapeutic Touch and believed in the afterlife. She thanked me for the messages; she felt they were important for her daughters to hear. Her ex-husband, she told me, who was killed in a car accident, had given me the message. The name I relayed was that of a granddaughter born *after* he passed.

When our class began, we each received a booklet to study over the course of the day. The information was all new to us and triggered many questions. We learned that stress caused by negative emotions — such as loss, fear, anger, anxiety, worry, and doubt — disrupts and weakens the flow of "life force energy" and can block the body's natural ability to repair and protect itself.

Someone asked what life force energy was, and I listened intently for the meaning of the phrase. The body is alive because of the "life force energy" that flows through it. The teacher explained that, for some of us, keeping it flowing freely was often complicated. Reiki healing, a hands-on method to channel healing energy, would allow the blockages to be cleared so we could keep our life force flowing. Then we would stay healthy.

Just as happened when I encountered chakras for the first time, I was learning how important it was to treat the body, mind, and soul as a whole in order to remain healthy.

The rest of a very long day was spent learning and practicing this form of spiritual healing. When the day was over, I knew I would be back sometime in the future to continue with level two.

❊ ❊ ❊

**July 2000.** I planned to spend the next two months focusing solely on family. I decided I would take a break from my spiritual work. I hoped to resume a semblance of the normalcy I had enjoyed prior to October 27, 1998, when my world fell apart. But with my new spiritual life purpose, I was unable — and unwilling — to completely distance myself from the spiritual side of my life. I was drawn like a magnet to bookstores in search of spiritual material to read that would increase my knowledge and understanding of "the other side" and the "afterlife."

I discovered a few books dealing with the subject of near-death experiences. One such classic, titled *Life After Life*, by Raymond Moody, M.D.,

Ph.D., was published in 1975 after the physician interviewed more than 100 people who shared the details of their near-death experiences with him. The people Dr. Moody interviewed had all been declared clinically dead by medical personnel but later came back to life. Each person told Moody what happened during the time they were clinically dead.

Dr. Moody compiled a list of consistent experiences described by those he interviewed. His list included the sensation of floating out of the body, seeing a tunnel with a brilliant light, reuniting with deceased family members, a feeling of euphoria, and having no desire to return to the body or earth. Many of the experiences detailed in the book sounded like what I experienced when I traveled astrally. Fascinating!

I felt the summer holidays should be spent with my family, but I was always conscious that I wanted to remain connected to the other side in a more subtle way. Although I took the month off from my automatic writing, I found friends with whom I could practice my Reiki technique. I knew I needed to practice so I wouldn't forget the different hand positions and symbols.

My husband's sister Norma and her three daughters arrived from France for a six-week visit with us. I sincerely wanted to enjoy their company. I decided the best way to feed my spiritual needs during this time was by reading. Since I knew Norma's belief system somewhat paralleled mine, I shared with her some of the events that had transpired since Kim's passing.

I told her I felt it necessary to practice giving messages from the other side so I could build confidence in my psychic ability and gain a greater understanding of the process. However, I admitted to Norma that I felt out of control.

Norma quickly responded that I could practice with her. This gave me the opportunity to do my very first "reading." I was nervous and wondered if I would be able to bring through facts about her life that I did not already have, data that would provide validation for both of us. My task was made easier since Norma had lived in France for such a long time that much about her life and the people in it were unknown to me. I prepared to give the reading.

Despite my nervousness, I began to meditate to enhance our connection to the other side. As Norma eagerly sat down, I took a deep breath. A torrent of words flowed out of my mouth. By the end of the session, the depth of the information was so startling that it knocked us both into stunned silence.

Mention was made of a past life Norma had lived. Years before, Norma told me, she had been given a glimpse of the same past life by someone she met in France. For her, it was a confirmation; for me, it was something else to contemplate, as I was still forming my belief in past lives.

Below are excerpts from the session that afternoon, as recorded by Norma in hand-written notes.

> Sandy: "A slim man, with blond hair has come forward. He is in his 40s, and I feel he is 'gay.' Name starts with a 'J' or 'G' with an 'r' in it. You can tell 'Nugrape' that he came, and he says hi."
>
> Norma: "Nugrape is a nickname that we gave to a good friend 30 some years ago. One of the young men in our big group of close friends was Graham. He came 'out of the closet' a few years ago, but only a few of us knew that he had declared himself 'gay.' He died after heart surgery about two-and-a-half years ago." *I asked Norma if she still saw this friend Nugrape and Norma replied she was planning to see him during this visit home. She wasn't sure if she would tell him.*
>
> Sandy: "An older man has come forward now. Name starts with an 'M.' He is short, stocky, balding, shy, and very quiet. Says he didn't like being old. Thanks you for looking after his son, Alain. Says he's often with his wife now, even if they were not very close [while he was alive]. Their life together was just a partnership. Hear 'five.' He wants to acknowledge five children or grandchildren."
>
> Norma: "He has five grandchildren."
>
> Sandy: "Two children?"
>
> Norma: "Yes, only Alain and his sister."
>
> Sandy: "Some miscarriages, too. I hear the number three. Do

you know about any miscarriages?"

Norma: "Yes, there were three."

Sandy: "I now hear a name like Morris — maybe Maurice — and now another 'M' name, too."

Norma: "The description fits my husband's father, who died in January, 2000. His name does start with an 'M' and it is Maurice. The most astonishing fact is that he always used to say, "It's not good to grow old." His marriage was an arrangement rather than a marriage 'd'amour!' His wife's name is also an 'M.'"

Sandy: "Would it be like Mimi?"

Norma: "Yes, it is. Wow! Mimi often says she can feel him near her when she's alone, in their home."

Sandy: "I am sure she does then." *I had no previous knowledge of Norma's father-in-law but I did know he had passed. I had never met Alain's parents and did not know their names. I was as startled as Norma when this information came through in such detail.*

Sandy: "In the year 2002, there will be big changes. Money coming. The numbers 'nine' and 'four' will be important. Something in Canada. This came up earlier in the reading, so remember this, okay. Year 2002, and four and nine."

Norma: "Ok, I will."

Following is Norma's final comment to me as she presented written copy for inclusion in this book. Year 2002 had already passed. *This last item didn't have any real meaning until I re-read my notes before submitting them for this book. In April (fourth month) Mom died, and I returned to Canada for three weeks at Easter. Don't know about the "nine" at the time of this writing. As for the money coming in, there is an inheritance from Mom and Dad's estate.*

I had done my first reading with success. I had turned one more corner and instinctively understood that it was a very big corner.

I spent the rest of July and most of August being as "normal" as possible. I still spontaneously received names and information in my head as I conversed with others, but I did not usually give them the messages. I just let them be. Not delivering them made it easier for me to stay focused on the physical side of my life.

❋ ❋ ❋

**August 2000.** It was the middle of August. Norma and her girls returned to France, and I returned to my spiritual journey. I checked out upcoming courses that I might take in September.

I knew of a woman in the next town who held meditation sessions in her home once a month. I gave her a call and learned that all her classes had an underlying Native American aspect to them. She dedicated one of the evenings to native drumming. Aware that I must allow myself to experience new concepts and ideas to see if they were right for me as I walked this spiritual path, I decided to attend a few classes.

In the interim I looked for a music meditation tape that focused on native drumming and found one called, "Songs from Mother Earth," featuring Eagleheart Singers and Drummers. I discovered the power this type of music held for me. It would take me deeper within myself when I meditated. So deep that I could only say: Wow!!

My friends Joanne and Jeanne had for some time talked of going to a "sweat lodge." I expressed an interest in going with them, and it all came together this month. When the evening came, we were told to wear layers of clothing that we could peel off as necessary.

As I drove to this country farm, an uneasy feeling came over me, but I ignored it. I waited by the car for my friends to arrive. We walked up to the area where we were to meet the people hosting the event. As we waited, my feeling of uneasiness increased; I wanted to leave. Something didn't feel right. My friends, however, looked comfortable and not at all nervous.

Should I honor my feelings and get out of there? Once we actually got into the sweat lodge, there would be no opportunity to leave.

The sweat lodge seemed to be nothing more than an old tent with blankets covering it. Should it be that way? When I saw the tent, I made my decision. I pulled my friends aside, apologized, and made a hasty retreat to my car.

Joanne called me the next day. "You okay?"

"Yes, now I am. But last night this feeling of uneasiness washed over me. I can't explain it but knew I had to leave."

"I found the evening interesting. The heat inside the tent was very intense, but I was never uncomfortable at all."

I had no idea why I had felt so nervous and out of place. Maybe I wasn't ready for the experience. It could have been the wrong place and time for me.

I decided that I wouldn't try this again, at least for a while. I had learned a valuable lesson. Honor your own journey, for it is as individual as you are.

I was still very much on a roller-coaster ride through my own grief. I needed courage to continue down the path to my spiritual enlightenment. I used positive statements or affirmations to help me eliminate my fears. I was now quite aware, thanks to books I read, that the more control I took of my thoughts, the more effective I became at manifesting what I wanted in my life.

I began to repeat inspirational affirmations throughout my day. One of the phrases I most often utilized was: "I have the power to create what I need in my life." What I needed most in my life was a connection to Kim. I focused on that thought and silently repeated it often: "I have the power to connect to the other side and Kim."

I bought the book, *Creative Visualization: Use the Power of Your Imagination to Create What You Want in Your Life*, by Shakti Gawain. Then I bought two of her tapes, finding that her voice soothed me as she incorporated mental imagery, affirmation exercises, and meditations. Her tapes were a tool to further my meditation skills and to feel more positive about others and myself.

I had often read we each attract to ourselves what we put out. I had a better understanding of this statement now. Since opening myself to the Light, I had received many valuable lessons.

As I challenged myself to remain open to new learning experiences, I found I was able to be more focused and deal better with my feelings of loss and grief. I was excited that September was just around the corner, so I could enroll in some more courses. In the meantime, I stayed busy with my own inner work through regular meditation sessions.

I had a realization that I was feeling a massive shift within me; my journey was somehow changing course yet again. I was torn between my yearning to understand and the fear of moving forward. I had a continual sense, a knowingness, of the presence of those on the other side.

This journey had given a new purpose to my life — *if* I was brave enough to pursue it.

Chapter 7

# Healing Communications

*The greatest good you can do for another is not just share your riches, but reveal to them their own.*

—Benjamin Disraeli

It was now the fall of 2000, and I was determined to find new avenues to further my studies and expand my abilities. This journey had given me hope and a purpose. It had carried me farther than I ever imagined. I strongly believed now that I was being led, lovingly but firmly, by my guides and Kim to continue my spiritual pilgrimage. It was imperative that I trust the process as it was unfolding and believe that everything would proceed for my highest good — and for the highest good of others.

I was apprehensive and often in awe of the power my guides exercised over me. I wasn't sure I wanted to venture further into the unknown than I already had. My mind, however, continued to be filled with thoughts and images when I least expected them. I seemed to have an almost continual sense of the presence of those on the other side.

One afternoon while having lunch with a friend from high school, I suddenly sensed two energies around her. I felt their presence but ignored them for a while because I was trying to have a normal, everyday lunch with an old friend.

Unbidden, two names flowed out of my mouth before I could stop them. Startled, she said they were the names of her grandparents who had died.

My friend was more than a little intrigued, so we stayed at the restaurant to talk about what happened. "You know, Sandy, just before the two names popped out of your mouth, you had gone silent and had a glazed expression on your face. You stared past me, as if seeing something over my shoulder." Before we left the restaurant that afternoon, I invited her to my home for a reading; she jumped at the opportunity.

The next day, she arrived at my door not knowing what to expect. Once we sat in the family room, information came quickly from her loved ones on the other side. After the session, we both expressed surprise over the amount of information that came through. Proof of their validity came through details about her family that I had not previously known.

The friend, with whom I had gone to both high school and teachers college, shook her head in disbelief and asked me what I was going to do with this "gift." I just shrugged my shoulders and answered that I felt I would be shown when those on the other side felt I was ready.

Later in the month, I joined a new meditation and learning group that I had previously investigated. One of my early readings was for a woman named Judy whom I met through this meditation group. The reading took place in my family room on October 13, 2000. Below are excerpts from this reading, as taken from her tape.

> Sandy: "Just relax, sit back, and mentally ask for your loved ones to come. Please don't give me more than I need. There is a woman stepping forward. She seems to be sort of the spokesperson and a 'mother vibration.' I get the feeling she is sending you immense love."
>
> Judy: "My mother is still living."
>
> Sandy: "Okay. This might be an aunt then. I get the feeling

she lived farther away from here. Does your mother live farther away from here?"

Judy: "Yes."

Sandy: "I feel she is connected to your mother. This would be your mother's sister? I sense distance and a suitcase. I see the number six. Did she cross six years or six months ago? I get a feeling of six. Were there six in your family?"

Judy: "No."

Sandy: "How about June?" *I was learning how to interpret the information I received. I was glad Judy knew that I was just learning.*

Judy: "She died in June. She may have died on the 6th of June."

Sandy: "That is why I saw the sixes. I have goose bumps."

Judy: "I have them, too. Mom has two sisters who have passed away."

Sandy: "Okay. I have the one that crossed in June. Does her name start with a 'B'?"

Judy: "Not a 'B' but a 'P'."

Sandy: "Okay. Great — I am just learning. I hear two syllables. It is different, so I may not get it. Does it begin with a 'PE'?"

Judy: "Yes."

Sandy: "I will leave it for now." *I later found out her name was Pearl.* "She wants to talk. Are you worried about your mother right now?"

Judy: "Yes."

Sandy: "That is why she has come first. Is it your mother that has arthritis? I feel pain in my hands. I feel it more in my hands than anywhere else. Her movement is affected."

Judy: "Sort of."

Sandy: "Is there another sister, and a brother on the other side? I hear four. There is a whole group here."

Judy: "There are four that have passed on."

Sandy: "Okay. Your mother is really going through something right now. She is very worried about her. Does she live with your dad? I feel they are together."

Judy: "Yes."

Sandy: "He has a good sense of humor. Some think too much of one, sometimes."

Judy: *Smiling.*

Sandy: "They still live in a house? It seems to be a small house with two levels but just a few stairs.

Judy: "Yes."

Sandy: "She is going to step back and a man is going to step forward. Sort of sounds like Harry. Is there a Harry or Henry there?"

Judy: "Hmm."

Sandy: "This man has passed recently. Name has two syllables. He seems to be around 50."

Judy: "A bit younger than that."

Sandy: "Is this a brother for you?

Judy: "Yes."

Sandy: "You have felt him, and you know it, he says. Is it just about a year now?

Judy: "Yes."

Sandy: "You were very close. He is showing me you were very close. You were quite a bit older. You were more like the mom."

Judy: "Yes."

Sandy: "He was sick, very sick. This wasn't quick. It was slow.

He shows me you were with him when he passed. You were right with him, he says."

Judy: "Yes, I was."

Sandy: "He said he bugged you a lot, too. Actually he said he bugged the hell out of you. True?"

Judy: *Laughing,* "That would be an expression he would use."

Sandy: "Harry is the first name I heard, and I will stick with that. Is this close?"

Judy: "His name is Terry."

Sandy: "Thank you. I am learning. It was close, though. Did he live with you?"

Judy: "Yes, for a while."

Sandy: "He says 'to get himself together.'"

Judy: "Yes, to get himself together. *Laughing.* Can he hear me, too?"

Sandy: "Yes, he can hear you, so talk to him. Did he pass toward the end of November?"

Judy: "November, yes."

Sandy: "I sense a . . . black car. This has lots of meaning for you, he says. The car he had when he crossed? It was important to him. He liked his car."

Judy: "Yes."

Sandy: "He says he never really grew up."

Judy: "He had too many older sisters to look after him." *Laughing.*

Sandy: "He has a good sense of humor. He liked to talk. I get the feeling he would have liked to talk more than he did. Are you from down east? He is showing me the ocean."

Judy: "Yes."

Sandy: "He is showing me a house now that is near the water.

He is showing me a front porch with a few steps up. There is a front hallway with lots of family pictures. Now he is showing me a kitchen. There is a wooden table in the kitchen and the bedrooms seem to be on this floor."

Judy: "Lots of pictures in the hallway, wooden table in the kitchen, and the bedrooms are on this floor. Yes."

Sandy: "From the front door you can see the kitchen straight through. I see a turn in the hallway."

Judy: "Yes. This is so amazing!"

Sandy: "He is impressing pictures on my mind. He is very good. He is showing me a small window in the kitchen, looking out onto the back. The sink is there at the window."

Judy: "Yes, the sink is there."

Sandy: "Wow! Okay. He spends time here, he says."

Judy: "Okay, they would like to know that."

Sandy: "Is this your parents' home?"

Judy: "Yes."

Sandy: "They have a back patio with a railing. Terry is showing me all this. He wants you to know that he is around them. Who was musical?"

Judy: "My son is!"

Sandy: "He plays a few instruments."

Judy: "Yes, a few."

Sandy: "A piano, for sure. He is doing the keyboard. Now he is doing Elvis, so he must play a guitar, too. Terry has a good sense of humor. Is your son 30?"

Judy: "Yes to the guitar. He will be 30 on his next birthday."

Sandy: "Okay, I hear an 'R.' Does your son's name start with an R?"

Judy: "No, but there is an R in it."

Sandy: "Maybe I can get it from him later. Your son is married?"

Judy: "Yes."

Sandy: "Your son lives in Ontario? I hear an hour and 45 minutes."

Judy: "45 minutes to an hour."

Sandy: "Okay, and Terry is saying, 'has a good job!' Terry is saying he is much wiser over there. I really like his energy. He must have been well liked."

Judy: "Everyone loved Terry."

Sandy: "You're in a house? He shows me a house in a subdivision. Fairly new, I feel. I get impressions. Showing me that you are the gardener and your gardens are nicer this year."

Judy: "I never gardened before, really. I have done it since Terry died."

Sandy: "So now you are doing it! Well, it is thanks to him you are now in the garden." *Laughing.* "Do you have some kind of swing in your backyard? It looks like a covered something."

Judy: "Yes, we have a gazebo in our backyard."

Sandy: "There is something else big in your backyard. You don't have lots of grass."

Judy: "We have a pool."

Sandy: "You don't use your pool a lot, he shows me. Actually, what he said was 'she could bulldoze it for all she uses it.'"

Judy: "It wasn't a nice summer, Terry. Okay?" *Laughing.*

Sandy: "You have a daughter?"

Judy: "Yes."

Sandy: "Your daughter is younger than your son?"

Judy: "Yes."

Sandy: "She is single. He shows me a diamond ring. Was she

engaged at one time?"

Judy: "She just got engaged."

Sandy: "Oh, he showed me the diamond ring. Wow! He will be at her wedding. Will it be next year?"

Judy: "Supposed to be. She just got engaged Monday."

Sandy: "Wow! That is why he showed me it. He knows."

Judy: "I haven't even had a chance to call everybody."

Sandy: "This proves to you that he is watching. He is talking about where she got engaged. I don't get the feeling that he proposed where they lived. It was some place much more romantic. I get the sense of open. I get the sense of area and space. I will just let it go for now and maybe it will just pop into my head when I am not trying so hard. He is with you when you are gardening. You will be able to sense him there. He loves you. He loves all of you. You are a close family. Not a lot of hassle. He says 'blessed.' You had a good childhood. He had a good childhood."

Judy: "Yes."

Sandy: "Are you starting a new path? He says you are. 'A giving of the heart,' he says."

Judy: "Okay."

Sandy: "He says you are a healer. Are you going to do healing with your hands?"

Judy: "Possibly."

Sandy: "He is going back to your daughter. He says he is not finished there yet. He wants to tell you a date, but don't tell her while she is planning it. It is like the last weekend of August. I am almost wondering if it is Labor Day weekend or it could be the weekend before. There will be an issue about the color of her gown. This will be a big issue for her."

Judy: "Really? I don't know yet."

Sandy: "She is a little off the traditional path. It is almost like he is a little more traditional than her. She hasn't picked her bridesmaids yet. I see three bridesmaids. I have a feeling that she will pick a different color as opposed to a light blue or light green. Maybe purple. I sense a dark color like deep blue or a purplish. It will be a rich color and more striking. I feel it will be a church wedding."

*Since the engagement had just happened at the time of this reading, these facts were not known yet. It wasn't until Judy, getting ready to lend me her tape for this book, listened to her tape again. She confirmed that the wedding was indeed scheduled for the last half of August, that her daughter was having three bridesmaids, and that her bridesmaids' dresses were purple. The most surprising to her was the information about the white wedding dress. Because of her daughter's light complexion, the experts advised her against traditional white for her dress and suggested ivory or a newer color called diamond white. She decided to go with the diamond white. The wedding, however, will be in a hall not a church.*

Sandy: "Were they somewhere high when he proposed to her? I sense high. I got the sensation of floating up high."

Judy: "Yes."

Sandy: "There is a plane involved. Were they in a high building like the CN Tower?"

Judy: "Yes."

Sandy: "Did they fly where they went?"

Judy: "Yes."

Sandy: "That's where the airplane came in. He really planned this. I mean really planned this!" *Pause.* "They went to New York?"

Judy: "Yes."

Sandy: "Like the Empire State Building? Oh, Wow. That is

amazing."

Judy: "That is exactly where they were. Wow!"

Sandy: "Terry says he was there, he was watching, and he was the first one to see it. So tell her that her uncle was the first one to see her engagement. He is going to step back now. I am getting tired. He is around you. Says there are lots of family members there. I am seeing a whole group of them. He sends lots of love. He will be with you on the day of his passing. Thirteen, I sense a 13. Did he pass on the 13th of November?"

Judy: "Yes."

Sandy: "He said you needed to come [for this reading], to get through this month. He is pulling back now."

Feeling the healing messages that Terry gave his sister Judy that day brought me a level of joy and contentment I had not felt in a long time. Helping Judy receive some much-needed messages also helped me.

The fact that Terry was safe on the other side meant Kim was safe on the other side, too. I wondered if Kim and Terry had met each other. It was a comforting thought.

Since this reading I have had the pleasure of "meeting" Terry a few more times. Judy is from a very large family and more of her brothers and sisters have come to me to connect to Terry and other loved ones who have passed over.

I continued to practice readings whenever I had the opportunity. The following week, I met a woman named Fran in the same meditation group. It was the way I met her, however, that is important to mention.

Twenty of us sat in a circle. Native American music played softly in the background while incense burned. We had just completed a short meditation when I felt my attention being drawn toward her as she sat across the room. I couldn't seem to take my eyes off her. I would catch myself staring at her and hoped Fran didn't notice me watching her. I sensed the presence of an elderly man in spirit around her. It felt like he was trying to get my attention. It was a strong sensation. After a few minutes of this, I felt compelled to approach her.

I introduced myself and asked if I could give her a message from someone on the other side whom I felt was standing behind her. Words just flowed from of my mouth.

This is her version of the short message given to her: "There is an older man, like a grandfather in spirit, giving me a name like Mark, but more foreign. He seems to be speaking another language. Just give me a second. It is like he is speaking Bulgarian or something."

I couldn't believe the word "Bulgarian" came out of my mouth, but Fran's reaction was instantaneous! She almost fell off her chair.

"Oh, my gosh! That's my grandfather. His name is Marco and he was from Bulgaria."

The name of the country startled both of us. The reason she was taken so much off guard, Fran explained, was the fact that just moments before I had approached her, she had been thinking about being an Orthodox Jew with roots in Bulgaria.

We settled in beside each other as I explained that I was beginning to receive messages from those on the other side. She reacted to this information with interest, so I felt compelled to invite her to my home for a reading.

*This ushered in a series of practice readings that I was to give over the next few months. As I practiced, I trusted what I heard and understood that I had opened a reliable connection to the other side.*

We set an appointment for October 24. Fran became the second "official" client to come to my home for a reading. While enlightening for her, it was still a learning experience for me. For a second time, her grandfather came through, this time with messages for her mom and information about her daughter Kelly.

To this day, Fran and I have maintained a friendship, believing we were meant to meet each other on a personal level at that first class gathering. I was relieved that she had not had a significant loss in her life. She had not known her grandfather in life. Because she was not grieving the loss of a close loved one, Fran appeared to be a "safe" client. I was still too raw from my own loss to handle clients who were similarly wounded.

This ushered in a series of practice readings that I was to give over the next few months. As I practiced, I trusted what I heard and understood that I had opened a reliable connection to the other side. I enlisted the help of my friends to bring me clients interested in a loving reading. I insisted, however, that they not refer anyone who had lost a child. I needed to be confident in my ability and sure that I could connect with accuracy before I was ready for that.

I had experienced the heart-wrenching pain of losing a child and was acutely aware of the responsibility placed on me if I were to deliver messages from a child in spirit. I prayed that I would possess the strength for this journey.

I openly talked to my guides, asking them to help me hear the messages accurately. One evening, in the midst of a moment of panic and insecurity, I sat down and clearly told them what I needed from them.

"I need to hear names, facts, and validations in these readings. If I can't find the children who are on the other side for the parents who eventually will come, then I don't want this journey. I am not strong enough to walk this path without these validations."

My skepticism, when I first had readings from the mediums I contacted nearly two years before, had required substantial validations. I remembered how my logical mind tried to discredit the information. I remembered thinking this whole process and experience was not rational. My logical left brain told me Kim *couldn't* be talking to these mediums.

On the other hand, I recalled the sense of peace I felt when I accepted that the mediums could not *know* the details they told me. The information *had* to come from Kim; to think otherwise became the illogical alternative.

Receiving validating facts meant the difference between someone *thinking* their loved ones had connected and *knowing* that they had. I wanted no part in hurting those whose hearts were already shattered.

I prayed for guidance and strength, worried about how all this would ultimately impact my own family. My work was now becoming more public. Doug had always been supportive; however, I was not so certain other members of our immediate families would welcome the idea that I was a medium who gave spiritual readings.

It was exceedingly easy to find people willing to let me practice my mediumship abilities. The information brought through during these sessions was detailed and repeatedly astonished both the client and me. Apparently, I was doing a credible job as the best conduit I could be for those on the other side who wished to impart their messages.

In these early readings, I found I connected to young people who had passed. The children who came through in that stage of my development as a medium were always connected in some *distant* way to the person I was reading for.

For example, during one of these readings, I felt a young boy step forward. He told me he had been struck by a car while walking down the street. I felt he had been on the other side for some time. He gave me his name, which I announced. Until the name came through, the lady sitting in front of me did not realize who he was. It turned out her husband had a brother who passed many years earlier. Yes, he was struck by a car. She had never known him but knew his name. It was the name I brought through.

In another reading for a teacher friend, her father stepped forward. After he completed delivering his messages, I felt the presence of a young boy. He shared that he had fallen on the school ground and died. He was even more specific as he gave the details of his passing. He explained that everyone thought he had suffered only a minor head injury and that he would be okay, so they sent him home. He passed away a few days later. My friend knew who this boy was but had not known him when he was alive. She was both surprised and pleased that he had stepped forward.

Over the next several months, reading after reading brought through information that validated the presence of my clients' loved ones on the other side. I increased my ability to use my sixth sense and reach beyond the limits of our physical world. I understood and trusted that I was connecting to deceased loved ones who would impart previously unknown information to me to pass on to their families. It was just as my mentors — Lou, Sharlette, and others — had done for me when I so needed such confirmations. Payback.

My clients were eager to share their personal experiences with me at the conclusion of each reading. They often would tell me about times when they had seen, sensed, or felt the presence of a departed relative or friend. They had kept these experiences to themselves because they feared they had imagined them. They also frequently expressed a fear of being labeled a bit crazy. I knew how they felt and told them their unease was understandable, in fact, universal — until they could acknowledge their spiritual lessons.

Once my clients realized that contact with the "so-called dead" was more common than they thought, they opened up and revealed that a tremendous burden had lifted. I discovered I just needed to initiate the discussion. I found that those who have had their own experiences with spirit entities had a great need to talk about what occurred and were grateful to have others confirm their sanity.

Continuing with my spiritual development, I enrolled in a second-level Reiki class with Carol Baltkalns as my teacher. The group was small, intimate, and eager to learn and practice the techniques. During the course, I brought forth messages for each person from their loved ones on the other side. I had been gaining confidence in my ability over the last several months, so by this point, acting as a conduit came easily.

In order to keep expanding my expertise, I needed to practice what I had learned about Reiki healing and the techniques involved. Doug built me a healing table. He also constructed a "reading and meditation room" for me to use — in our basement.

So now, thanks to Doug, I had my room and my own Reiki table. Having a private spot away from everyone and everything was wonderful. I would no longer have to wait until the house was empty to do my readings or practice Reiki on my friends.

Regardless of whatever class I enrolled in, my intention was always to improve my connection to the other side. To achieve this I needed to reach and maintain a higher level of consciousness. Increasing my knowledge through studies was one way to achieve this higher consciousness; meditation was the other.

*Meditation was the way I listened to Kim and my guides. . . many people talk to their loved ones on the other side and feel their presence. Yet, frequently, they don't take the time to listen to the feelings and messages their loved ones send back. By quieting my mind, I learned to hear, sense, and feel them.*

Meditation was the way I listened to Kim and my guides. I discovered that many people talk to their loved ones on the other side and feel their presence. Yet, frequently, they don't take the time to listen to the feelings and messages their loved ones send back. By quieting my mind, I learned to hear, sense, and feel them.

As word of my mediumship spread via acquaintances and friends, my phone began to ring. One evening a woman named Clare called to ask me about my work. She was very emotional during our telephone conversation; I set up an appointment for two days later.

As I prepared for the reading through a meditation technique that I now enlisted prior to every reading, I was nervous. I hoped that my nervousness would not be evident. I was taking a big step out of my comfort zone. My other readings had been for friends and acquaintances I knew to be open to the other side, or for women I had met in my learning classes. Their participation in these groups told me they were spiritually open. Clare, on the other hand, had heard about me at a party one evening and inquired about the work I did.

She was in a whole new category. Knowing this heightened my anxiety. Clare admitted to me on the phone she wasn't sure if she really believed in an afterlife, but she desperately needed to and wanted to.

I felt her urgency and pain. Was I getting myself into something I could not handle? Would I disappoint Clare? Would I break her heart? I had no idea who she hoped to connect with. In my heart, I was terrified it could be a child. I didn't think I was emotionally ready yet to facilitate this type of contact.

A woman of about 35, Clare looked very nervous when she arrived 15 minutes early on November 7. I took her into my new reading room and tried to make her feel as comfortable as possible. I secretly had my own nerves to calm down but could not let my anxiety show.

I explained to her there was no guarantee the person or persons she was hoping to contact would come through. Just as I could not tell *her* what to do or say, neither could I make anyone in the spirit world communicate if they chose not to. I asked her to put her wants and needs aside as much as humanly possible — not believing for a moment that she could really do that — and allow the messages to come through the way her loved ones on the other side wished them to. I was struck that I now repeated what other mediums had so often said to me: "I am merely the vehicle through which your loved ones can bring their messages."

With that said, I took a deep breath and began. The transcript below is taken from her tape.

> Sandy: "There is a lady stepping forward. I feel a deep pain in my stomach. I feel this lady passed of cancer in the stomach area. She seems to be older than you. She is your mom or a lady like a mom. She is of that generation so it could be a mother-in-law, too. Is your mother on the other side?"
>
> Clare: "Yes."
>
> Sandy: "I feel it is your mom, but let's wait and see. Again, I feel a pain in my stomach area."
>
> Clare: "My mom passed of liver cancer."
>
> Sandy: "This will be your mom, then. She makes me feel like you are number one. Are you the oldest?"

Clare: "No. I am the only."

Sandy: "Okay, thanks. I hear a name like James or Jamie."

Clare: "My son is Jamie."

Sandy: "There is another 'J' name, too, connected to you."

Clare: "My daughter is Jennifer."

Sandy: "Well, your mom is saying hello to your children. I feel there are only two."

Clare: "Yes."

Sandy: "Your mom is showing me a hospital room. I feel she passed in the hospital but she is saying 'thank you' for looking after her. It's okay that she went to the hospital."

Clare: "I tried to keep her at home but I just couldn't, and I had to put her into the hospital. She died two days later."

Sandy: "She says 'you did the right thing.' You were with her at the time of her passing?"

Clare: "Yes."

Sandy: "She knew you were there. I feel that she was in a coma-like state and couldn't respond to you."

Clare: "Yes. I didn't know if she knew I was there."

Sandy: "She is telling you that she knew you were."

Clare: "I am so glad. I did all I could."

Sandy: "Now I feel this lady has not been gone long. Shows me the number three. Has she been gone for three years or did she pass in March?

Clare: "No to both."

Sandy: "Well, she is showing me a three and is circling it."

Clare: "Oh, she passed on the third of April. Would that be it?"

Sandy: "Yes, I believe that is the three. Now she is showing me a soccer ball. It is black and white. Looks like a soccer ball to me. Mean anything?"

Clare: "Yes, both my children play soccer."

Sandy: "Well, she is showing me a BIG trophy. One of your children must have won a tournament?"

Clare: "Oh, yes, my daughter did, but Mom never got to see her play."

Sandy: "I think she just told you that she did!" *Clare was crying softly now, but I had to stay focused on the connection I had with her mother.*

Sandy: "Is somebody a nurse? I see a hospital but feel someone works there and is not in it as a patient."

Clare: "My mother was a nurse before she retired." *Wow! I thought to myself.*

Sandy: "Well, she's hanging out in the garden now. Shows me flowers all around her."

Clare: "That's my mom. She loved to garden. It was her favorite pastime after she retired."

Sandy: "Now I feel a man with her. She has someone of her generation with her. Brother or a husband. He has been there longer."

Clare: "My father passed before Mom but not long before."

Sandy: "Okay, but don't give me too much information, because the more I can give you without any information, the more validation it is for you."

Clare: "Okay, sorry."

Sandy: "I hear a name like Don, could be Dan but a 'D-N' name."

Clare: "My husband's name is Dan, but we are separated."

Sandy: "Your dad is stepping forward and says, 'Dan.' I think he liked him in life."

Clare: "Yes, they were buddies."

Sandy: "I feel that he knew you were broken up and needs to

tell you that."

Clare: "I hid that from him when he was so sick."

Sandy: "Well, I think he wants you to know that he is aware of the situation now."

Clare: "Tell them I love them."

Sandy: "You can tell them yourself. They can hear you."

Clare: "Thanks. How do I know they are around me?"

Sandy: "They are showing you that today, don't you think?"

Clare: "I miss them. I am all alone."

Sandy: "I hope this helps you to know that they are around you and your children."

Clare: "I think it will."

Sandy: "Now, Mom seems to be in control of this reading."

Clare: "That's funny. She always was in control."

Sandy: "Still is, I guess. She is with someone who had a head injury of some sort, as I feel pain in my head. I think a fall to the head. Not sure! I feel a falling sensation, and I am still learning the signs."

Clare: "Well, her brother fell when he was drunk and smashed his head open. He died shortly after."

Sandy: "Oh, wow. That would be it. Who is 'one of four'?"

Clare: "My mom was one of four."

Sandy: "Only one brother with her?"

Clare: "Yes, as far as I know. One of her brothers we never saw much of. I think he is still living, but I don't know for sure."

Sandy: "Okay. George?"

Clare: "That is her brother, the one we don't see."

Sandy: "Makes me feel that she can now. Your mother likes to talk. Think she did here, too."

Clare: "That is for sure."

Sandy: "She is showing me a house. I think it is their house, but she says she still goes there. Is their house not sold?"

Clare: "No, I live in it."

Sandy: "Well, she knows and said she still goes there. I feel you were living there before she passed."

Clare: "Yes. I moved in just after Dad passed." *I thought this reading was going very well, and I was starting to relax a bit.*

Sandy: "I see a green couch. I feel it has been moved or shifted recently or put in a different room."

Clare: "Well, I just moved a green chair into the basement, but not a couch."

Sandy: "I guess that is what she means. Maybe she will show me more. Now I see a couch with a hole in it."

Clare: "That's exactly why I moved it out of the room. My cat got at it."

Sandy: "Guess your mom knows. She is letting you know today that she is okay and is still connecting with you. Open to the sensations and you will realize that your mom is still around you."

Clare: "How do I learn to connect?"

Sandy: "What worked for me was meditation. Finding a group to meditate with would be a good start. Your mom is making me feel like, 'stop talking and get on with this.'"

Clare: "That is so much like Mom."

Sandy: "I hear a smashing sound, like a window breaking, but I feel it is in the house. This was a loud crash of something that would maybe startle you."

Clare: "Don't know what that would be."

Sandy: "I hear it again, so it must mean something."

Clare: "Jamie broke the lamp the other day when he was jumping around."

Sandy: "I guess she knows that, too. One of my favorite aunts was Rita. Do you have any connection to the name?

Clare: "Yes, my mother's sister is Rita."

Sandy: "I feel the connection with your mom pulling back. Remember, she just leaves me, she doesn't leave you. Now I think this is your dad who is coming forward. Maybe Mom had to leave before Dad could come through. He is showing me a red car."

Clare: "Their car was red. Still sits in the garage. Does he want me to sell it?"

Sandy: "I don't think it is about that. Just his way to say, 'I am here.'"

Clare: "Okay."

Sandy: "Mom holds out a black and white cat. Says she has it with her. Hear 'Sh' kind of name. Would that be a cat of yours that has crossed?"

Clare: "Oh, my gosh! No, but it is a cat of theirs named Sally."

Sandy: "Well, she has that cat with her."

Clare: "That's good. Dad never liked the cat much, though."

Sandy: "Then I guess that's why Mom said she had the cat and not Dad." *Laughing.*

Clare: "Can they tell me what I am to do? I feel so lost."

Sandy: "They are letting you know that they are around you. Talk to them. They know that you are struggling right now. I don't feel they will tell you what to do, but I hope that hearing from them will help to give you more peace."

Clare: "Can you ask them?"

Sandy: "I feel your mother is giving you a hug but no advice. Sorry."

The reading continued but Clare did not receive any advice about her future. Her parents on the other side did talk about the break-up of her marriage and her children. These very private messages I will not share.

At the conclusion of the reading, Clare was grateful for the connection we made with her parents. She explained that her parents were her best friends and that with her marriage break-up she was becoming depressed. As an only child, she felt very much alone. She said this would help her to know they were still around her, guiding her from the other side.

*I was shown that the other side was really in control; I merely functioned as the vessel to bring their messages through.*

I felt joy in knowing that I was successful in connecting Clare to the parents she missed so much. She left my home feeling more at peace than when she arrived. I gratefully thanked my guides on the other side for their help and Clare's loved ones for their desire to come through.

I was shown that the other side was really in control; I merely functioned as the vessel to bring their messages through. They did not tell Clare what she should do in the future but offered validations to let her know they could see what had happened in her life since they passed.

With each reading I gained more confidence in my abilities. I continued to meditate daily and found new spiritual groups to attend that would further advance my skills. I was continually grateful to my guides, Holly and Raphael, for aiding me along my journey and so thankful for the realization that Kim was also around me as I walked this new path. I could now balance what I knew to be true about the other side with my intense grief over losing my daughter.

This spiritual work was important. It was not a cure for grief, however, and I was acutely aware of this. Though I missed Kim terribly, this journey had given me the strength to live again. I vowed I would continue these readings. I was going to dedicate my-

*This spiritual work was important. It was not a cure for grief, however, and I was acutely aware of this. Though I missed Kim terribly, this journey had given me the strength to live again.*

self to help others who were grieving because of the loss of a loved one. I was not yet aware, however, that by helping them I would be brought to a new level of peace within myself.

During the ongoing evolution of my readings, I had the good fortune of giving a reading to a woman named Sue. We scheduled the reading for November 20.

It was quickly apparent that Sue liked to talk. She chattered away as we headed downstairs into my reading room, telling me that she had heard about me from a friend who had been in a Reiki class with me.

Sue was such a friendly lady with a warm smile; I was drawn to her immediately. I hoped, however, that she would chat a lot less during the course of the reading. As I prepared, I felt it was important to mention this fact.

"Please keep your responses short and do not add any information," I firmly instructed.

Sue nodded. "I understand."

During the course of this session a few different people came through. I sensed the energy of a younger woman who felt like a sister to Sue. Sue responded that her best friend was on the other side. When I uttered the name Joan or Joanne, I saw tears in her eyes. The reading brought through a lot of information about Sue, her family, and her friend Joanne.

Sue had come hoping to hear from her best friend; I was glad this had happened for her. Sue was very excited and happy with the validations. Sue really did like to talk and was not shy about telling her co-workers about her session. Unbeknownst to me, Sue worked for a company called Purity Life Health Products Limited, a leading health products distributor. Due to the nature of the business, a large number of employees were devoted to expanding their own spiritual awareness. Soon my phone was ringing on a more regular basis from other employees who worked with Sue.

I was about to become intertwined with these women from Purity Life, and it is thanks to them I found myself taken to a new level of spiritual awareness, one that far exceeded my expectations. Eventually I met David and Elyse Chapman, owners and founders of the company.

It was through Purity Life that I met Karen Green, Sharon Kerr, and Sylvia Christensen, who exposed me to many new concepts and ideas related to alternative health and natural healing. This began for me a journey to understand more. Eventually I took some classes taught by them on the subject. I was quickly realizing that this was another avenue I needed to pursue to continue to grow in my spirituality.

I knew it was inevitable that one day I would find myself sitting across from someone who had suffered the loss of a child. That day came on November 27, 2000. I could see that my new client, Gloria, was nervous as we walked downstairs to my reading room.

I could feel her relax as she looked around the room. She scanned the bulletin board where I had neatly arranged articles and pictures. She commented on the angels spread through the room. I had lit incense before she arrived. She commented about the pleasant fragrance. It pleased me that my carefully designed room made her feel comfortable.

As soon as the session began, I felt an older gentleman step forward. He brought with him a younger man who, I soon discovered, wanted to talk. Her father had brought her son.

*The healing that took place in my reading room that day was immeasurable for both of us. As a result of connecting this mom with the son she had so tragically lost, I felt a deep sense of inner peace. So did she. . . I was so very grateful that I was able to help this bereaved mom and her family.*

I tried not to get caught up in my own emotions. Just bring through the messages, I reminded myself.

The young man named Michael, accompanied by his grandfather, revealed his name, details of his family, and information about his passing. He gave messages for his siblings. When the session ended, Gloria and I cried together.

The healing that took place in my reading room that day was immeasurable for both of us. As a result of connecting this mom with the son she had so tragically lost, I felt a deep sense of inner peace. So did she.

I thanked all those on the other side for helping me make this most important connection. A wave of relief passed over me. I was so very grateful that I was able to help this bereaved mom and her family.

When Gloria left, I went into Kim's room. Her bedroom remained much the same as it was when she was still with us. As I sat on her bed and hugged her big white teddy bear to my heart, I thought about Kim and the changes in all of our lives since her passing. For the millionth time, I reflected on the life that used to be and would never be again. As Kim's mom, I had needed to know where she was and that she was really okay — the driving force for my journey into the Light.

*. . . I cried long and hard for the daughter I lost. Wiping away the tears, I knew I was ready to begin another new chapter in my life. I knew — without one ounce of doubt — that connecting bereaved parents with their deceased children was what I was meant to do with my gift of Light.*

As I sat on her bed, I cried long and hard for the daughter I lost. Wiping away the tears, I knew I was ready to begin another new chapter in my life. I knew — without one ounce of doubt — that connecting bereaved parents with their deceased children was what I was meant to do with my gift of Light.

This reading contained some personal, very moving information about Gloria's son and her life, much of it too personal to share. Gloria has consulted with me a few more times since that first session and is aware of how her reading impacted my own healing journey. She and her son Michael will always have a special place in my heart.

I wondered when another bereaved parent would hear about me and decide to come. I had to have faith that their children would step forward with messages for them; otherwise, I would have made myself crazy with worry. I believed that other bereaved parents would soon find their way to me. I knew, as a bereaved parent myself, that bereaved parents banded together for comfort. No one else can really understand the depth of our despair.

I spent a great deal of time in meditation asking for strength and guidance with my "spiritual consultations." I was now calling them that since it sounded more professional than "readings."

I also contemplated the idea of teaching a guided meditation class for beginners. I was trained professionally as a school teacher, so organizing the teaching material would be easy. It was such a natural progression, but I wondered if enough people would be interested in such a class. I was soon shown the answer: I found myself surrounded by people who were opening to spirituality, interested in making their own connections.

When my clients and acquaintances asked me how I began to develop my abilities, I always responded that meditation was the key. "Learn to meditate," I advised.

"Please show me how to start," they invariably pleaded.

Within days of my decision to teach meditation, I had ten very interested women eager to take my course. I was excited to share the meditation techniques I had learned. I enlisted the help of my friend Sue, since we planned to teach the class together.

I walked through this new door very naturally. The classes were held at my home. The excitement that all my students experienced as they felt themselves connecting to the unseen energy from the other side was incredibly rewarding. Eight weeks turned into ten. Still they wanted more.

I laughed. "You have opened yourself up and begun your own healing journey. How far you go is up to you." These were words I'd been told just months before.

I had aided them in their understanding that they, too, could connect to their guides and loved ones on the other side. They did not need me to do that

*Impossible as it was to believe, Kim had been gone for two and a half years. I had become a spiritual medium. That fact also seemed impossible to believe.*

for them. I warned them that it was hard work and suggested they find another meditation group to join.

It was now the summer of 2001. Impossible as it was to believe, Kim had been gone for two-and-a-half years. I had become a spiritual medium. That fact also seemed impossible to believe.

I still had so much to fathom about the process. Understanding the signs and feelings I received took practice. How to interpret these signs and feelings required patience on my part. As word spread, the number of spiritual consultations I did per week increased.

My own passion for this work impelled me to continue my studies. I attended more workshops. One such workshop was hosted by Dr. Doreen Virtue, a spiritual clairvoyant and conventional doctor of psychology who works with the angelic realm. She has written many books on the subject of angels. A few of my friends and I had the opportunity to attend one of her angel workshops in Toronto.

The topic of angels piqued my interest. Were they really all around us waiting to help us if we asked? I read her books titled, *Angel Therapy: Healing Messages for Every Area of Your Life* and *Connecting With Your Angels*. I enjoyed both of these books immensely. I had previously read her book called, *The Lightworker's Way: Awakening Your Spiritual Power to Know and Heal*. It was the book that had cemented my belief in miracles after I found my lost ring on the night table.

While browsing through the New Age section of a bookstore, I spotted the book, *Touched by Angels*, written by Eileen Elias Freeman. I felt uplifted as I read her beliefs. In this book she shared what she had learned about the spiritual nature of angels, both personally and through a network she initiated called "The Angel Watch Network," which provides information on angel activities today.

I was comforted to learn that angels bring healing into our lives, and when needed, a sense of direction. I came to believe they help us, guide us, and want us to understand that heaven is not as far away as we think. We can bridge the barrier between their dimension and ours.

All of these concepts encouraged me to continue on my journey, because bridging the barrier between their dimension and ours was exactly what I had passionately devoted my life to since Kim's death. I had achieved my goal and now worked to show others how thin the veil really is between the two dimensions.

More and more bereaved parents began coming to me for spiritual consultations. In each case, I would successfully connect to the child they desperately wanted to hear from. I decided to offer a special class strictly for bereaved parents who had been to see me. This was my way of giving back for the help I received from others along my journey.

Ten bereaved parents were eager to participate. Two couples were part of the group. It was nice to have the men there, too. I asked that they bring a small donation that would be sent to the Mothers Against Drunk Drivers organization, better known as M.A.D.D. I knew that two of the women planning to attend this class had children who were killed by drunk drivers.

This class would introduce them to a few different meditation techniques to practice. I hoped they would find one they felt comfortable with and could practice at home. My hope was that their meditations would initiate their own connections to their children or other loved ones on the other side. I anticipated a long, full day.

Participants arrived wearing comfortable clothes and carrying pillows. Only one couple had tried meditation previously. We spent the morning practicing the meditations and discussing what each person felt, sensed, or saw. We shared names of tapes, CDs, and books that were meaningful to each of us. After lunch we had another short meditation. All were surprised and pleased with the sensations and feelings they experienced. We spent more time in discussion, knowing we could learn so much from sharing our experiences with others. Such discussions helped us understand that our paths are as individual as we are.

At the end of the day I did some spontaneous readings. I had hoped this would happen. I was not surprised that doing all the meditations opened me up so I could receive messages. However, this was my first experience with a session involving an entire group.

Two months later I held a second class for another group of bereaved parents who had come to me for spiritual consultations. It felt so good to help others. I knew Kim was proud of me for what I was doing; she'd so often told me this was our mutual mission.

As my mediumship work spread by word of mouth, I was getting busier. I was blessed to meet many spiritual people who encouraged me to continue to do this work and not let fear take over. It was the following reading for a husband and wife, however, that made me realize, once again, how valuable my work really was. It was meeting bereaved parents like Rob and Wendy Lindsay that helped me truly comprehend why I must continue giving spiritual consultations.

The two of them sat down with me on November 28, 2002. The following is a partial transcript as re-captured via their tape recording of the session.

> Sandy: "I have a man stepping forward connecting to me and pulling me toward you. (Going to Rob): You have a father on the other side, and I feel like Dad is going to control this reading."
>
> Rob: "Yes."
>
> Sandy: "You have a mother living that he wants to acknowledge?"
>
> Rob: "No."
>
> Sandy: "Then he wants to acknowledge another woman living, could be a second wife for him. I feel he was with her for a long time."
>
> Rob: "Yes, for 24 years."
>
> Sandy: "That is a long time. I feel like he remarried not because of divorce, but because your mother had passed. There will be a lot happening here for you today."
>
> Rob: "Yes."
>
> Sandy: "Your father is acknowledging a brother. There are

three of you in your family."

Rob: "Three children?"

Sandy: "Yes, in your family."

Rob: "Yes."

Sandy: "Then there must be a sister, too."

Rob: "Yes. She has passed as well."

Sandy: "That's why we are pulling over to you! Someone passed of cancer in the stomach area. There is a short 'D' name like Dave or Don."

Rob: "There are two 'D' names connected to me."

Sandy: "Okay. Your sister has been gone for a while. I feel she was sick, and she was quite young when she passed, maybe a teenager."

Rob: "Dianne was 24."

Sandy: "Okay, not quite so young. Now he is acknowledging a 'J' name, could be a 'G' but would sound like a 'J.'"

Rob: "Dad's name is John."

Sandy: "There may be another John he wants to acknowledge or maybe a Jack. But I think another one." *This was not acknowledged until later in the reading.*

Sandy: "He doesn't want to be called John. I feel we don't have it quite right. Your dad wasn't called John? Was he called by another name? Because he doesn't want to be called that."

Wendy: "That's him for sure, then. He was called by another name. Do you want us to tell you?"

Sandy: "No. Let him work on it. There is a young man here. I feel you have lost a son. He is showing me a younger female, too. Like a daughter for you. I feel you have lost one of each. Two children?" *I didn't think I had this right. I couldn't fathom that they had lost two of their children. I was to find out that they had lost their only two children.*

Wendy: "Yes."

Sandy: *I was trying to stay calm and focused, but my heart was breaking for them.* "Know your dad has brought both of them with him. Is your daughter older?"

Rob: "No, but she has been gone longer."

Sandy: "Okay. Thank you. He is acknowledging a quick passing."

Rob: "Yes. It was quick."

Sandy: "She is showing me her head so I think she hurt her head. She is making me pay attention to my head. I feel like your dad was a talker here. He likes to talk. So many men come through who are not talkers, but I feel that your dad was not that way. So he is doing quite well. He is going to lead the way, I feel. He is saying 'car accident.' I think we are with your daughter, because he is focusing on her first. She was your first loss?"

Wendy: "Yes."

Sandy: "She was driving the car. She does not take responsibility for this, however. Someone hit her; someone did this to her. She is very strong that it was not her fault."

Rob: "Yes. This was not her fault."

Sandy: "Okay." *I found out later she and her boyfriend were killed by a drunk driver.* "She is standing with your dad. The two of them come together."

Wendy: "Okay."

Sandy: "It was another car that hit her, not like a train or anything."

Wendy: "That's right."

Sandy: "Bigger than hers! But it was another vehicle."

Wendy and Rob: "Yes, that's right."

Sandy: "She passed quickly, but not instantly, and you worried about her hurting. She says she didn't. There was a man [on the other side] there to get her, but I don't think it was your dad, Rob. She makes me feel like it was another man of your dad's generation, though. Rob, did your dad pass before your daughter?"

Rob: "No."

Sandy: "Then she is acknowledging another man of your dad's generation."

Wendy: "That was probably my dad."

Sandy: "Okay, thanks, but he was still Grandpa to her?"

Wendy: "Yes."

Sandy: "She never made it to the hospital and passed at the scene."

Wendy: "Yes."

Sandy: "There was another person who passed, too, in this accident. He was older than her."

Wendy: "No, same age."

Sandy: "She says 'older.'"

Wendy: "Well, yes, by a few months."

Sandy: "Well, she insists older. She says they are together. He was a boyfriend of hers? Not married, I feel."

Wendy: "More than a boyfriend. He was a life partner for her."

Sandy: "But 'not married,' she says — very strong in that. She says: 'No ring!'"

Wendy: *Laughing.* "We were wondering about that."

Sandy: "She is saying, 'Michael.' Who is that?"

Wendy: "A previous boyfriend, before Jonathan."

Sandy: "Please don't give me names. But that is the other John your dad was talking about at the beginning of the reading. Jonathan is the same as John for me. Must be acknowledging Michael as a way to bring up a memory for you."

Sandy: "Now I feel your sister, Rob." *I was feeling a lady more of his generation so I felt it was his sister.* "She passed in a hospital, I feel, because I am seeing a hospital setting."

Rob: "Yes."

Sandy: "And before her mom. She is making me feel that your mom had lost a child in her lifetime. I feel this pain, and I know this pain."

Rob: "Yes."

Sandy: "There is a 'six' connection to a month, or a day of a month."

Wendy: "Don't know."

Sandy: "Keep it, if you don't understand it."

Wendy: "I think his sister's birthday was in June."

Sandy: "Now acknowledgment of a March birthday. I see a candle."

Rob: "My dad's birthday was in March."

Sandy: "Must be letting us know they are all together. Now I am seeing a two. That is a February or a second of any month. I am being pulled towards you, Wendy."

Wendy: "Oh! My birthday is in February."

Sandy: "That is why I am being pulled towards you now."

Wendy: "Actually there are three birthdays in February in my family."

Sandy: "Okay. There is a 'C' or 'K' name that I hear… like Catherine."

Rob: "Kathleen."

Sandy: "Also on the other side, and to you, Rob."

Rob: "My mother's sister is Kathleen."

Sandy: "A Mary name, too. Also pulled to you, Rob."

Wendy: "That would be his grandmother, Mary Ellen."

Sandy: "Well, they are a big group. Okay. I am hearing an 'L' name now."

Wendy: "That would be our daughter, Laura."

Sandy: "Now your son is stepping forward." *I should not have jumped to that conclusion, as there were two young men on the other side. Laura's boyfriend had also passed. This shows my inexperience as a medium.*

Sandy: "A young man is stepping forward. He shows me a car accident, too. He was driving the car, too."

Wendy: "Yes."

Sandy: "I feel it was a single vehicle accident, like a roll over, and he went off the road. He hit something off the road. I feel a bang. Like he hit a tree or something."

Rob: "A telephone pole."

Sandy: "I feel it might have been raining."

Wendy: "Yes. It was raining."

Sandy: "I know this is hard, but this is the validation to let us know that they are okay. He says hello to a girl you still connect to. I feel someone you just saw that was a friend of his."

Wendy: "They were just at our house the other day." *They told me later that she and her husband brought their young family to help them celebrate what would have been Tim's 34th birthday.*

Sandy: "Now I feel the female connection stepping forward. Laura says she has a small chocolate-colored dog with her. Maybe black, but dark in color."

Wendy: "Not a cat?"

Sandy: "No, a dog! Did you have a dog called Blackie?"

Wendy: "My dad had a dog named Brownie."

Sandy: "Well, that would be it."

Wendy: "My dad was really close to that dog!"

Sandy: "It was dark black or dark brown?"

Wendy: "Yes. It was chocolate brown and little."

Sandy: "Yes, little. Must be your daughter's way to show your dad is close to her, by talking about his dog."

Sandy: "Now, I hear a Tom kind of name. A 'T-M' name. Maybe Tammy or Tim."

Wendy: "Tim is our son's name!"

Sandy: "Oh, your son's name is Tim. They are acknowledging something similar to each other, like birthday, for example, or a passing. Something they share in common. Is this your son and daughter?"

Wendy: "Yes! Tim and Laura both have birthdays in October."

Sandy: "I feel there is a 4th of October or four things in October."

Wendy: "Yes. My mother's birthday and an anniversary in October, too."

Sandy: "Okay. That would be four things then. Now they are talking about a red van. This could be burgundy, but definitely a red shade. They are showing this vehicle at your house, I think. Like someone just coming to your house in this kind of car."

Wendy: "Yes! We have friends from Northwestern Ontario, and they were just visiting in a burgundy van. Neat!"

Sandy: "They just came to your house not too long ago. It was in your driveway. They say that you were also in this car. You went somewhere in this car. There were four of you. And recently, like a few weeks ago?"

Wendy: "Yes! We did!"

Sandy: "This is their way of letting you know that they are around you. By talking about this recent visit, they show you they remain connected to both of you. It is your validation that they are close. They are acknowledging a restaurant. Did you go out to eat with them while they were here?"

Wendy: "Yes. That is where we went in a burgundy van." *Rob and Wendy explained after the session that the visiting couple were very special friends. As a teenager, the lady used to babysit Tim and Laura. She had become a very close family friend, and they thought of the woman and her family as their family. They found it amazing and wonderful that their recent visit was acknowledged in this reading.*

Sandy: "I feel there is a black or dark truck, now. Maybe involved in one of these accidents. I feel this might be connected to your daughter. A guy was driving the other vehicle. He was alone."

Wendy: "Yes."

Sandy: "And he passed, too. I feel a lot of heat here. I think things blew up."

Rob: "Yes. The truck did."

Sandy: "Oh. Okay." *My heart was aching for them, but I had to remain focused, so I tried the best I could to take my emotions out of this reading. As a bereaved parent myself, it would have been so easy to get caught up in their pain. I took a deep breath and refocused.*

Sandy: "They are showing me a house now. Talking about a house and taking me to the basement. They are pulling me towards you, Rob. I feel that you were just in the basement fixing something and there would be a water connection to this. It would have been very recent."

Wendy: "Yes. If he would have been home, Tim would have been helping."

Sandy: "You were just fixing something that had a water connection to it. This was downstairs in the basement, because I feel myself going down the stairs."

Rob: "Yes. I was."

Sandy: "I feel that Rob is down there a lot and that Tim is with you down there. I understand that to mean you spend a lot of time downstairs. Do you have a room down there, Rob?"

Wendy: "His office is down there."

Sandy: "And 'with you, Dad,' he says. You are still in the same house. Says he knows this house. He is showing me two computers now, both in the same room, I think, and maybe a laptop, too. Do you have three computers?"

Wendy: "Yes, we do."

Sandy: "But two of these computers, the ones that are stationary, are in the basement? One might be off to the side and maybe is not working."

Rob: "One is not being used."

Sandy: "Okay. Now, Wendy, there is a writing connection to you. Do you have a publishing company? I feel a big writing connection. Not only do you write a journal, for example, but there seems to be a book connection to you as well."

Wendy: *Laughing.* "Yes." *I found out after the reading that they are both journalists, travel writers, in fact. They write for magazines and newspapers, and they have also contributed to grief support books.*

Sandy: "And I feel you have done this since Laura's passing because I feel this is recent, and she wants you to know that she knows about this. She is aware of this book. I feel it is spiritual in nature and about her. Not a facts-and-figures kind of book. You had your hand in this book and she is mentioned in this book. Has this book been published?"

Wendy: "Yes, it has."

Sandy: "You will have to tell me about this book after the session."

Wendy: "I actually have brought you a copy of this book today."

Sandy: "Wow! I guess that is why they had to mention this book. Your mother is living, Wendy?"

Wendy: "Yes."

Sandy: "There is a man here who had a heart problem. Is that your dad? That's how he passed?"

Wendy: "Yes."

Sandy: "He is sending lots of love to your mom. I feel they were married when he passed. Not separated or divorced. I feel he has been gone a long time and equating this timeframe to your mom, Rob. I feel that both of them have been gone a very long time. Although I feel you were adults when they passed."

Wendy: "Yes, we were."

Sandy: "I feel one of your children was born before your dad passed."

Wendy: "Both were born."

Sandy: "Okay. Now where is the Eve or Evelyn connection?"

Rob: "My aunt. She just passed about three weeks ago."

Sandy: "Well, this must be their way of saying she is with them. She was old and ready to go, I feel. Must have been in her eighties and would have been sick."

Rob: "Yes. She was in her eighties."

Sandy: "Now, did you superimpose some words onto some pictures? I don't quite know what they mean by that. There's got to be words as well as pictures that are superimposed in some way. Is there a web site for your kids? They need to talk about the web page and say thank you for this. I don't know if you have superimposed both of them on there. Is there a web page you have done in honor of them?"

Rob: "Yes."

Sandy: "You can do that?"

Rob: "Yes. What we have is a picture of the lake where Jonathan grew up. Above the lake we created "Laura and Jonathan" in the sky, like clouds, and added words across the bottom of the picture. When we open the computer, this comes up on the screen.

Sandy: "Oh! Wow! And she is superimposed on the clouds! 'You did this, Dad,' she says."

Wendy: "Yes, Rob did this."

Sandy: "This is her way of saying she knows and that she sees what you do. What they want you to take with you today is a knowing that they are still with you and not that far away. Now they are acknowledging a trip you are taking soon. I don't feel in an airplane, but rather by car and there are more than just the two of you going?"

Wendy: "Yes, this is business related and it is a group of us. We are going soon."

Sandy: "Well, have a good time. You were a writer before Laura passed, but I feel you will be speaking soon, and Laura is acknowledging this. She is talking about a speaking engagement."

Wendy: "I will be speaking next week on this topic." *Wendy explained after the session that only a handful of people knew she had been asked to speak to a university group about the COPING Centre, a non-profit support group for those experiencing grief.*

Sandy: "They know it and will be with you, because I feel this is so hard for you. You are more comfortable with the writing. Again, they are showing you they know what you are doing at the present time."

Sandy: *I felt they were starting to pull back and the reading was coming to an end.* "Now remember that when this reading is over, your loved ones just leave me and *not* you. Know that this is their chance to prove they stay connected to both of you. They

> want you to go home and continue this relationship knowing and believing and having more faith in this connection."

The spirit messages were not finished, however, and the reading did go on for a while longer. I felt that I needed to continue as long as their loved ones remained connected to me and as long as I could accurately bring the information through. Finally, when I felt Laura, Tim, and all the others pull back and disconnect from me, I knew this reading was at an end.

The three of us chatted for a while and, as bereaved parents, shared our grief, pain, and loss. I honestly couldn't understand the depth of their loss. The incredible sense of loss and immense grief I felt when Kim passed had incapacitated me. They had lost *both* Laura and Tim, in two separate car accidents. How had Rob and Wendy survived such a disaster? I marveled at their strength.

I had to hope that the connection we made with both of their children today would help them know they were still very much with them.

They handed me a copy of the book that Laura had mentioned in the reading. The book is called *Afterglow: Signs of Continued Love* and includes stories of comforting coincidences from those who grieve. It was the first book of a series planned by publisher Karla Wheeler of Quality of Life Publishing. Her company works with hospice organizations, providing publications to help ease the way for those who are dying and grieving.

*There are two major synchronicities about that book. First, a beautiful photograph of Laura and Tim as young children canoeing on a lake at sundown graces the front cover of* Afterglow. *Second, when I was searching for a publisher for* My Gift of Light, *wanting to be certain the publishing team was both spiritually based as well as sensitive to the many facets of grief, Wendy suggested I contact Karla. As a result, Quality of Life Publishing is the publisher of the book you hold in your hands.*

I was in no rush for Wendy and Rob to leave, as we created a strong bond with each other that day. Since that day, a comforting friendship has blossomed.

After Rob and Wendy left, I thoughtfully pondered the strange and unusual work I was doing now and the personal journey I had taken since the loss of Kim. I had to trust that this was all meant to be and that what I was doing would provide a coping tool for people grieving the loss of a loved one.

I asked Rob and Wendy if they would like to include some of their own comments as to how this reading affected their lives. I am pleased to include their insights:

> **Wendy:** My first reaction to Sandy's reading was exceeding joy. When our son was killed five years after our daughter, I remember saying I could "maybe" cope with not being able to see and touch my only two children, as painful as that was, if only we could hear from them sometimes. Why couldn't there be emails from heaven — or phone calls — at least on birthdays and special occasions?
>
> I guess we got the next best thing via Sandy. It does not replace our desire to have them physically here with us. It does not give us back our hopes for the future, but it helps tremendously to know they care, are still near, and can feel our love. The confirmation is very healing and comforting.
>
> I am firmly convinced that the messages Sandy related were from our children and family members who have passed. There is no other way she could possibly have known so many personal details regarding our immediate family circle.
>
> In my journal on Wednesday, November 27, (the night before meeting Sandy for the first time), I wrote to my children, "How I hope we get to hear from you tomorrow. Would you please tell us what you are doing now? I can't believe you just float around doing nothing. Do you come and go from this earthly plane? Can you see us and what we are doing? Do you see your earthly grandparents? We so very much want to communicate with you and send you our love."
>
> Many of my questions were answered the next day, thanks to Sandy's reading. My journal entry the evening of November 28

was, "Our reading with Sandy was like a phone call from Heaven! Thank you! It was so wonderful to hear from those we miss so much."

I phoned every person mentioned in the reading, and you wouldn't believe all the happiness it brought. We thank Sandy for the joy she has brought to so many.

**Rob:** Part of the reason I felt a little more comfortable having a reading with Sandy was the knowledge that she had lost her own daughter in a car crash and had not done mediumship work before that. We had been to see a few mediums before this reading with Sandy. One medium in particular was Rosemary Altea, who has written several books, including the bestseller, *The Eagle and the Rose*, and is on the international lecture circuit. We could not get a private booking to sit down with her, although she did tell us during an autograph session after one of her public readings, (where we were hoping to hear from our son) exactly how our daughter was killed, the type of vehicle she was in, that there was a fire, and so on. So we were somewhat preconditioned to believe that some kind of connection could be made between our world and the spirit world.

As our reading with Sandy continued, there were just so many details that were not available anywhere publicly *that were dead-on accurate* that I abandoned my skepticism and simply enjoyed the moment. If we could no longer talk with our children, we could at least hear from them and confirm that there was something beyond the grave.

One thing I would suggest to anyone going into a reading with a medium is to get together a list of important dates, particularly for family members who have passed, including birthdates, anniversaries, and death dates. It's a lot easier to check a list than it is to try and remember your granddad's date of death when it was 30 or 40 years ago.

I had brought comforting messages from Tim and Laura to their mom and dad. I was grateful for that. The process of knowing and understanding how this is possible did not happen for me overnight. Rob and Wendy would now have to begin their own journeys. I prayed they would learn how to tap into their own inner abilities to hear and sense Tim and Laura. Until that time, I would make myself available to them. I would aid them in any way I could as they opened themselves to the Light.

*I had found my purpose in life. I was finally ready to let go of my earthly relationship with Kim and embrace the new relationship we had now. I understood that I could use my psychic talents to help others deal with their grief. I was now strong enough to deal with the skeptics I would come across in my work. How ironic, because I was a skeptic myself only a few years ago!*

I had found my purpose in life. I was finally ready to let go of my earthly relationship with Kim and embrace the new relationship we had now. I understood that I could use my psychic talents to help others deal with their grief. I was now strong enough to deal with the skeptics I would come across in my work. How ironic, because I was a skeptic myself only a few years ago!

I had personally experienced the healing power that communication from loved ones on the other side could bring. My work as a spiritual medium was too important to let my fear of being different stop me. I had to trust that Kim and my guides would direct me in my healing work. I hoped to become a catalyst for others to know they could develop their own abilities, too.

I recognized that every one of us has the ability to connect in some way to our own loved ones who have crossed over. I believed with all my heart that through my readings I could aid others to awaken to the Light within themselves.

Chapter 8

# MY RETURN TO LIFE

*In the book of life, every page has two sides: we human beings fill the upper side with our plans, hopes, and wishes, but providence writes on the other side, and what it ordains is seldom our goal.*

—Nisami

Life after death will always remain a mystery to those on this side of the veil. I have learned, however, that connecting to loved ones who have crossed over to the other side can create hope at a time of greatest despair. The death of a loved one, especially the death of one of our children, forces us to search the depths of our souls for life's meaning. In the face of such devastating loss and heartache, we must devise new core values to live by.

As we search for answers, spirituality can provide a doorway to this understanding and to new hope. I know it changed my life, the way I view this world, as well as my belief system forever.

When we learn to reach beyond our five senses and attune to the non-physical — or unseen — influences around us, we awaken to an expanded consciousness. Only then can we truly believe that our children and other loved ones who have passed still exist and are okay.

This new understanding can help us to get up every morning when our earth lives have been drained of meaning. As we work through our grief and take those first hesitant steps back into life — as we all must eventually do — spirituality can play a significant role in the coping process.

*As we work through our grief and take those first hesitant steps back into life — as we all must eventually do — spirituality can play a significant role in the coping process.*

This book has acquainted you with my journey to the Light, so you know the path I took as my coping process unfolded. I hope you will consider putting your own feet on a similar path.

A session with a competent medium can open your eyes to the reality that your children or loved ones on the other side remain connected. They are closer than you may ever have imagined and eager to let you know they are still present in your life, are well and, yes, happy.

A session with a medium cannot take away your grief. It might, however, ease your heartache by showing you that someday you will reunite with your loved ones. My belief is that the true purpose of a medium is to open our eyes to this fact and encourage us to learn how to fashion our own connections with the spirit world.

I doubt we will fully comprehend the enormity of it all until we ourselves cross over. I believe the full scope of the life of the eternal spirit lies beyond our human capabilities to understand. We have to put aside our logical mind and accept the truth that there is more around us than what we see with our physical eyes. The phrase I use most often now with my clients is, "It just is! Believe they are close. They have proven it to you today."

Grief is so very personal; all who grieve must do whatever they feel will be most beneficial. I believe no single book or person can make anyone's grief disappear. Only by focusing within ourselves — by going on our own journeys after the loss of our beloveds — can we adopt the coping skills we need.

We must confront our grief, learn how to move through it, and eventually embrace the truth that because of our loss, we are forever changed. We become so transformed by the work of grieving that we awaken to the fact that events or possessions that used to be important to us no longer are. Our once-ordered life is in chaos. As a result, we open ourselves to self-exploration. As we begin our grief journeys, we feel impatient. We crave to understand how contact is achieved between ourselves and those in the spirit world.

Please remember that psychic signs are usually very subtle. Your sixth sense may give you "an impression" of someone near. You may notice a scent of a loved one who recently passed. You may actually feel a comforting touch or see a movement out of the corner of your eye. Because these signs are so subtle — or enigmatic — and seem to be contrary to our logical left brain, it is easy for us to ignore them or believe they are just wishful thinking.

Dreams are another avenue utilized by those on the other side to bring their messages through. Please pay attention to any dreams that are vivid and lucid. If you wake up with the "knowingness" that your loved one has come for a visit, don't discount it because "it doesn't make sense." Believe and know that love is the bond that makes this link possible. Our beloved ones in spirit are comforting us in our sorrow by showing us how thin the veil is between our two worlds.

When it seems that the process of your spiritual transformation is moving forward much too slowly, you may serendipitously encounter a "miracle" that strengthens your personal faith in the journey. When you open yourself to endless possibilities, you are more apt to acknowledge and believe these signs.

When we on this side of the veil become more sensitive to the presence of unseen energies, we are transformed by the experiences. We increase our awareness of our right brain, the intuitive side. This can be an exciting time. If you are grieving the loss of someone who was very important to you, such experiences can also bring you peace at a time you feel peace is unattainable. I know they did for me.

Different losses generate different needs and impact us in various ways. The loss of an aging parent is not like the loss of a spouse. The loss of a friend is not like the loss of a sibling. Each loss brings its own degree and type of grief. It is the intensity of that grief that can open the door to a deeper meaning of life.

The death of a child is a death out of the natural order. As Kim's mother, I obviously expected to die before she did. The emptiness, torturous pain, and disillusionment with life that resulted felled me. As I have repeatedly said, the magnitude of my loss turned my entire life — and my belief system — upside down. Once the natural order had been torn apart, I had no choice but to discover a new way to look at the world — a way that would return me to well-being and, someday, happiness. I chose spirituality as one of the avenues to pursue to make sense of this sudden and devastating loss.

Grieving the loss of a child, however, lasts a lifetime. May I remind you to be gentle with yourself as you look for solace. You must allow yourself to express your feelings of grief. It is important to talk about your loss, your feelings of emptiness, your anger and pain. All these emotions are a normal part of the grieving process.

I found a grief counsellor I felt comfortable with, one with the personality and expertise to support me. I also began regular visits to a local psychiatrist. I needed a place to scream, cry, and talk, talk, talk. I took advantage of every available avenue.

I went to two very wonderful support groups in our area. Bereaved Families of Ontario and The COPING Centre were instrumental in aiding me through the initial stages of my intense grief. COPING stands for Caring for Other People in Grief. It is run by both professionals and volunteers who have experienced the depth and breadth of this journey in their own lives.

My husband and I attended a couples group at the COPING Centre in a nearby town. I did not realize how much I needed to be part of a group until I arrived that first night. Talking with others who had lost a child opened my eyes to the fact that men and women grieve in very different ways. Doug and I learned to be more understanding of each other's grief process.

I joined a group of bereaved moms affiliated with Bereaved Families of Ontario. It was important for me to find a venue where I could talk as much as I wanted about Kim and about the incredible person she was. I was drawn like a magnet to other parents who had lost children. I felt they were the only ones who could begin to understand the anguish of my loss. When I attended that first meeting of bereaved moms, I really believed that even they could not understand the depth of *my* pain.

I was very selfishly immersed in my own pain. Kim was such a loving daughter, had such admirable goals and aspirations, and loved life with such passion that I felt she was cheated out of the wonderful life she worked so hard to set up. I believed that no one could have suffered a loss comparable to the one my family and I had endured. Our family of five was perfect and our life blessed. Our family of four was just not complete. A part of *me* had died with Kim. I was overcome with such intense anger and such immense pain that I truly felt I could not live through it.

As I listened to these bereaved mothers that first evening, I was awakened to the reality that I was not alone. I listened to the details of the loss of their children and, amazingly, rose from my numbness to feel *their* pain. I understood why I was there. As I put my arm around one of the moms, I was able, if just for a moment, to set aside my own feelings of loss and reach out to comfort her.

How valuable it was to sit among a group of people who could personally understand my feelings! It was a place where we did not have to hide our grief but could safely share it with one another. It was here that I learned to publicly express my grief and extend compassion to others who had lost children.

I found that my new spiritual beliefs slowly seeped into these professional and traditional avenues of healing. I shared my experiences with my psychiatrist first — and am so thankful I did — since he introduced me to Bonnie, who served as a catalyst to my early learning. Eventually I also told the psychologist my husband and I consulted together.

When I joined the mothers' group through Bereaved Families, I shared the reading I had recently received from Sharlette. They were fascinated and asked questions about my experience. A few of them had their own readings. We talked about our beliefs and the hope that our children were still around us.

Becoming aware of the spiritual dimension brought me understanding of where Kim now existed. I became driven to understand how contact between the two worlds could be initiated and then strengthened. As I continued to learn how closely these two worlds were interwoven, I became aware that we can *all* connect to this unseen world *if* we do the work required to make this connection.

If you feel driven to follow this path, do everything you can to develop your connection to the other side. Many ideas and suggestions have been mentioned in this book to help you begin your journey. The journey is not automatic. It requires concerted thought and deliberate action.

Read some of the countless books available on the subject to gain knowledge of the other side. Join meditation groups in your area. Find a spiritualist church to attend. Go online and discover spiritual websites and chat lines where you can talk about spiritual issues. Take courses offered by spiritual teachers who will help you develop your own inner abilities. Pay attention to spiritual companions you meet along the way who offer you encouragement and friendship.

Tune into your own feelings. Go within yourself and pay attention to your intuition. Take responsibility for your learning. It's important that you seek out learning experiences that will increase your awareness of your higher self and the other side.

Set time aside for meditation and prayer. Self-enlightenment happens when you spend time alone and focus on your thoughts. Realize the importance of daily renewal. Take a walk in nature. Find what brings peacefulness to your soul. Actively pursue your own path to enlightenment, but know that along the way, you may mistrust your own perceptions because they are too hard for your left brain to grasp. Remember: when your analytical mind creeps in, it brings doubts. Our analytical minds are wonderful, but don't let yours rob you of your spiritual knowings. Honor yourself and your journey.

Fear may be the strongest deterrent on your journey. Fear of the unknown and fear of ridicule from others are powerful forces. Only you can find your way through this fear. Allow, trust, and believe that *all* is possible.

My spiritual journey is now a lifelong path, one woven with pain and tears from the tragic loss of my beloved daughter. It is a journey that will continue in honor of Kim. I will continue to work hard to raise my vibration so I become a clearer medium. I will continue to strengthen my perception of the signs I receive for others so I can better relay the messages.

In helping others connect to their loved ones who have gone to a new realm of existence, I found the strength to move forward with my own life and once again become a loving wife to my husband and mother to my other two daughters. I have finally let go of Kim's physical being and embrace the new relationship we miraculously now share. I have, at last, returned to life on this plane.

I know there will always be sad and painful days of missing Kim for the rest of our lives on earth. The knowledge, however, that Kim is still with us in so many different ways brings me a sense of peace that allows me to move forward with my life.

Someone once said that hope is the "enduring feeling that life makes sense." This spiritual road I have traveled has brought me to a new place of hope. Thanks to my spiritual enlightenment, I totally put my trust in the fact that Kim is fine and lives on in another dimension. One day, when it is my time to leave this physical plane, we will meet again — that I know for certain.

*The bonds of love are never severed. Love is what enables and maintains the links between our two worlds.*

I take comfort in knowing we never truly stop living and that what we on the earth plane call "death" is anything but. My understanding is that we take our characteristics, habits, and memories with us. In spirit, we are free to develop our souls. We continue to grow, remember, and love — both here on earth as well as on the other side.

My wish is that by sharing my very personal journey with you, it will aid you on your own path as it twists and turns through your loss and grief. It takes a great deal of courage to find your way back into life. You will never be the way you were before, but you will learn to live with your loss and regain your abilities to function and be happy.

I believe that our children and other loved ones on the other side of life will help us to find our way if we allow them to. The bonds of love are never severed. Love is what enables and maintains the links between our two worlds.

I pray that by sharing this journey and my gift of Light, I bring new perspective and hope to others who have lost loved ones. My sincere hope is that reading my story will inspire you to embark upon your own journey of discovery. May it open your heart and nourish your soul.

Appendix:

# Communication through Automatic Writing

*Remain open. There is something bigger than you know going on here.*

—Iyanla Vanzant

As I promised in Chapter Two, I will now delve deeper into automatic writing, which was my preferred method of connecting to the spirit world early in my pilgrimage into the Light.

I readily adapted to this form of communication with the other side in which I allowed information to come through my hand as it held a pen to paper.

I quickly discovered that loved ones who have made their transition from the earth plane to the afterlife could communicate with us in a variety of ways. Automatic writing appeared to be one of these ways. By this time I had begun to interact through the Internet with many men and women who had faith in this form of communication.

Although there may be no way to conclusively prove that automatic writing is a real and true communication from the other side, I have determined to my satisfaction that it is. Some skeptics believe it is information from our subconscious mind and nothing more. My experience, on the other hand, has convinced me it is much more.

Through experimentation and information on the subject gleaned from reading, I drew my own conclusions and made up my own mind as to what I believe. I have free will, which includes the power to choose what is right for me to believe or do at each stage of my earthly journey. What is appropriate for me might not be appropriate for someone else.

On the advice of a mentor, I went in search of a book on the importance of "psychic protection." I explored reading material that explained what might happen, what I could expect, and ways to achieve a connection with the other side. However, in retrospect, I should have done all this at the beginning of my process.

Today, I definitely do not recommend that anyone attempt automatic writing the way I did — uninformed and oblivious to the dangers I could encounter. I never took time to investigate what might happen. I had already begun my communication with the other side before I read my first book on the topic of automatic writing. I was driven by a single intention: to hear from Kim. I believe I was protected by a power much greater than I so I would continue my pilgrimage into the Light without fear.

Ruth Montgomery, a bestselling author who died one day before her 88th birthday on June 10, 2001, was renowned for her landmark series of work with automatic writing. Her book titled, *A Search For the Truth,* describes how she went from being a highly regarded political reporter who covered the White House and the State Department — very much the skeptic — to doing automatic writing herself. She was on a first-name basis with six presidents and is a past president of the prestigious National Press Club. Ruth describes how her guides took over her hand to impart messages and information to her. She recounts her personal journey into the world of spirituality and into the unfamiliar territory of automatic writing. In the end, she authored 16 leading-edge books on spiritual or metaphysical subjects.

Ruth's work encouraged me to move forward with my attempts at automatic writing and to be patient with myself. In the beginning, I learned you may not feel that your writing makes much sense or that it offers you any credible information. But with practice, the words flowed more easily. I dated my writings, then kept them for future reference.

I believe automatic writing can be a reliable method to bring through communication from the other side. It has been proven to me by countless validations. Too much of the information I received this way was verified through others, making it impossible for me to doubt the authenticity of the process.

I have included a small sample of my writings in this book. These personal writings span the period of eight months — from March of 1999 to the end of October 1999 — that directly parallels the events I have shared in the chapters covering that timeframe. I have chosen for clarity's sake to give them their own chapter in this book since they speak for themselves.

As I previously mentioned in an earlier chapter, I made my first attempt at automatic writing on March 10, 1999. My writings started slowly but produced startling results. For six nights I went into Kim's bedroom and sat with pen in hand, waiting expectantly. On the seventh night, March 16, my hand moved in such a way that I knew I myself had not moved it. This movement generated just a few scratches across the paper.

The following evening I received the first few legible words. They were: "*Sandy, you can help me.*" That is all. I had asked for contact with my daughter; yet this is what I got. I reasoned that this wasn't Kim but had no idea who it was.

I had located someone on the Internet the week before who did automatic writing. I now went in search of her. I had many questions. When I found her — by searching various sites for her name, I asked her: "How can I find out who this 'spirit' was?" She informed me that all I need do was ask. That was my first lesson: Automatic writing is a two-way conversation.

The next evening, as I prepared myself to write, I did just that. As my hand began to move, I received a name. The name "Paul" was scribbled on the page and along with it, the name "Ruth." The person coming through from the other side seemed to be my husband's brother-in-law who had passed 20 years earlier.

You can imagine my shock! I did not know what to think. How could this be? I couldn't comprehend what had just happened and literally ran down the stairs to show my husband.

He thought it was exciting. I thought it was eerie. I was definitely stepping into unfamiliar territory. Could Paul really be coming through my hand to bring a message to his family? Shaking my head in disbelief, I carefully put away the page displaying these few, almost illegible, words. I did not sleep well that night; my head was a jumble of unanswered questions.

The next evening I gingerly ventured back into Kim's room, thanks to some coaxing from my husband, to attempt this technique at least one more time. As I prepared to connect to the other side, I asked for Paul to come through with a piece of information I did not know. This, I reasoned, would be a means of verification that it was Paul who connected with me.

When my hand once more began to move across the paper, I was given two pieces of information. I wondered if these facts were true and if I could verify them. I enlisted the help of my husband who made a telephone call to Paul's wife, Ruth. Doug planned to find out if the information was true without letting Ruth know the reason for his inquiry. I leaned forward on the edge of my seat. By the time they had finished their conversation, the information was verified.

Doug and I exchanged looks of disbelief.

On the next page are samples of two of my earliest writings.

Mar 17/99

You can help me

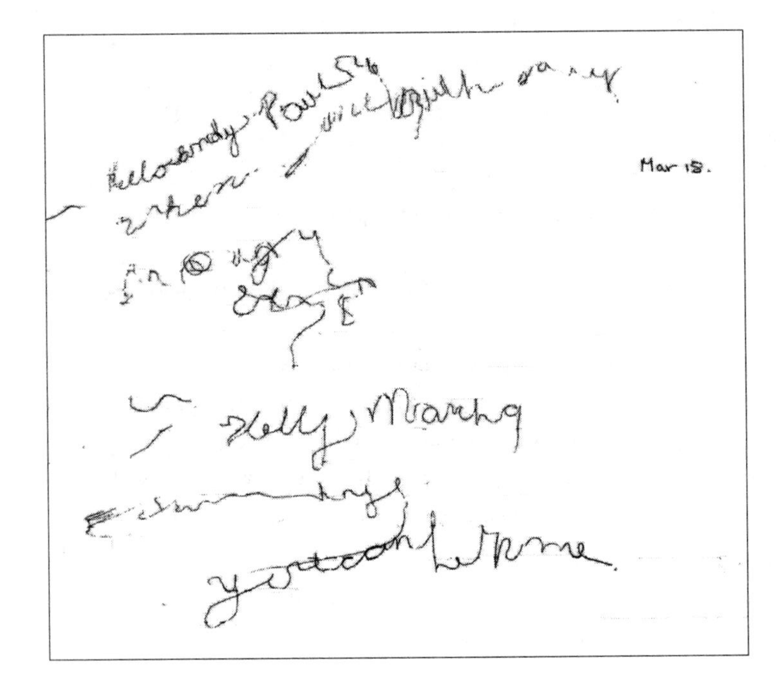

Mar 15.

I knew I needed to gain more understanding of the process of automatic writing and its implications; however, I did not stop. Opening myself to the mysteries beyond this plane of existence felt strange and more than a little frightening. I knew that if this were the way to communicate with Kim, I would keep trying until I received a message from *her*. Since it was very early in my journey, I did not totally believe in such a thing as "the other side." Receiving those first messages from Paul certainly made me wonder.

I reflected, with a measure of sadness, on the puzzle of why I had heard from Paul and not Kim. Did the messages really come from Paul? If not, where did they come from? Paul had passed over about 20 years earlier, and it had been some years since I had thought about him. I reasoned, therefore, that I had not "made up" the messages. I had pleaded for contact with Kim yet I had supposedly made contact with Paul. I was baffled by the connection and by the messages.

Almost every evening for the next few months I went into my safe spot — Kim's room — and asked for her to come through in my automatic writing. Almost every evening I received a response, but not yet from Kim. I was determined not to give up and tried to have faith that I would hear from Kim when she felt I was ready.

My writings were scribbled and not always legible. As I opened myself to this other world, my writings rapidly improved and appeared to come in full sentences. I was fascinated!

After a few weeks, Paul ended his communication, and the messages I received came from others. Still nothing from my daughter. I became extremely frustrated that they were never from Kim.

Looking back, I am not sure what made me strong enough to continue in spite of all my fears. Communication with Kim was my driving force, far stronger than my trepidation. The fact that I persevered proved the depth of my desire to connect with Kim. Still, this was a scary, nearly irrational, thing to attempt.

In one of my early writings, when I was unaware of who from the other side was making the connection with me, I was mystified by a name that came through. *"Raphael, here."* I reread the message, scanning the words for something recognizable as a message from Kim. No, not Kim, I thought sadly. Who, I wondered, was Raphael, and why did he not tell me who he was?

I have since come to understand that the spirit or guide will not give you more information than you can deal with at one time. Because I was still uneducated on the subject of spirit guides, I was not ready to hear that Raphael was one of mine. I have come to understand that if you are not ready to hear the information, they will not share it with you.

I had enough to deal with: my times of intense grief, our suffering as a family, Kim's birthday that was approaching, and all the new spiritual happenings in my life. I had all I could handle. It wasn't until months later in August that I found out who Raphael was.

During my discussions about automatic writing on the Internet, I heard people voicing concerns about this type of communication. When someone asked me what prayer I used to protect myself, I pleaded stupidity and mumbled that I used none. I was informed that I needed to pray for protection by surrounding myself in "the white light of God" and to pray that "only my highest and best purpose be served." I learned it was imperative to always ask for protection.

I did not understand what I was protecting myself from. I had heard of "dark entities" and wondered if such things actually existed. I was told to protect myself before each session, so that is what I did. I urge you to do the same without fail.

This presented a conflict for me: I had to ask for protection from a God I wasn't really sure I believed in. As I was driven to continue this form of communication because of my need to hear from Kim, I asked God for protection — just to be safe.

It was at this time that I finally went in search of a book that would help me understand what I was doing. By now, I knew I was definitely receiving communication from the other side. Once I experienced this truth for myself, I grew confident enough to trust in the process and believe in myself.

It was up to me, however, to study and learn more about this form of communication.

Initially, during my automatic writing sessions, it felt as if my hand was moving all by itself. I was always in a totally aware yet relaxed state of mind. I was, however, unaware of what I was going to write. The energy in my hand seemed to be one different from my own. It was such a strange sensation that I often wondered if my sanity was questionable.

Before long I became cognizant of the fact that the words would appear in my head just before I wrote them down. They did not feel like part of my own thoughts. This mystified me, and I struggled to understand it.

Sharlette, now my friend and mentor, helped to answer some of my questions about this whole procedure when we chatted over the Internet. I could ask her anything and, consequently, bombarded her with questions. Sharlette always responded with love and patience.

As the months went by, I continued doing all my automatic writing in Kim's bedroom. It was a quiet place where I wouldn't be interrupted. I held pen in hand, a pad of paper ready, as I settled into a comfortable writing position. I would go into a light state of meditation by taking a few slow, deep breaths. Trying to set aside my immense sadness was the most difficult aspect of my process. Every time I prepared to write, my mind would immediately flit to thoughts of Kim and how much I needed her to come through. I believe this extreme need occasionally blocked my ability to relax into the state necessary to receive communication.

It was my need to contact Kim that brought me to this place on my journey, but ironically it was this same urgency that threatened to block my success with this form of contact. Eventually, my ability to achieve automatic writing became more consistent. As the words flowed more freely, I had to remind myself not to judge or analyze the words that appeared on the page. When I was done, I would read what my hand had written. As I became calmer and more relaxed, I became more centered. Only then, could I trust the process.

I reasoned that the better I could quiet my mind, the more superior my connection to the other side would be. I diligently practiced meditation. To be honest, I had never meditated before I began this spiritual journey. I would never have believed that I would use this as a tool to find my way to Kim. I meditated before each attempt at automatic writing. For me, meditation and automatic writing went hand-in-hand.

Nonetheless, practice was necessary for me to gain skill and become a good meditator.

I was learning the importance of the proper breathing techniques to employ during these meditation sessions. I had read that proper breathing deepens and strengthens one's meditation because it helps to clear the mind of everyday thoughts and focuses awareness at the highest level. My goal was to connect with my higher self, my spirit guides, and my loved ones on the other side — especially Kim — as well as to bring about the development of my sixth sense.

I knew that the clearer I could hear spirit messages, the more chances I would have of hearing Kim. I would soon discover that the time and effort to learn proper meditation techniques paid off: I connected to Kim.

When Kim first came through in my writings, I was, of course, very emotional. Was this really her? Could she really talk to me in this way? Her message was short and simple. *"I love you, Mom. Tell Dad it is great here. I love him. I came to him in a dream. Wow, Grandpa is here. I live, Mom."*

As I re-read the words that jumped off the page, tears flowed down my cheeks. This is what Kim had said to her dad during my telephone reading with Sharlette, just weeks before. *"Tell Daddy. Not dead."* If I believed that Kim was relaying the messages through Sharlette, and I did, and she was using Sharlette's hand to relay her messages, why couldn't I believe she would do the same for me?

The thought that Kim had been with me brought a flood of tears. I did not write for a few days while I tried to get hold of my emotions. Instead, I bought a journal and wrote back to her. I poured out my feelings, my aching loss. I wrote all the things I would have said to Kim if she were standing in front of me.

On April 9, Kim came for the second time. Oh, how I wanted it to be her! She imparted some personal information then ended this writing with, *"This is so strange — to have you write for me."* My writing was huge, slanted, and only four lines; the words filled the whole page.

I cried for a long time and wondered if I would ever believe one hundred percent that these messages came from Kim. I had been told it might take some time before I got there; in the meantime, I should record these writings and date them. Then, someday, when I looked back on these writings, I would see the verifications and know they were from Kim. I wanted that confirmation to come soon.

Rereading the information channeled through in my automatic writing often brought a host of conflicting emotions to the surface. Tears and smiles were often intermingled. Most of the time the messages brought me immense hope and great comfort. One of these times occurred when Kim talked about her grandmother who had been sick. Kim wrote, *"Grandma will be okay as it isn't her time to go yet. She is stubborn and she will take her time to come to us."*

This was the longest writing I had received to date. Kim ended it by saying, *"Keep writing and I will keep coming. You are reading my thoughts now. We are getting pretty good, aren't we? Yes! I wrote this, Mom."*

I sat down and had a splendid cry.

The day I went to see Shawna Ross back in February, I had been told that one of my guides was named Holly. On April 28, I received what appeared to be my first message from her.

*"Hi, my name is Holly. I am your spirit guide. I am very tall, slim, dark hair, some say pretty. My last death was from a shooting in New York."*

Now this was a thought-provoking message. What did she mean by her "last death?" How and where did this come into my thoughts? Strange, I thought, very strange.

I remember reasoning that if I ever got a second confirmation of the name Holly, I would really have to think about this message again. I was such a skeptic.

This verification came from Joanne and Jeanne later in June. We met at Chapters bookstore to have a cup of coffee at Starbucks. To my amazement, they informed me that, through automatic writing, they learned that the name of my guide was Holly. With this confirmation, I believed that something bigger than I understood was at work here. My heart beating like a drum in my ears, my mind at last embraced this new idea as truth.

Up until this time, during my automatic writing attempts, I had asked only for Kim and other loved ones who had passed. Through my conversations with Joanne and Jeanne, I was awakened to the reality that I could ask for my guides and angels to impart their wisdom as well. I immediately began to do this and was startled to notice how the content of my writings changed. I began by asking my guides what they would like to teach me. The information I recorded in my automatic writing sessions immediately became more inspirational and loving.

My friends surely were correct when they explained that our spirit guides, angels, and loved ones are waiting for the opportunity to aid us along our life's journey. However, we must always *ask* for their love, help, and knowledge.

As I began to have a more personal relationship with my guides and angels, they shared a great deal of knowledge about their world. I was given glimpses of their "home" and what our journey on the earth's plane is really all about. As my guides Holly and Raphael began to send their wisdom through my writings, I quickly noticed they each spoke with their own distinct style. The ways in which they spoke were very different from Kim and the other loved ones who had visited me to deliver their messages. When I read over the material from my guides, I realized that the information they gave me was very wise and deep. This information certainly was not coming *from* me, only *through* me.

One such writing occurred on June 21:

> *"This is Raphael. Be guided by your heart. Trust in the power within you and you will find the faith and strength to continue this connection to those of us who love you. We are not as far away as*

*you might wish to believe. We are here vibrating at a different pace. We are close now to aid you on your healing journey with love and caring. Your fear will prevent you from moving forward. When you begin to understand that all is in Divine Order, then you will come to a realization that there is no need to fear. What is not love is fear. Trust in yourself, in God, in the God within you and you will become free from fear."*

When I put my pen down. I picked up the paper and began to read what had come through. I pondered the words that stared back at me. Then I read them again. What was Raphael trying to make me understand about fear? Was there really no reason to be fearful? Was all in Divine Order? What exactly was Divine Order? I was hoping my guides would continue to enlighten me. I was not disappointed.

My next experience, which followed very quickly on the heels of the last one, seemed to continue the message and answer my question on Divine Order. The very next evening Raphael began to impart his wisdom:

*"My dear, begin to understand that there are spiritual laws that govern our existence. Understand, too, that there are natural laws that govern our existence. Become more familiar with the existence of these laws and you will understand Divine Order. Realization will come that there is no reason to hold fear within you. Fear does not come from the outside. Comprehend this and you will grow in your search for the truth. I have given you much to ponder and so I will take my leave."*

I picked up the paper I had written this message on and thought to myself, yes, you sure have given me a lot to think about. Now I wondered where I would find out more about these spiritual and natural laws Raphael had written about. The fact that I did not fully understand what had just been written helped me realize this information came from a source other than myself.

I headed off to the bookstore once more in search of books that might help me understand what Raphael had talked about. As I glanced over some of the books on the shelf, one particular title caught my eye: *Seven Spiritual Laws of Success: A Practical Guide to the Fulfilment of Your Dreams*. I took the book, went to the coffee shop in the bookstore, and sat down to skim through the pages. I felt that this was the right book for me to buy. I had never heard of this author, Deepak Chopra, M.D., but noticed he had written many books.

When I talked to Joanne and Bonnie about Chopra, they both expressed amazement that I had never heard of this bestselling author on spiritual matters. I reminded them just how new I was to all this.

I was now communicating with my guides on a regular basis through automatic writing and began to sense the subtle differences in their energies. As much as I wanted Kim to connect with me through my writings, I was comforted by the fact that Holly and what appeared to be other guides were there, too, and that someone was looking out for me. I was excited. I was beginning to feel the presence of my guides. At first it had been hard to believe in something not visible to the naked eye. This was a real journey of faith.

This connection to Kim and my guides brought out a whole range of emotions. On one hand, I had succeeded in finding my daughter, and we were communicating with each other. However, the reality was stark: Kim was not here in this world with us.

One of the new emotions to surface was anger toward Kim for leaving us. I was seeing a psychiatrist who provided me a safe avenue to work through this feeling. I yearned for any contact with Kim, wanting her back with us, even though I knew this was impossible. I still struggle with this desperate desire. I will always miss the physical Kim that I gave birth to. Always. However, I knew I would take Kim any way I could have her, so I continued my connection and worked on my feelings of anger.

As my circle of new acquaintances continued to grow, and we shared our personal stories, we realized we were destined to meet. We were all on this new journey together, learning from each other. We found in each other the support we needed to grow spiritually. I appreciated being able to share my automatic writing experiences with Jeanne and Joanne.

I still had many doubts about the validity of my writings. It was difficult not to. Yet I progressed so rapidly that I was having a hard time accepting it all. Trusting the messages was my biggest hurdle. Faith in this communication from spirit came only after I received confirmation of the information.

On June 20, 1999, Kim came through very strongly. It was a different sensation, very powerful. She took over my hand to relay this message to me:

> *"When are you going to really believe me, Mom? We are forever together. We have work to do. We can help so many, but you must believe first. When you do, you will be successful."*

The amount of information coming through from the other side was increasing. I noticed my handwriting changed with different writers. I would sense a shift in the energy around me when someone else would come in.

On June 30, 1999, Holly wrote:

> *"Careful that you don't let yourself make mistakes in your work. We will help you meet more people who can further you on your journey into the Light. This is Holly and more will be revealed to you as you become ready to receive these important messages. They will help to enlighten many in your world. More later."*

On the next page is my actual writing. This illustrates how my writing style had changed from my first communications in the month of March.

On July 4, I received a message from someone called Raphael. I had been given this name a few times in some of my earlier writings but didn't yet know who this was. I knew Holly was my guide. I wondered if Raphael was another guide. Did we each have more than one? I wanted Holly to be my guide because I was so comfortable with her and already trusted her.

This is what he wrote:

> *"Raphael here. Love will help your healing. Feel your cheek, your neck. I am here."*

June 30/99

All
Careful ~~that~~ you don't let yoursef make mistakes in your work. We will help you meet more people who can further you on your journey into the light. This is holly and more will be revealed to you as you become ready to recieve these important messages that will help to enlighten mamy in your world. More later.

I would have to find out who Raphael was. Shawna had taught me I could ask him myself, but I didn't always trust the messages yet. I wanted to get confirmation of this name through someone else.

In another writing on July 5, Kim gave me some wisdom to help me along my journey.

> *"Are you ready, yet? We are here to help you learn. My mission is to help you. You are ready to work with us now. You need to start a learning circle. Ask Bonnie to help."*

What did Kim mean?

By now there were five of us eager to learn. Did Kim want us to get together in a learning circle? We discussed the possibility of a weekly gathering to practice meditation. In books I was reading, I found information about how to start a learning circle. We decided that getting together would be an excellent way to keep us focused on our journey and give us opportunities to practice meditation. Our knowledge was limited, but we agreed to help one another. I began to make meditation tapes to use. Kim had suggested I ask Bonnie to lead us.

I didn't yet know Bonnie that well and did not immediately ask her. After a couple of weeks, the five of us realized we needed a teacher. I had no idea if Bonnie was even interested or if she had the time, but I decided I would at least ask. Kim had urged me to, and I liked Bonnie and felt comfortable around her. As mentioned in an earlier chapter, Bonnie led our group for six weeks. As our knowledge grew, so did our desire to know more.

This was the time my writings stopped for a period of about three weeks. Finally, on July 28, I got another message from my guide Holly. Now I was beginning to focus not only on Kim, but also on "the other side" in general and all that encompassed. In my journey to find my daughter, I had discovered something bigger than I could ever imagine. I had ventured into this unknown world as a means of finding some peace and understanding about our devastating loss. Now I had to re-evaluate my entire belief system.

During my writings one evening, I invited Holly to join me to impart her messages and wisdom. This is what she said:

*"My name is Holly. When you are calling me, I am at your shoulder. We are going to help you to connect with the spirit world. Angels of healing surround you, as healing is your greatest need. Kim is rubbing your neck right now and saying, 'Tell Dad that I miss him and I look at Dad in my heart.' Kim wishes to talk now so I will step back."*

Next I connected with my daughter. The words that came through always brought my emotions to the surface since they were so indicative of Kim's personality. As I tried to stay focused, I received this message:

*"Hi, Mom. You were afraid this would end, but you just had to catch up to your gift. It was scaring you, but you are really ready now. This makes me happy. This is our plan together."*

I noticed the handwriting when Holly imparted her wisdom changed when Kim was connecting. As I went over my dated sheets of automatic writing, I studied the different handwriting styles.

On August 9, Raphael appeared again:

"*Well, my dear, I am here to guide you along your spiritual path. What you wish to know I will help you to understand. Believe in yourself and all will be made clear.*"

Now I understood: he must be a guide.

To learn more about these guides I went in search of another book and chose *How to Meet and Work with Your Spirit Guides* by Ted Andrews. This book presented several exercises to open up communication with our spirit guides. He asserted that we are being contacted and surrounded by our guides and deceased loved ones all the time. If we would just acknowledge them and pay attention to the clues they give us, we would be more aware of them. How right he was!

Another book I felt guided to read at this stage of my spiritual enlightenment was simply titled *Spirit Guides*, by Iris Belhayes. It is filled with information about who these guides are, where they come from, and various ways for us to contact them. Though receiving contact through automatic writing, I yearned to learn how to improve my connection plus discover other modes of communication.

On August 16, I was finally given validation through Sharlette that I had a guide by the name of Raphael. I had not told her that his name had come through in my automatic writing. Sharlette informed me, during one of our frequent discussions over the Internet, that I had a guide named Raphael. He was more powerful, more "full of Light" than Holly. His purpose was to help with my enlightenment.

This was the proof I needed to believe I heard the messages accurately and clearly. I reasoned that I wasn't unconsciously making up the information in my writings because Sharlette had given me this same name. When I asked her about Holly, she reinforced the fact that we have more than one spirit guide with us. "They each have different roles to play in our spiritual awakening. As there are different types of people here, there are different kinds of guides there. Some have more wisdom that others — are more of the Light — and all have specific tasks." I had so much to discover and to learn.

On August 18, I received guidance from an energy that called himself Archangel Raphael. The tone of this writing was different from all the previous ones. When I re-read the message, the words were startling, the tone especially powerful. This was his message:

*"Give yourself to the Light and ye will continue to grow. Blessed be the earthly form that gives their heart to God for ye shall be blessed. Healing, this is part of your journey. I will help you. You understand now that only the earthly body dies. Love is eternal. Love is forever. Your spirit continues on forever, growing closer to the God spark.*

*"You are doing well. I am pleased for you, for your soul. I bring you God's love, God's devotion. Now you must let it enter your heart. Open your heart and let God enter. He is all. He is goodness and Light. Feel His love."*

As I had never been a religious person, I had to do some major thinking about this message. Who was Archangel Raphael? He didn't sound like my guide Raphael. Could this be an angel? If so, then what I had read was true:

angels could also impart their wisdom to us.

I went in search of information on the archangels. Bonnie had just the book I was looking for: *How to Work with Angels*, by Elizabeth Claire Prophet. I realized that the more I learned to work with the angels, the more effectively they could help me on my personal level. What a feeling of comfort that information gave me!

On August 30, I received new insightful information. In one of my writings, Raphael explained to me a very important reason we must always ask for protection before we open ourselves up to all that is out "there."

Raphael wrote: *"Make sure to see the Light of God. Most souls go to the Light; but some, due to things wrongly done in your plane of existence, do not immediately progress to the Light. If they are sorry for their earthly wrongs, then they can be helped to go to the Light in time. Some, however, don't realize that they have to atone to themselves, their own soul. They place themselves in their own lesson levels here on our plane. Some don't want to believe they have crossed and attach themselves to people from the earth's plane that have opened themselves to the spirit world. The White Light of God, therefore, protects you from these souls."*

Wow! Because this was obviously important information, I knew it was not from my own knowledge. I had never heard of this before. Now, fear about opening to the spirit world awakened in me. During the early stages of my automatic writing, I reasoned, someone must have been protecting me. Now I adopted the habit of protecting myself before every session.

I needed to understand more about the art of protection. While browsing, I noticed many books about the importance of psychic protection. Now, I decided, was a fine time to read them.

Having knowledge *before* diving into this unknown territory would have been the smarter way, but I had not been rational at the onset of this journey. I was in grief. I was driven by our loss of Kim who had so much to live for and was taken away so suddenly. I had to find some answers that made sense to me. I couldn't wait to investigate. I just acted. I am confident that Kim, Holly, and Raphael were the protectors who watched over me during my earliest experiences.

I decided it was time to start asking Kim, Holly, and Raphael some deeper questions. I craved understanding. As I settled in one evening and prepared to write, I asked Kim to please answer this question: "Was this predestined that you and I communicate in this way? Can you explain this to me?"

This was the surprising answer I received. *"Mom, I choose to step back and let Raphael explain this to you. I love you all."*

Then Raphael began to write in his familiar style. *"My dear, you are first a soul and only secondly a person having an earthly experience. I know this is hard to comprehend, but believe this is true. Kim is a very wise soul because she is from the Love and Light of God, as we all are, but she has had many earthly experiences. The two of you have spent lifetimes connected. Don't doubt this information."*

Realizing there was a pause in the information, I silently asked, "What are my lessons in this lifetime?"

Raphael responded with, *"You know more of them now. You are to begin to help people — many people — with your gift. Do it with love and good purpose and it will bring you fulfillment."*

The writing abruptly stopped. I put down my pen, closed my eyes, and permitted myself time to reflect on this information. Overwhelmed and shaking my head, I wondered what all of this meant.

I now received messages from Kim on a regular basis. Many of my writings from Kim were very emotional and extremely personal while some of a less personal nature reflected much wisdom. When she arrived I could sense it was her. The personality that came through was just so Kim.

*"How's life? Exciting, eh! Your Kim, here. Wow, what an adventurer you are. Never were before, but you sure are now. You can feel me, Mom. I am writing this. It is nice to still be able to do this. Wow, Mom, your love is so wonderful. Thank you for this immense love, Mom. It fills me up and lifts me up. Remember we are a team. Always, Kim."*

On August 31, I was surprised to receive a message for Sharlette while doing my automatic writing. This was a new experience for me. I was used to the messages I received being for *me,* but now I wrote information to give to Sharlette. Spirit is truly amazing!

I knew I must relay this message but wondered if it would mean anything to her. I came to understand this as a lesson for me to trust the messages I received. By having to share this message with Sharlette, I was shown, once again, that I could hear the messages accurately and clearly. Sharlette confirmed the information in my writing. I had taken another, more confident, step into the Light.

By September, after only six months of automatic writing, I was receiving very detailed information. Some of my writings ran to three or four pages. I was sometimes writing twice a day. I was driven by a passion only a mother in grief can understand, to remain focused and open to all that I was experiencing. It was my link to Kim.

I didn't want to face the first year anniversary of Kim's death or the court appearance, both of which were fast approaching. The only comfort I had was in keeping my connection to Kim and to the other side. I immersed myself in my learning; consequently, much was shown to me in my automatic writing. It was a month of both intense grief and valuable spiritual growth.

I was about to find out Kim and Raphael had plans to teach me new and exciting things. The first example of this happened during my regular evening writing on September 2. As I prepared myself to write, I felt a new and different sensation overtake me. Kim wrote:

> *"Mom, you are so smart. Mind is a wonderful thing. Clear it and we come to you. When you pray, I like it. I am writing. I finally have control over your hand. We are all okay here."*

Although Kim had often come through in my writings, this was a different sensation and different handwriting.

I had always felt a pressure on my hand while writing, but this time I felt *she actually was my hand*, as if she and I were one. The writing was completely different, too. How I ever kept my focus I will never know, but I did.

I didn't want the feeling to end, but all too soon the sensation was over.

Hours later, after many tears and much thought, I finally fell asleep exhausted. I did not experience this sensation again until September 13.

The next evening as I settled down to write, I marveled at the fact that I could ask questions. I decided to start the session with a question for Kim. I had been worried about something for a while now and wanted to ask her about it. Kim, as a fourth year business student at Wilfrid Laurier University, had been accepted into the International Business Program and was chosen to go to France. She was so excited! This would have been a wonderful experience for her. I was sad that she did not live to experience this wonderful opportunity. I wondered if she was sad that she didn't get to go.

This was her response to my question:

> *"I have been all over the world. I can now, but I have already done that, so it is not important any more. Your world is for you and all the others. I thought about all my earthly wants and desires, but love was the most important. I radiated positive energy there. That was the most important purpose of my journey. Your journey is just beginning. Don't be sad, Mom. I am right here with all of you."*

As I digested this information, emotions rushed over me like waves on a beach. Tears rolled down my face as I reflected on Kim and the amazing person she had been. She definitely had the ability to bring out the best in people. As I thought back over the day of her funeral and all the people Kim had influenced at the tender age of 22, I knew this to be true. Her happiness and positive outlook on life were contagious. She loved, she laughed, and she lived every moment to the fullest. These characteristics, however, made her passing even more tragic for all of us left behind.

The journey I was now pursuing helped to ease some of my grief. It had to! How could it not? I was still, amazingly enough, talking with my beloved daughter. I reasoned that if I could talk to her, she was not "dead," just somewhere else. Indeed, she was very much alive.

I wanted her here so badly, but I had to find comfort in knowing she was still around us. I rode a roller coaster — up one minute with this new understanding and down when an immense wave of pain struck.

On September 10, this profound evidence enlightened me:

> *"Make sure to love. Saying it does not mean you live it. Share your love. Show your love. Draw close, help each other and live your earthly life. Kim, your daughter is here, is fine and lives on. God gave us eternal life. Know this. Trust in this knowledge. Your growth brings you closer to her. She is! Trust! Follow your spiritual path, but continue your lessons on earth, too. You need both lessons, all lessons to progress your soul. We love you and will help you now that you have asked for our guidance. This is Raphael, my dear. Your grandmother is here with us now. Resting and understanding. When she is ready, she will come to you again. All in God's time, my dear. Raphael."*

On September 13, I received another lesson from the other side.

This experience shows the trust Raphael and I had built up over our months together. It had been six weeks since I had received his name from Sharlette, but he had made his presence known to me for much longer than that. Since I was writing on such a constant basis, I became accustomed to his unique energy. Each time he arrived, I felt a strong, warm sensation — a very loving feeling.

I felt a new sense of peace knowing loved ones, guides, and angels were all around me, guiding me and watching out for me. I had given both Kim and Raphael my permission to become one with my body whenever they felt I was ready for it. Kim had already done this earlier in the month; now it was Raphael's turn. A sample of his writing follows on the next pages.

My handwriting changed as I felt the sensation of Raphael blending with my body. As I allowed Raphael to share this experience with me, a powerful, loving feeling enveloped me. I believe I was given a lesson this day to advance my understanding.

Did not write on Sept 12/99.

Sept 13/99
(Am)
Amazing
a lesson for me!

Nurse arrives I come to you
now you will feel my presence just
like now. Those are the signs
that I am here with you. What
better way for you to help yourself
grow and to help others with your
knowledge. This is from God. This
is his will, his love. Use this knowledge
to help others. I am entering
your body become I with you,
feel the different I am
using your hand. Feel this
new energy It is my loving
energy. Feel me feel me leave
(Yes) now you are writing, Feel
your energy now. Different from mine
(Yes). Now I will sometimes join

your body, sometimes join only the
mind. Do you understand. Pen down
just feel my presence entering, breath,
concentrate then feel me leave and
stand in front of you.
What did you feel. Write it down,
focus... its OKay relax I know it is a
strong sensation... (chillbumps, cold... shivers)
pressure on chest... breathing rythm changed
.... ~~left~~ you leave from the top of my
head... pressure lifted.. breathing returned
to normal ...warmth returned did not see you infront of
me but I was very emotional Thank you Raphael
for this learning, thank God for his direction
-I know it is you Raphael by the feeling
I get am I right? ... yes my
dear you are right. (Thank you,
thank you...)

You are ready to come to our world
again ... to join up again. Trust .. believe
Hazel will help. call her ... We are waiting
to advance you in this direction. Rememb
I will help you with God's blessings.
It is time for your next step in
learning. Love & Light as Sharlette
say Raphael

Wednesday, September 15, 1999, will be etched in my heart forever since this was the day my grandmother, Gladys Gallant, came and took over the writing for me. The only other communication I had received from her was when Kim had shared the message on her behalf. Now she came to talk to me directly.

Although this is a personal message to me, I wish to share it with you. Grandma could not write when she was alive on earth. She had taught herself to read but had never mastered the ability to write well. Now, in spirit, she could write.

> *"Grandma here, finally. I have to learn how to do this for you, my daughter. Always said you were more like my daughter than granddaughter. I am here. I am with you. I love you, too. Nice here. I was scared to die. Don't know why, now. It was time. All in the right time, honey. You know some of this reality now. Not before, sorry, but you can ask me your questions now, for I hear them clearly. Prayers hold power; remember that."*

"Thanks, Grandma, I will," I silently responded, adding I was sorry for not believing in all of this before. I had wanted to talk to her about my newfound faith and understanding after Kim had passed, but because she had a stroke shortly before, I never had the chance to. I knew she heard me now.

On September 26, I received more information from Raphael. He wrote:

> *"My dear, you are listening to your true self. You are advancing. It is now time to continue to open your three upper chakras. To do this, meditate and, as you do, visualize them opening up from throat to head. Visualize and feel the colors of each. Ask us to keep them balanced and invite God's Divine Light into these chakra points. You now understand. You are listening to us. You hear us so clearly now. Slowly, you will open up these chakra points to hear, see and feel us even more than you do now. Continue to affirm God's love within you. You are worthy of this love. Your inner knowing is becoming stronger with each new miracle. They are miracles, day-to-day miracles, because you are asking. We, with immense love, are listening to your outpouring of love to God, to us. We cleanse you and continue to shine our love and understanding to you, your higher self, your perfect self. Feel the warmth in the area of your crown chakra. Close your eyes and feel. Breathe in the White Divine Love God is sending you through us, your guides and angels. Yes, angels from God."*

I felt a shift in energy and found out why as this writing continued:

> *"I am your angel of strength as your loss has been so great and the time so difficult now. Your strength through God abounds and you are filled with the power within you, God's power, God's devotion. Your Kim is Love and Light. You are also of this Love and Light. Find strength in this knowledge. Pray for others to see this love and receive this inner awareness. My name is Ericka. Feel my energy as it merges with yours. Ask for me when you need renewed strength and I will make myself known. Love eternal, Ericka."*

As I reread the words written by spirit, I realized that I had just received a message from my angel. I had chill bumps all over my body, my new sign that someone from the other side was close. I thanked my angel Ericka and went to sleep.

By the end of September, I had more understanding of our spirit guides and angels and their roles in our lives. I reminded myself of what I'd learned: Accepting their existence allows us to open our souls and allows them to participate in our lives. This is what happened to me. I discovered they are all waiting for the opportunity to make themselves known. Once I began to ask, I did, indeed, receive.

Holly had been the first guide to make herself known. Then Raphael appeared, and, through him, I was able to access a greater wisdom. Kim was also one of my guides, a fact amazing in itself. A message received from Archangel Raphael taught that anyone can receive guidance from any one or all of the archangels if they just asked. I knew, as well, that I had an angel of strength named Ericka helping to guide and comfort me. In my writings, I was starting to write, "we are," implying there were many on the other side who wished to help me grow in my learning. I learned they are there for all of us.

Thirsting for knowledge, I picked up a book written by Barbara Mark and Trudy Griswold called *Angelspeake: How to Talk with Your Angels*. This book is a guide on how to connect with your angels. They explain that when they say "angels" they refer not only to angels but also to guides, masters, teachers, and loved ones from the other side. I discovered I had been doing all the steps this book detailed. I highly recommend reading this book, since it is filled with information we all need in order to understand what happens during this process.

I learned some important information about automatic writing from this book. I had been puzzled about the different sensations I felt during my automatic writing. On page 50, the authors wrote, "Hear the words come just a second before they are written. You will hear. Do not worry about it making sense. Just write what you hear as you hear it."

As I reviewed my writings, I knew this was not how my writings had started. I had not heard the words; instead I had felt what seemed like someone putting pressure on my hand. I had no knowledge of what was going to be written before I wrote it. Was I not doing what was called automatic writing? I was confused.

Then I read on page 51, "The angels call this process of recording information automatic dictation. Automatic dictation is simply recording the information as it is being given to you through your thoughts. Basically, you write what you hear. You are fully conscious, aware, and in control of yourself. Don't confuse this with automatic writing, which is a different method entirely. In dictation, you are fully conscious of what is being given to you. In automatic writing, you are not aware of the information as it is being sent."

Further study has brought me to understand that if you write — whether you hear the words then write them or if you are unaware of the words you write — all of these types of communication can be categorized as "automatic writing."

I now understand that I have done both. Most of the time I feel someone has taken over my hand, but sometimes I am writing words that "appear" in my head. With both methods, since they are not my words, I quickly forget what is being written. When I read over the information, it is as if I am seeing it for the first time. With both techniques, I am always fully conscious but in a relaxed, meditative state, one similar to the feeling I get when I am driving along a straight, boring stretch of highway. I "zone out," even though I remain conscious.

I had heard it was possible to sit at the computer and type rather than hand-write messages. Perhaps, by typing, more information could be imparted in a shorter period of time. I wasn't sure if this would work for me, as most of my automatic writing took place when those on the other side guided my hand.

I reasoned using the computer would work when I was just writing the words that appeared in my third eye, the area just above and between my eyes. I could never anticipate in advance which technique I would be using until I began a session. My guides were definitely in control.

When I was ready, I sat in front of my computer, set my fingers on the keyboard, and waited. I expected to hear messages and then type, but again, they had something different planned for me. I felt a cold breeze at my back; before I had time to think, my fingers started moving. I did not have control of my hands as my fingers stroked the keys.

Raphael appeared first. This was what he typed:

> *"My dear, you are a great teacher. We are proud of you. We love you. Use this knowledge with love. Love is all. Love is the universal answer. Hold it in your heart."*

Then my fingers stopped and Raphael was done.

On September 30, I sat at my computer to update my logs when I heard, *"Write these words now."* I was taken completely by surprise, as I had not prepared myself to write. The words had never come this way before. This felt like a command. As I continued to update the logs, I heard again, *"Write these words, now!"* This command was very clear and very loud. Guess they want me to write, I thought.

As I said my prayer of protection, I opened up a new file and filled it with what they said. Although I was expecting them to take over my hands, this did not happen. I waited for my hands to start moving. They did not, but words were coming like a banner across my forehead. I started typing. I heard:

> *"You are working for us now. We are working for God. Listen to us please and we will help you to advance. Raphael here. Glad you decided to try it again on the computer. It is right. You can hear us very clearly now. Your mission is to help others. Hope you understand that this is a gift right from Him. Follow your heart and you shall be free. We are all here for you. Ask for more and you will receive more. We love you and protect you always. Kim is with you right now as you write this. Believe it to be true and you will feel this warmth that surrounds your shoulders."*

There was a pause in the flow of words as someone new stepped forward with messages. I heard:

*"Mom, good for you! Typing right on. It is so clear. Learning, learning, Mom. Always learning. Just like me, Mom. We are here to help you and to love you."*

Then she was gone and Raphael continued:

> *"You are goodness. We wish to let you know that so many have messages for their loved ones, and you will help to give them strength. Comfort is in the knowledge that there is so much more than you, on the earth's plane can comprehend. You are not to understand (it all), just know it to be true. Trust God. Trust Him. For He is all-knowing and all-loving. He wishes to impart this wisdom to his people on the earth plane, for there is much still (for you) to learn. Understand that this is God's truth, the truth, the only truth."*

The words stopped as abruptly as they had started. I definitely realized that I had begun a journey that I was not going to be able to stop. I, thankfully, did not want to.

As I shared these computer writings with Doug, he noticed something. The words that were written by them — when they took over my hand — were free of any typing errors, while the ones in which I typed the words I heard had plenty of mistakes. This was an interesting observation, one I myself probably would not have noticed.

I preferred to write my messages by hand, however, because I liked seeing the different handwriting produced. I could often see a distinct writing style when they were guiding my hand. I decided I would go back to writing the messages by hand.

Trusting the messages was my biggest hurdle. When I just let my hand relax and allowed the energy to come through, my guides, angels, and loved ones on the other side helped me do the rest. I learned to just write and, later think about the messages. I discovered clearing my mind of my own thoughts was the best way to make the connection. I learned to meditate, breathe effectively, and listen to the words as I heard them.

On October 9, I was introduced to another angel. The words in this message were similar to only one other message:

*"When you pray to us, you know we listen. God listens. We take your prayers directly to Him. Praise Him and all will become clear. Now it is time to understand more of your life... others who need great healing, also. This is your journey — to help them connect to their loved ones who have gone to join God. Trust the messages; write only what you hear. The verifications will come through. Clearing you own mind of your thoughts is your job. The better at this you become, the clearer the messages. Never think: Does this make sense?*

*"Remember they are not for you to judge, just to give. Meditation is what you must practice more. Quieting your mind on command. It is helping that you are working on more positive thoughts. Remember all is for a purpose. All conflict is for your learning. Send your loving thoughts out to those not so loving, those that are consumed with selfish thoughts, and you not only clear yourself of negativity but you show them that love emanates from you. They will unconsciously absorb your loving rays and, in return, they will be more loving. Now it is time for Raphael to appear. Please continue to talk to us as you need to. We send your questions directly to God. Love and believe that the God Spark is within you and you shall continue to be enlightened."*

Then this angel — this energy — was gone and Raphael picked up the writing in his familiar style. I had read that angels are sent directly from God, that they have never lived on earth. I would have to find out more about angels, but for now I had enough to think about with a new awareness of my guides, my changing beliefs in God, and my contact from the other side.

Mine is a continuing journey with so much to learn. I went in search of another book and picked up one called *Touched by Angels* by Eileen Elias Freeman. This book piqued my interest on the topic of angels. One paragraph that caught my attention read, "Angels bring healing into our lives, and when we need it, a sense of direction. They can instantly help clarify our doubts and uncertainties because they see the whole more surely than we do; they see with God's eyes. And when we let an angel touch our life to heal us, we can become instruments for spiritual healing for others." I was now able to connect to my own angels and was comforted.

This was the month that I was going to attempt astral travel for the first time. The circumstances that brought this about were mentioned in an earlier chapter. I was worried about attempting this out-of-body adventure and wondered how much success I would have.

One evening I decided to ask Kim to talk about it. This is the message she gave me on October 11, the day of my canceled appointment with Hazel.

*"The deeper the connection, the closer to us you are, Mom. Astral travel soon. Patience. You must meditate, prepare your body for this special energy work. You know it will be soon. Please be patient. Not today, Mom. I know you want it, but today is not right for you. Ground yourself for this day. Strength I give you. Immense strength. God has given you Ericka. Don't forget to call on her. She is your angel. Devoted to you by God, for God. Remember you are loved deeply, completely by God's Light and, by me, of course. Love you forever, always. Love my family. Be together and know I am with you. Kim."*

How do I adequately share with you my feelings when Kim was with me, talking to me, sharing her new life with me? I know the power love gave me — as it gives to all — the energy to accomplish all things and create my own miracles. I had found my daughter, and she was okay. I had my miracle. But oh, how I wanted her to physically be here with us again.

Over the course of these eight months I enjoyed quantum growth in my spirituality, primarily through these writings. When I became overwhelmed by the immensity of what I was doing, I would withdraw from my automatic writing for a few days.

During these breaks, I read. I trusted that my journey was as it was destined to be, and, when I needed more understanding and wisdom, I would feel the need to take a break from my writings. I felt guided to each new book I needed to read. I had heard about Betty Eadie and her book titled, *Embraced by the Light*. While walking in the bookstore one afternoon, I noticed a young lady sitting quietly and reading. She had shoulder-length hair and reminded me a bit of Kim. As I took a second look, I saw the book she was reading: *Embraced by the Light.*

When I tried to buy the book, I was told no more copies were available in the store at that time. My friend Judy Hunt lived right around the corner, so I decided to drop in. As I explained to her that I had put my name on a waiting list for a copy of this book, she chuckled. She disappeared upstairs and returned with Betty Eadie's book in hand to loan it to me. I just love synchronicities!

By the middle of October I was told that I was ready to advance on my spiritual journey. I wondered where this journey would take me now. I felt a new sense of peace within me. My guides and Kim had made references to the fact that I would give messages to others.

I worried about turning this corner, about giving messages from the other side to those who had lost loved ones. I knew I could break their hearts if I didn't get the messages right. I felt that, as I continued to develop my psychic abilities, my responsibility to use it only for the highest good of all would increase. My intentions must be pure and honest.

I knew the devastation of loss and the comfort these messages had brought me. Could I write for others and bring them the same solace with information that came through? I had to be sure I could hear the information accurately and clearly.

It was, by this time, October 1999, and my automatic writing was changing. I was now being guided to channel information for others and not just for myself. I feel the decision as to whether or not I was ready to turn this corner was taken out of my hands. Divine Order and Kim were at work once again.

Automatic writing served as only the first stepping stone on a very intricate path to my enlightenment. Having read the previous chapters, you know that I encountered many twists and turns and experienced many highs and lows as I proceeded on my personal journey. Each stepping stone laid out a path to Spirit that now forms the new structure of my life. I am eternally grateful for *My Gift of Light.*

# Recommended Reading

*These are the books that I read and often reread along my spiritual pilgrimage.*


Altea, Rosemary. *Proud Spirit.* New York, William Morrow & Company, Inc., 1997.

Altea, Rosemary. *The Eagle & the Rose: A Remarkable True Story.* New York, Warner Books, Inc., 1996.

Anderson, George and Barone, Andrew. *Lessons from the Light: Extraordinary Messages of Comfort and Hope from the Other Side.* New York, Berkley Publishing Group, 2000.

Andrews, Ted. *How to Meet & Work With Spirit Guides (Llewellyn's Practical Guide to Personal Power).* St. Paul, M.N., Llewellyn Publications, 1992.

Belhayes, Iris and Enid. *Spirit Guides: We Are Not Alone.* San Diego, ACS Publications, 1987.

Browne, Sylvia and May, Antoinette. *Adventures of a Psychic: The Fascinating Inspiring True-Life Story of One of America's Most Successful Clairvoyants.* Carlsbad, C.A., Hay House, 1998.

Cayce, Edgar. *Auras: An Essay on the Meaning of Colors.* Virginia Beach, A. R. E. Press, 1991.

Chopra, Deepak. *Seven Spiritual Laws of Success: A Practical Guide to the Fulfillment of Your Dreams*. San Rafael, C.A., Amber-Allen Publishing, 1995.

Dalai Lama. *An Open Heart: Practicing Compassion in Everyday Life.* New York, Warner Books, 2001.

Dalai Lama and Bstan-'Dzin-Rgy. *Dalai Lama's Book of Wisdom.* New York, Thorsons/ Element, 2000.

Eadie, Betty and Taylor, Curtis. *Embraced by the Light.* New York, Bantam Books, Inc., 1994.

Edward, John. *One Last Time: A Psychic Medium Speaks to Those We Have Loved and Lost.* New York, Berkley Publishing Group, 1999.

Freeman, Eileen Elias. *Touched by Angels.* New York, Warner Books, 2001.

Gawain, Shatki. *Creative Visualization: Use the Power of Your Imagination to Create What You Want in Your Life.* New York, Bantam Books, Inc., 1997.

Guggenheim, Bill and Guggenheim, Judy. *Hello from Heaven!: A New Field of Research, After-Death Communication Confirms that Life and Love are Eternal.* New York, Bantam Books, 1997.

Mark, Barbara and Griswold, Trudy. *Angelspeake: How To Talk With Your Angels.* New York, Simon and Schuster Adult Publishing Group, 1995.

Martin, Joel and Romanowski, Patricia. *We Are Not Forgotten: George Anderson's Messages of Love and Hope from the Other Side.* New York, Berkley Publishing Group, 1992.

Martin, Joel and Romanowski, Patricia. *We Don't Die: George Anderson's Conversations with the Other Side.* New York, Berkley Publishing Group, 1989.

Montgomery, Ruth. *Search for the Truth.* New York, Ballantine Books, 1982.

Moody, Raymond and Kubler-Ross, Elisabeth. *Life after Life: The Investigation of a Phenomenon — Survival of Bodily Death.* San Francisco, HarperCollins, 2001.

Moody, Raymond and Perry, Paul. *The Light Beyond.* New York, Bantam Books, Inc., 1989.

Prophet, Elizabeth Clare. *How to Work with Angels.* Corwin Springs, M.T., Summit University Press, 1998.

Reed, Henry and Cayce, Charles Thomas (Editor). *Edgar Cayce on Channeling Your Higher Self.* New York, Warner Books, Inc., 1989.

Reed, Henry. *Your Mind: Unlocking Your Hidden Powers.* Virginia Beach, V.A., A.R.E. Press, 1997.

Roman, Sanaya; Packer, Duane; and Armstrong, Gregory (Editor). *Opening to Channel: How to Connect with Your Guide.* Tiburon, C.A., H J Kramer, Inc., 1987.

Stack, Rick. *Out-Of-Body Adventures.* Columbus, O.H., McGraw-Hill, 1988.

Van Praagh, James. *Talking to Heaven: A Medium's Message of Life After Death.* New York, Penguin Group, 1997.

Van Praagh, James. *Reaching to Heaven: A Spiritual Journey Through Life and Death.* New York, Penguin Group, 1999.

Vanzant, Iyanla. *One Day My Soul Just Opened Up: 40 Days and 40 Nights Toward Spiritual Strength and Personal Growth.* New York, Fireside/Simon and Schuster, 2002.

Virtue, Doreen and The Angelic Realm. *Angel Therapy: Healing Messages for Every Area of Your Life.* Carlsbad, C.A., Hay House, Inc., 1997.

Virtue, Doreen. *Connecting with Your Angels: How to See, Talk, and Work with the Angelic Realm.* Carlsbad, C.A., Hay House, Inc., 2004.

Virtue, Doreen and Hay, Louise L. *The Lightworker's Way: Awakening Your Spiritual Power to Know and Heal.* Carlsbad, C.A., Hay House, Inc., 1997.

Wagner, Angelica Eberle and Fisher, Murray. *Are You Ready for a Miracle with Angels?: A Practical Guide to Understanding Angels in Everyday Life.* Miracleworks, Inc., 2000.

Webster, Richard and Krause, Marguerite (Editor). *Astral Travel for Beginners.* St. Paul, M.N., Llewellyn Worldwide, Ltd., 1998.

Webster, Richard and Maupin, Mike (Editor). *Aura Reading for Beginners.* St. Paul, Llewellyn Worldwide, Ltd., 1998.

Williamson, Marianne. *Illuminata: A Return to Prayer.* New York, Riverhead Trade, 1995.

# *Tributes to and Memories of Kim*

*The inspirational passage on the next page was found taped to Kim's desk at Microsoft. It was sent back to her family from one of her bosses with a note attached.*

> *"I found this on Kim's desk and have shared it with others at Microsoft. For me it depicted Kim's outlook on life and I will always carry it with me."*

*Everyone who knew Kim recognized this is truly the way she lived her life.*

# The Station *by Robert J. Hastings*

Tucked away in our subconscious is an idyllic vision. We see ourselves on a long trip that spans the continent. We are traveling by train. Out the windows we drink in the passing scene of cars on nearby highways, of children waving at a crossing, of cattle grazing on a distant hillside, of smoke pouring from a power plant, of row upon row of corn and wheat, of flat lands and valleys, of mountains and rolling hillsides, of city skylines and village halls.

But uppermost in our minds is the final destination. On a certain day at a certain hour we will pull into the station. Bands will be playing and flags waving. Once we get there so many wonderful dreams will come true, and the pieces of our lives will fit together like a completed jigsaw puzzle. How restlessly we pace the aisles, damning the minutes for loitering – waiting, waiting, waiting for the station.

"When we reach the station, that will be it!" we cry.

"When I'm 18."

"When I buy a new 450SL Mercedes-Benz!"

"When I put my last kid through college."

"When I have paid off my mortgage!"

"When I get a promotion."

"When I reach the age of retirement, I shall live happily ever after!"

Sooner or later we must realize there is no station, no one place to arrive at once and for all. The true joy of life is the trip. The station is only a dream. It constantly outdistances us.

"Relish the moment" is a good motto, especially when coupled with Psalm 118:24: "This is the day which the lord hath made; we will rejoice and be glad in it." It isn't the burdens of today that drive men mad. It is the regrets over yesterday and the fear of tomorrow. Regret and fear are twin thieves who rob us of today.

So stop pacing the aisles and counting the miles. Instead, climb more mountains, eat more ice cream, go barefoot more often, swim more rivers, watch more sunsets, laugh more, cry less. Life must be lived as we go along. The station will come soon enough.

*Kim's Graduation from High School*

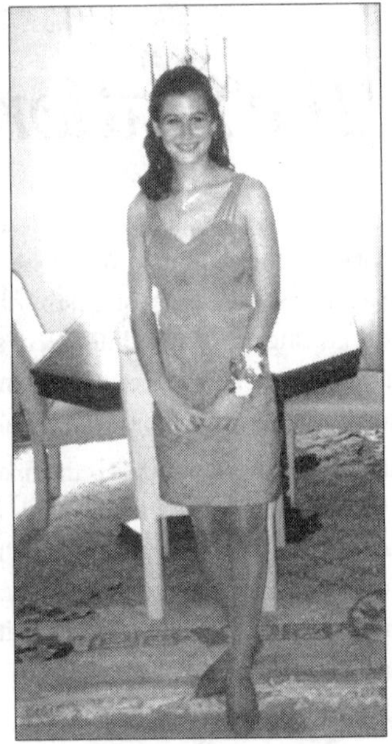

*Kim dressed up for High School Graduation*

*Kim at 22 years old Summer of 1998*

*The more casual Kim. She never really fully relaxed. She usually had something she was studying in her hands.*

Cord

WEDNESDAY, NOVEMBER 4, 1998

In memory of Kim Wiltshire

Published in Wilfrid Laurier University's
student newspaper,
*The Cord*, Volume 39, Issue 14
November 4, 1998

---

*Written by Nina, Jeannette, and Prabha,*
*three of Kim's closest university friends*

As we sit down to write this article, it's so hard to know where to begin. How do you fit 22 years of living on to one single page?

Kim Wiltshire was born on March 15, 1976, in Ontario. She grew up in a very strong and supportive family, sharing close relationships with her parents and two sisters Kerry and Kristy.

Kim always set goals for herself and then did whatever it took to meet them. Being accepted to the business program at WLU was the first of many goals she would achieve as a student.

Kim's determination and drive to succeed were a constant throughout her academic career. She was a well-rounded student and worked hard to achieve good grades in all of her classes.

Kim wanted to be a part of the co-op program and worked hard during her first year to ensure she was accepted. However, things did not stop there; every work term, Kim set her sights on the top jobs available. She always had numerous interviews and was the first choice of many employers. This led to very successful placements with Bell Mobility and Microsoft.

Kim knew that there were no boundaries for learning. She had a strong desire to travel and experience new things, which led to her decision to apply for an international exchange. She was accepted for the winter term and was to leave for France this January.

Although her academic and professional life was very important to Kim, her social life had equal priority. She knew exactly how to balance school work and partying and always made sure she had time for each. Kim was rarely in front of the TV without having a textbook in her lap. On the other hand, she was also rarely at the bar without a beer in her hand!

Kim's love of life and good times made her so much fun to be around. She had an amazing ability to make friends immediately with everyone she met. It didn't matter if you hadn't been introduced to her; if she wanted to know who you were she just went up and asked you.

Kim's friendliness and sense of fun were made evident to many Laurier students on last year's reading week trip to Puerto Plata. From playing volleyball during the day to partying at night, Kim made many new friendships that continued beyond the holiday.

Kim's friends were an extremely significant part of her life, and she loved to spend time with them. No matter what you were doing with her, you always knew that you were important to her. She didn't hesitate to introduce her friends to everyone she knew because she wanted everyone to be able to have a good time together.

Good times with Kim almost always included laughter. Kim loved to laugh and be silly; she wasn't afraid to be childish when the time was right. It's funny how someone could be so mature and yet so immature at the same time and always know the appropriate time for both.

Kim loved her life at Laurier. The fun started right away in the first year, living on the first floor of Bouckaert Hall. She got along with everyone and made many friends immediately. Kim rarely missed a Thursday night at the Turret; however, the only dance you would see her do there was the running man or her own "point your index finger in the air and bounce" dance.

After first year the four of us and Sarah moved to our first house on King Street. We became famous for our seasonal pot-luck formal parties, which half the second year population attended. The following year we moved to James Street. Although our house party days had diminished, the fun and good times continued. Living together had made us all closer than we had ever thought possible. We were more than friends, we were a family.

Those of us who were lucky enough to have known Kim will always remember her as someone who had no regrets in life. She crammed more things into 22 years of living than some people do in an entire lifetime. She gave true meaning to the phrase "live life to the fullest."

Kim has touched so many lives, it's hard to imagine what life is going to be like without her. Although she is no longer with us, she will continue to live in the hearts and thoughts of those who love her.

# About the Author

SANDY WILTSHIRE was an average mom who never gave much thought to spiritual matters such as life after death. She considered herself an agnostic and skeptic when it came to new-age, religious, or spiritual topics.

But when her daughter was killed by a reckless driver, Sandy fell into the depths of despair and depression. With every fiber of her being, she longed to know that Kim was okay and that her lively, loving spirit did not die with her body. Sandy began to immerse herself into books about angels, after-death communication, automatic writing, astral travel, and other metaphysical topics.

As she opened to ways to communicate with her deceased daughter, she found herself becoming a channel for reaffirming messages from others who had crossed over to the other side.

As she learned to trust her new "gift of light," Sandy began to hold private readings with those who are bereaved — especially parents — bringing words of love and hope to anyone cast adrift in the seas of sorrow. She believes this is her soul's purpose and that her own unfathomable pain has served as the gateway to help others.

Sandy lives in Ontario with her husband and their two daughters.

# How to Order

Quality of Life Publishing Co. specializes in gentle grief support books and booklets for readers of all ages. Here's how to order *My Gift of Light* and other publications:

**BOOKSTORES:** Our books are available at retail and online bookstores via Biblio Distribution.

**ONLINE:** **www.QoLpublishing.com**
Purchase online using your Visa, MasterCard, Discover, or American Express card.

**EMAIL:** **books@QoLpublishing.com**

**PHONE:** **1-877-513-0099**
Toll free in the U.S. and Canada
or call 1-239-513-9907

**FAX:** **1-239-513-0088**

**MAIL:** **Quality of Life Publishing Co.**
P.O. Box 112050
Naples, FL 34108-1929

***DISCOUNTS.*** *Be sure to ask about* ***substantial discounts*** *available for bulk orders.*